Praise for *Great Again*

"At a time when its competitive position is under siege from emerging economic powers, America requires an insightful and compelling call to arms from an experienced messenger that refocuses our policy makers on what is really at stake in revitalizing innovation and nurturing start-ups. There is no one more qualified to be that messenger than Hank Nothhaft. This is a visionary book."

—Richard Hart
Managing Director, Deutsche Bank Technology Group

"Why did we have the money a generation ago to fund schools and interstate highways, but today we cannot even fix a few broken bridges? Why does prosperity seem to be a fading memory for most of us, even as ever greater riches accrue to an ever smaller few of us? Hank Nothhaft poses tough questions and then tackles them head-on. He brings the perspective of his life as the son of a steelworker, Naval Academy graduate, and creator of wealth and jobs through new, innovative businesses. Here is a genuine must-read for innovators, businesspeople, policy makers, and anyone who cares about building a healthy economy for *all* of our citizens again."

—Morgan Chu
Partner, Irell and Manella LLP
voted the Outstanding Intellectual Property Lawyer in the
United States in the first Chambers Award for Excellence

"Hank Nothhaft is the rare CEO who adroitly straddles the intersection of innovation public policy and the actual business of innovation itself. He is one of only a handful of technology executives engaged on Capitol Hill who understand the challenges today's innovation companies face, and because of that he has been able to work effectively with policy makers to craft and advance policy initiatives that benefit our country."

—Manus Cooney
Partner, American Continental Group, former
Chief Counsel, U.S. Senate Judiciary Committee

"At last we hear the true voice of start-up entrepreneurs—the men and women who create the jobs and breakthrough innovations that power American economic growth. Hank Nothhaft's message in *Great Again* will be embraced by people coast to coast, no matter what their political persuasion is. Let's hope the politicians are listening."

—Jeff Brody
Founding Partner, Redpoint Ventures

"This is an important book. *Great Again* describes policy changes that will help keep America competitive, growing, and strong."

—Curt Carlson
CEO, SRI International (formerly
the Stanford Research Institute)

"Ask any experienced Silicon Valley entrepreneur and they'll tell you that America is putting too many obstacles in the way of the innovation golden goose—the start-up businesses that are the source of all breakthrough innovation and job growth. *Great Again* offers a very dramatic inside look at the root of our problems and offers workable solutions everyone can get behind."

—David Ladd
venture adviser and former Partner, Mayfield Fund

"*Great Again* offers a breakthrough vision on innovation as a rallying point for restoring America's economic vitality."

—Damon C. Matteo
Vice President and Chief Intellectual Property Officer,
Palo Alto Research Center (PARC)

"Jobs, jobs, jobs—it's all about jobs. For this reason, *Great Again* is an absolute must-read. Why? Because Hank Nothhaft has left the politics and ideology to the talking heads and laid out practical, honest, concrete, and sensible ideas for rebuilding our economic vitality, our middle class, and our democratic society."

—Kevin Rivette
author and IP strategist, 3LP Advisors

"Hank Nothhaft is a combat veteran who has led many successful campaigns in the trenches of the high-tech business world. In *Great Again,* he shines a bright light on the intersection of innovation, intellectual property, and job creation. Everyone with an interest in building a more vibrant economy should definitely read this book."

—Norm Fogelsong
General Partner, Institutional Venture Partners

Great
again

Henry R. Nothhaft
with David Kline

Great
again

Revitalizing
America's
Entrepreneurial
Leadership

Harvard Business Review Press

Boston, Massachusetts

Library of Congress Cataloging-in-Publication Data
Nothhaft, Henry R.
    Great again : revitalizing America's entrepreneurial leadership / Henry R. Nothhaft, with David Kline.

    p. cm.
    ISBN 978-1-4221-5857-9 (alk. paper)
1. Small business—United States. 2. New business enterprises—United States. 3. Entrepreneurship—United States. 4. Technological innovations—United States. 5. New products—United States.
6. Industrial policy—United States. I. Kline, David, 1950- II. Title.
    HD2346.U5N69 2011
    338'.040973—dc22

                                                           2010051665

The paper used in this publication meets the requirements of the American National Standard for Permanence of Paper for Publications and Documents in Libraries and Archives Z39.48-1992.

To my wife, Randie, my sons, Hank and Ryan, and my parents, who made my

American Dream possible.

—Henry R. Nothhaft

To my mother, Ruth, who raised three boys with nothing more than love and

courage. This one's for you.

—David Kline

Contents

Acknowledgments

Writing a book is really hard work. This was especially true of the writing of *Great Again*, which required us to bring to life a world unknown to most people—the world of the high-tech innovator and entrepreneur, with all its daily human dramas and struggles. An even greater challenge was to comprehend the economic forces that are slowly but surely bleeding out the wealth of our nation and destroying the middle class—and then to marshal the evidence and practical, achievable remedies needed to break through the partisan gridlock in Washington so that our nation's innovation leadership and economic health can be restored. There is no way we could have even come close to achieving this goal without the advice, counsel, argument, debate, support, and assistance of a staggering number of very smart people.

Among the many veteran entrepreneurs, CEOs, venture capitalists, deal makers, and "tribal elders" of Silicon Valley who helped make this book a reality, we wish to thank (in no particular order) David Ladd, Jeff Brody, Steve Wozniak, Daniel Burstein, Gary Lauder, Pascal Levonsohn, Conrad Burke, Andy Bugas, Brian deHaaf, Chet Kolley, Curt Carlson, Damon Matteo, David Lazovsky, Eric Hippeau, Vern Norviel, Greg Galanos, James Beldock, Tim Bacci, Alfred Lin, Ken Goldman, Rocky Pimentel, Matt Howard, Rich Barton, Richard Hart, Peter Waal, Kathleen Kelleher, Belgacem "Bel" Haba, and Carl Guardino. Especially helpful in suggesting people to interview and providing feedback on the book itself were John Peters, Craig Mitchell, my son Hank Nothhaft Jr., Robert Yung, and Gary Griffiths.

We also offer special thanks to Richard McCormack of *Manufacturing & Technology News*, professors Willy Shih and Gary Pisano at the Harvard Business School, United Steelworkers union president Leo Gerard, and Gregory Tassey, chief economist at the Commerce Department's National Institute of

Standards and Technology. Their breakthrough research, analysis, reporting, and advocacy—in defiance of more than thirty years of wrong-headed thinking by economists and Washington policy makers—have paved the way to our nation's dawning realization that high-tech manufacturing is as essential as high-tech innovation to America's economic future and the continued survival of our once-great middle class.

We wish to express our profound gratitude to America's independent inventors and small business innovators, without whom this nation could never have developed the most successful economy in the history of the world. It is they, working alone or in small entrepreneurial start-up firms, who have invented virtually every great new industry of the last hundred years, and it is their work that provides the foundation for literally all net job growth in the United States. We wish to thank in particular Larry Roberts, the man who really did invent the Internet forty-four years ago and is still hard at work improving it, Segway inventor and National Medal of Technology winner Dean Kamen, new medical treatment pioneers Dr. John Kao and Dr. Andrew Perlman, the prolific and esteemed environmental technology inventor Roger Hoffman, and, last but not least, Mirk Buzdum and his ninety-two-year-old partner, Dick "Cappy" Capstran, of Cappy's Concepts. Cappy has been reinventing the tools of everyday life since he was a fifteen-year-old boy in the Great Depression of the 1930s, and it doesn't look like he has any intention of quitting any time soon.

One cannot praise innovators, however, without also acknowledging those who fight for their interests—and therefore the nation's best interests as well. So allow us to offer our thanks to David Kappos, undersecretary of commerce and director of the United States Patent and Trademark Office (USPTO), who took a huge cut in pay to come to Washington to try to repair America's "innovation agency," and in the process reminded us what good government and public service looks like. We also wish to thank retired Chief Judge Paul R. Michel of the U.S. Court of Appeals for the Federal Circuit, who spends his retirement and his considerable prestige not relaxing on a beach someplace but tirelessly advocating on behalf of inventors and a strong and balanced patent system. In addition, former USPTO directors John Dudas and John Doll, as well as Arti Rai, the Elvin R. Latty Professor at Duke Law School, each offered wise counsel on important issues addressed in this book. Many thanks also to Gene Quinn, patent attorney and blogger extraordinaire at *IP Watchdog,* voted the top intellectual property blog of 2010, who can always be counted on to stand up for entre-preneurial innovators.

A special acknowledgement is in order here for the breakthrough writing of reporter John Schmid of the *Milwaukee Journal Sentinel,* who was the first to expose the tragic human and economic cost of an underfunded patent office that leaves millions of jobs and thousands of new products and med-ical treatments undeveloped. Schmid's editors at the *Journal Sentinel* also deserve a nod—they were way out in front of the rest of the mainstream media on this issue.

For our chapter on the global war for talent, we must thank especially Farzad Naimi and his wife Farahnaz, who gave generously of their time and emotion in sharing with us the details of their struggle for true love, freedom, and the American Dream. We are also grateful for the help provided by immi-grant entrepreneurs Velchamy Sankarlingam, Hao Zhou, and Hongyu Ran, among others. We wish to also acknowledge the cutting-edge research and analysis of Vivek Wadhwa, professor at Harvard, University of California–at Berkeley, and Duke on this issue, as well as that of economist Richard Florida, author of *The Flight of the Creative Class.*

Speaking of research—whether of the academic, journalistic, or practical real-life varieties—we also want to thank economist Scott Shane for his work on fast-growing "gazelle" start-ups, Louis Vintro of semiconductor equip-ment maker ESI for his surprising proof that America absolutely can compete with Chinese labor—and at American wages, too—and law professors Robert Merges and Ted Sichelman, two of the coauthors of the ground-breaking 2008 Berkeley Patent Survey. We are indebted to the Ewing Marion Kauffman Foundation and the Information Technology & Innovation Foundation for their unsurpassed research on "innovation economics" and entrepreneurship, and to the U.S. Small Business Administration for its outstanding treasure trove of research into the truly outsized role played by new and small busi-nesses in the nation's innovation leadership and economic performance.

We must also single out for special mention the extraordinary work of eco-nomic historians Naomi Lamoreaux, B. Zorina Khan, and the late Kenneth Sokoloff on the development of America's unique patent system, which was deliberately designed by the Founding Fathers to be the first in the world to enable ordinary citizens without access to wealth to participate in invention. Simply calling them "historians" seems inadequate though, because, by dig-ging into dusty patent records and other documentary evidence of nineteenth century life, they have managed in much the same way as archeologists or novelists to bring to life the motivational environment for America's "Great Inventors"—and in the process, to reveal the secret of our nation's economic success.

Then there are the many counselors, advisers, and enthusiastic supporters who helped to guide us on our journey of discovery in this book. Manus Cooney, former chief counsel to the Senate Judiciary Committee and one of the most thoughtful and effective lobbyists in the nation, was irreplaceable in helping us understand the way things work (or don't work) in Washington. Also invaluable was the wise counsel provided by Barney Cassidy, Julie Seymour, Bruce Mehlman, David Schairer, and Julie van Amerongen and Jeff Klein, authors of *Working for Good: Making a Difference While Making a Living*.

First-class research assistance, economic analysis, and a critical editorial eye throughout the eighteen-month-long writing process were provided by Jennifer Powell and Troy Apparicio. To uncover the human cost of the deindustrialization of my hometown of Sharon, Pennsylvania, we are indebted to Alexander Ellis Landry of the U.S. Census Bureau, Rima Selius, reference librarian at the Community Library of the Shenango Valley, and the editors and reporters at the Sharon *Herald* newspaper. Barbara Wadors, meanwhile, made our busy lives manageable while we worked on this book—no small feat.

A few words about our editor at Harvard Business Review Press, Ania Wieckowski. If ever there was an editor who brought out the very best in her authors—who pushed them to dig deeper, think harder, and explain better without ever trying to restrict their freedom to write with passion or in their own fashion—she was it. All her writers should thank their lucky stars for her.

As for our agent, Jim Levine of the Levine/Greenberg Agency in New York, he was (as always) a man of few words throughout the long effort. But when he did speak, it mattered. No fluff, no hype—just sound advice and an exquisite handle on the world of books and publishing.

It is no exaggeration to say that this book would not have been written had not Kevin Rivette urged me one day to stop complaining about the worsening state of affairs in Silicon Valley and do something about it. He then introduced me to David Kline, perhaps the one person with the talent and experience to help me accomplish this mission and guide the book through the rocky shoals of publishing. Kevin and David had previously collaborated on what is still the most influential book on intellectual property ever written: *Rembrandts in the Attic*.

Finally, on a more personal note, I want to thank my brother Carl for his suggestion some fifty years ago that a military academy might offer me a path to a wider world of knowledge and accomplishment than I might otherwise find in a steelworker's life. And indeed, the U.S. Naval Academy and Marine Corps did teach me the skills and values I needed not only to succeed, but also to never forget where I came from or lose sight of what this nation has given me.

For both my coauthor and myself, our final acknowledgment must go to our families—to our wives and our children—whose patience, forbearance, and support are more important to an author in the grip of a book deadline than the casual reader might ever imagine.

Introduction:
The Lost Decade

I've been a high-tech entrepreneur and CEO for more than thirty-five years. During that time, I've been privileged to take part in some of the most exciting technological breakthroughs of the postwar era. I helped grow the first commercial Internet company (Telenet) in the 1970s, helped develop the first voice mail and voice-data networks in the 1980s, and in the 1990s, led one of America's largest Internet service providers to a multimillion-dollar initial public stock offering (IPO) and then a billion-dollar sale to XO Communications. Then, in the early 2000s, I was CEO of a company called Danger that developed the first hugely popular smartphone with social networking capability, branded the T-Mobile Sidekick. We sold the company to Microsoft in 2008 for several hundred million dollars. My new company, Tessera, is at the forefront of semiconductor miniaturization technologies that enable the creation of ever-smaller cameras, cellphones, and other electronic devices.

All told, I have helped to create more than six thousand jobs and return $8 billion to investors. So obviously my work experience has given me some firsthand insight into a subject that many academics are only now beginning to study more closely—namely, the surprisingly powerful role that small start-up businesses play in job creation and economic growth.

But it's my life experience growing up as the son of a steelworker that has taught me the vital importance of this issue for the future of the middle class and, indeed, the fate of the nation.

Consider the questions on so many people's minds these days:

Why is it that two-income families can barely make it today, whereas when I was young, a middle-class family could usually do fine on just one income?

Why did America once have money for schools and GI Bills and interstate highways, but today can't even repair a couple of broken bridges without putting our grandchildren in debt?

And why does prosperity seem to be a fading memory for most of us, even as ever-greater riches accrue to an ever-smaller few of us?

The answers I offer in this book may surprise you.

I grew up in Sharon, Pennsylvania, right on the Ohio line. My father and mother had both emigrated from Germany, searching for a better life. Neither of them had graduated from high school, but my dad had gone through an apprenticeship program and become a skilled lithographer. He got a job at a U.S. Steel Products plant a few miles southwest of Sharon, supervising the printing of logos and labels on cans and other products. He worked at U.S. Steel Products all his life.

I chose not to follow my father into the mills. Instead, I won an appointment to the U.S. Naval Academy, where I received a first-class college education and then served my country as a young Marine captain in Vietnam. After the completion of my service, I went on to graduate school with help from the GI Bill, where I learned the information technology skills that proved so valuable during my career as a serial entrepreneur and CEO of five successful companies.

It's fair to say that I have achieved a degree of wealth and success that my father could never have imagined for himself. But he most certainly did imagine it for me. That's because he believed in the American Dream.

And why not? Looking back at my youth in Sharon, I'm struck by how good life really was for working people back then. In those days, the citizens of Sharon enjoyed a prosperous middle-class existence. Almost everyone we knew owned their own homes. My family even bought a small vacation cottage by a nearby lake. And the local economy offered all that anyone needed to enjoy a decent, upwardly mobile life: good public schools, local hospitals and colleges, a bustling retail center, and plenty of jobs not only for factory workers, tradesmen, and service providers but also for doctors, teachers, lawyers, and professionals of every sort as well.

So why is it that life once worked so well for middle-class communities like Sharon, whereas today so many of them, including now even my adopted home of Silicon Valley, are slowly but surely being hollowed out and stripped of opportunity for the middle class?

Two reasons. In the first place, back then America led the world in scientific and technological innovation. Every major advance in science and engineering after World War II—whether in aerospace, semiconductors, computing, telecommunications, or the Internet—was achieved right here in the United States of America. And each one of these breakthroughs gave birth to a brand-new industry generating hundreds of billions of dollars in economic output and millions of new jobs.

Simply put, America was the global leader in innovation. And as economists have demonstrated—most notably Robert Solow, who won the Nobel Prize in Economics for his work on the sources of economic growth—technological innovation accounts for at least 80 percent of a nation's economic growth and increases in living standards.

But the second reason why life in Sharon was so prosperous is that those technological innovations were inextricably linked to the high-value manufacturing of new products and services. This not only provided well-paying jobs for manufacturing workers. It also served as a powerful economic force multiplier that increased purchasing power for the whole community and created as many as fifteen jobs outside manufacturing—in skilled trades, engineering, product design, transport and supply, and many service sectors—for every position on the factory floor.

That's what enabled the wealth created by technological innovation to be diffused *throughout* society and produce income gains not just for some highly educated elite, but for the masses of ordinary citizens as well. That's what created the greatest middle class in the world.

Beginning in the 1980s, however, our nation began to divorce innovation from production. In our arrogance and our naiveté, we told ourselves that so long as America did the "creative" work, the inventing, we could let other nations do the "grunt" work, the manufacturing. We did not yet understand that a nation that no longer makes things will eventually forget how to invent them.

Today, the innovation-fueled prosperity that Americans once enjoyed is vanishing before our eyes. Despite a few high-profile gadgets like the iPod and iPhone (both manufactured overseas using Asian components), the innovation engine that has powered the U.S. economy to unmatched prosperity for more than a century is beginning to fail, threatening the way we work and live. Real per capita income is down. Job growth nationwide is stalled (and so far unable to recover from the recession). And promising new start-ups—the creators of tomorrow's new jobs and new industries—are being ravaged by a perfect storm of dire business conditions and dumb government policies that make even Apple cofounder Steve Wozniak doubt that an industry-creating start-up like Apple could even get off the ground were it just starting out today.

Meanwhile, we hardly make anything any more, but instead buy everything we need from those nations that do. No wonder the $30 billion trade surplus in advanced technology products that America enjoyed just one decade ago has now become a $56 billion *deficit*.

Not a very smart way to run an economy.

And as our nation spins its wheels, seemingly unable to generate the new jobs or new breakthroughs we so badly need in alternative energy, gene therapy, cancer treatment, and other scientific and technical fields, Europe and especially Asia have begun to capture the leadership of crucial emerging technology sectors—and the jobs that go with them. China now dominates the $30 billion solar power industry, even though the first device to convert solar energy to electricity was patented right here in the U.S. at AT&T's Bell Labs in 1957. South Korea's LG Chemical is producing the rechargeable lithium-ion batteries that General Motors uses in its Chevy Volt electric car. Singapore now leads the world in some of the most promising areas of biotech and medical research. And even in high-tech industries that America dominated just a decade ago—computers and communications, software, semiconductors, next-generation LED lighting, and the advanced materials used in a wide array of consumer and industrial products—other nations have now raced ahead of us, to the benefit of their economies rather than ours.

As a report from the Information Technology & Innovation Foundation (ITIF) noted, of the forty most advanced nations on earth, the United States ranks dead last in the innovation progress it has made over the last decade.

But wait, you ask, isn't America still innovating? Just look at the emergence in recent years of all those exciting new social media ventures like Facebook and Twitter.

And it's true. A hundred different flavors of Twitter and Facebook have sprung up in the last decade, sparking new businesses and reshaping our lives in ways that will yield great value for society in the years ahead. Still, something vital is missing from this new crop of innovations.

Jobs.

Not that some jobs aren't being created in the burgeoning social media industry, of course. Clearly, some are. But employment experts say that most social media positions, at least within existing firms, are being filled by repositioning traditional public relations staffers into new roles.

As for employment at social media start-ups themselves, consider this: Facebook has 500 million users and on January 3, 2011, its market value jumped from an estimated $35 billion to a staggering $50 billion. By midyear 2011, it may top $70 billion. Yet it employs only 1,400 people.

By way of contrast, the $35 billion Sony Corporation employs more than 170,000 people, $50 billion Boeing employs 157,000 people, and the $70 billion Walt Disney Company employs 144,000 people.

But perhaps these comparisons are unfair. Sony and Boeing, at least, are manufacturers, whereas Facebook is a light-footed Web company.

So let's compare Facebook to another Web company—Google. At a comparable stage of its life, when it, too, was seven years old, Google employed 10,674 people.

And therein lies the problem with innovation today: for the first time in our history, the connection between technological innovation and job creation has broken down. And for the first time also, the wealth created by innovation is going mostly just to a handful of founders and venture capitalists rather than to many thousands of employees, not to mention the community at large.

In short, Facebook's market value-per-employee ratio may be a venture capitalist's dream. But it's a nightmare for a nation that has always depended on the job-creating magic of innovation for its prosperity.

Why Write a Book?

In a million years, I never would have imagined that I would one day write a book. Like most entrepreneurs, I've spent my whole life focused entirely (if not maniacally) on growing my little start-ups into successful market leaders.

But recently things changed. Over the last decade—many of us in Silicon Valley call it "the lost decade"—the innovation ecosystem for start-ups began to break down dramatically in the Valley and across the nation. Promising young entrepreneurs could no longer get their patent applications approved in a timely manner from the U.S. Patent Office and, as a result, could not obtain the venture capital funding they needed to develop their new products, services, or medical treatments for rollout to the public. Successful start-ups could no longer undertake IPOs and access the public markets for the large-scale funds needed to ramp up their hiring and R&D efforts. High-tech manufacturers—especially in technology fields we invented and once led—fled pell-mell offshore, taking with them the jobs as well as the R&D skills needed at home. And the once-vibrant heterogeneous culture of Silicon Valley, the bellwether of the nation's innovation future, began to hollow out and lose its middle-class character and upward mobility.

The American Dream made everything possible for me. So how can I stand idly by while the innovation engine that enabled my generation to advance in life sputters to a halt for the next generation? I am also no enemy of wealth, obviously. But how can I remain silent as the growing income inequality in our country reaches extremes that border on obscenity, or deny the threat that this poses to the future of the middle class and the democratic character of our society?

I am the son of a steelworker, and I did not work my whole life creating jobs and wealth just to spend my golden years in some Banana Republic of Silicon Valley.

So I decided to write a book.

A conceit, perhaps. But then isn't it a conceit any time an ordinary citizen lifts his or her gaze from life's everyday struggles to get involved in the national discourse? I've spent a fair bit of time in the last few years flying to Washington and lobbying senators and congressmen about how to fix the patent office and other matters. I've become a man with a mission, you might say. And as you'll read in this book, I discovered to my great surprise that an entrepreneurial voice really can affect the outcome of policy debates—especially because such voices are so rarely heard.

In writing this book, I enlisted as collaborator and coauthor the gifted Pulitzer Prize–nominated journalist and communications strategist David Kline. Together, we poured a year and a half of in-depth research, interviewing, and travel into the project. David brought far more than simply his talent for the human-scale narrative. He took my rough ideas, argued with me over them, and added quite a few ideas of his own. Together we synthesized it all into what I believe is a powerful road map for recovering our nation's innovation leadership and revitalizing our middle class.

The result of our effort is *Great Again*.

What's Different About This Book?

Several other books have spoken to the decline in America's innovation leadership in recent years. But *Great Again* is unique in three ways.

First, our book takes you into the very heart of our nation's entrepreneurial innovation community and lets you hear the uncensored voices of entrepreneurs, venture capitalists, and inventors themselves as they speak of their struggles and concerns. People such as Conrad Burke, CEO of the hot solar energy start-up Innovalight and winner of the 2010 Ernst & Young Emerging Entrepreneur of the Year award, provide an eye-opening view from the innovation trenches of the increasingly hostile environment faced by start-up entrepreneurs today.

We will also introduce you to some of the most respected "tribal elders" of Silicon Valley. Some are famous; others are less well known outside the community but no less experienced in the art of creating and nurturing new companies and new industries. From these veteran CEOs and venture capitalists, you will gain an insider's appreciation of precisely where and how the Silicon Valley model of entrepreneurial innovation—a model that every other nation is trying to copy—has ironically broken down right here in the United States, the land of its birth.

You'll also feel the frustrations of some of America's most prolific and dedicated inventors. Again, some are iconic figures in the innovation community, such as Larry Roberts, the guy who really did invent the Internet forty-four years ago, and Dean Kamen, developer of the first insulin pump, the first all-terrain electric wheelchair, and the first self-balancing people transporter, the Segway. Others, such as young Mirk Buzdum and his ninety-two-year-old partner Dick "Cappy" Capstran of Milwaukee, are little-known inventors struggling to forge an entrepreneurial future from America's Rust Belt decay. From them, you'll discover how the disgraceful underfunding of the patent office and the myopic cutbacks in government-funded basic research are leaving literally thousands of promising life-saving and job-creating discoveries stillborn.

Great Again is also unique in that we have made every effort to ensure that its critique of Washington's innovation policies is nonpartisan. To be sure, my coauthor and I each came to this project with our own biases and preconceptions—one of us from the right, the other from the left. But at our very first meeting to discuss this project, we agreed on a fact-based approach meant to ensure that the only thing that got into the book was the truth, insofar as rigorous research and multiple, independent sources could verify it. Our recommendations for reform thus stand outside the battlefields of today's highly partisan politics and focus on only those measures that real-world experience suggests will actually work to stimulate innovation and job creation.

If, for example, research and the testimonials of countless entrepreneurs even in liberal-minded Silicon Valley indicate that U.S. tax policies are way out of line with norms elsewhere in the world and are hurting start-up growth, then some liberals may need to recognize that making the fat cats pay their fair share is not the *only* purpose of taxation. As progressive governments across Europe have discovered, creative tax policy can also help struggling young start-ups—especially in vital emerging cleantech fields like solar energy—compete much more successfully in today's challenging global economy, thereby creating more jobs for society.

And if, on the other hand, the facts demonstrate that it's actually the short-term profit seeking of large corporations and not the supposedly excessive demands of Big Labor that are responsible for the massive off-shoring of jobs over the last thirty years, then some conservatives may need to shift their focus from undermining the already-diminished role of unions in society to instead getting the United States to match the successful incentives programs offered to manufacturers by other nations.

In truth, cluelessness about the specific needs of entrepreneurs is an equal-opportunity affliction in Washington. For every Democratic Congress that passes a health reform bill with new 1099 tax reporting rules that impose heavy new costs on small businesses, a Republican-led Congress passes a Sarbanes-Oxley law that requires small firms to implement the same costly accounting procedures meant to stop Big Business from pulling another Enron on us—even though small businesses pose zero risk to the overall economy. The only thing this 2002 law actually stopped, of course, was start-ups' ability to afford the vastly increased costs of going public, thereby crippling the IPO market and job creation (92 percent of which occurs after an IPO). It certainly didn't stop Wall Street from recklessly sinking the whole economy in 2008.

Yet there is every reason to believe that if only our political leaders truly understood the vital connection between start-up businesses and job creation, they could unite on specific measures to help nurture these innovative small firms. And this is where *Great Again* is unique once more. This book offers an entirely new framework for understanding how to revitalize the nation's technological leadership and restore the historic connection between innovation and job creation.

At the center of this new framework lies the entrepreneurial start-up. Nothing is more crucial to America's economic future than the high-tech start-up. That's because, as noted earlier, virtually all economic growth and increases in per capita income stem from breakthrough technological innovation. And as our research discovered, the only force in society that creates those transformational technological innovations—the kind that give birth to whole new industries and millions of new jobs—are small start-ups.

To be sure, a highly creative large company such as Apple can develop extraordinarily innovative new products—and even whole new categories of products, such as the iPod, iPhone, and iPad. But the evidence shows that except in one or two cases over the last hundred years, the only firms that developed breakthrough inventions that gave rise to whole new industries and millions of new jobs—inventions such as the automobile, the airplane, the semiconductor, personal computers, and the Internet with its $4 trillion-a-year economy—were small start-ups.

Surprising, I know, but true. Just as surprising is the new research from multiple sources that shows that start-ups are also the *one and only* consistent source of new job growth in the U.S. Until now, the conventional wisdom has always been that small businesses create most jobs. But thanks to a new Census Bureau database called Business Dynamics Statistics (BDS) that correlates job creation with the annual number of new business starts, we now know that it's not so much small businesses that create jobs but *new* businesses that do so (although most are obviously also small). *All* net new job growth in the U.S. since 1977, in fact, is due to start-ups. If you took start-ups out of the picture and looked only at established firms, job growth in the U.S. over the last thirty-four years would actually be negative.

As senior researcher Tim Kane of the Ewing Marion Kauffman Foundation put it, "When it comes to U.S. job growth, start-up companies aren't everything. They're the only thing."

Ultimately, then, everything depends upon start-ups: Job creation. Our standard of living. Our prosperity as a nation. The American Dream itself.

All of it depends upon technology start-ups being able to obtain capital, hire people, expand their R&D efforts, and grow into independent public companies that can create the breakthrough products, services, and medical advances that drive our national prosperity.

This is a staggering thought for policy makers to try to wrap their minds around.

The Road Forward

Once we grasp that essential point, the architecture of a solution reveals itself. And that is to identify and remove the most damaging roadblocks to start-up growth and success.

Before we focus on those roadblocks, however, I should say a few words about what's not in this book. We did not address the crisis in education, for example, despite the fact that America hardly needs the National Academy of Sciences to tell us, as it recently did, that our educational system is a mess and that we are not producing near the number of science and engineering graduates we need to keep the United States at the forefront of scientific and technological progress.

Education is a serious problem in the U.S., and sooner or later we will have to deal with it. But it's not clear at this time that anyone fully understands how to do that—or that as a nation we have the economic resources or the political unity to tackle it even if we did. Indeed, fixing education may simply be one of those "wicked problems," as author and innovation expert John Kao calls them, that do not, at least at present, permit of any immediate solution. Therefore we have not addressed education except incidentally as it pertains to other topics, such as the need to rebuild America's government-funded basic science research effort.

Instead, *Great Again* focuses on the five most crucial, interconnected, and eminently achievable reforms we could undertake that would make an immediate and dramatic difference in kick-starting the nation's innovation engine and getting job creation moving again.

Liberate entrepreneurs from start-up–killing tax and regulatory shackles. Chapter 1 documents how a critical mass of regulatory and tax burdens have combined with a breakdown of the Silicon Valley venture capital model to block many high-value, job-creating start-ups from getting funded, scaling up, and undertaking the initial public offerings needed to start hiring on a large scale and building new industries. A few simple reforms here could help regenerate the IPO market and the job creation engine that depends on it.

Fix the patent office so we can stimulate invention and entrepreneurship again. Chapter 2 shows how the chronic diversion of funds from the patent office, America's "innovation agency," is preventing thousands of promising start-ups from getting the patents they need to obtain venture funding and commercialize their inventions. Who, after all, would invest the huge sums required to develop a new medical treatment unless they had at least the promise of exclusivity that a patent offers? And what, other than a patent, can stop a giant corporation from stealing a start-up's discovery and either crushing that start-up or burying its competing invention? Our estimates are that simply clearing the backlog of applications at the overburdened and underfunded patent office would create as many as 2.25 million jobs by 2014, not to mention getting thousands of innovative new products and medical treatments out to the public.

Offer meaningful incentives to bring high-tech manufacturing back to America. Manufacturing is the vehicle through which the wealth created by innovation is dispersed throughout all of society and not just to a tiny elite. Yet despite the widespread myth that America can succeed simply by specializing in innovation and letting others do the production, chapter 3 vividly documents the human cost to the middle class of our nation's thirty-year fetish for offshoring manufacturing. For contrary to the conventional wisdom, new research proves that when manufacturing leaves, R&D always follows. But can we really compete with Chinese labor? Absolutely, and as Germany shows, at U.S. wages, too. We need only do what every other nation but America has done: offer meaningful tax and other incentives to bring manufacturing home. I won't deny that our trading relations with some countries are unfair. But ultimately the most effective response to their manufacturing and export power is to develop our own once again.

Ease immigration rules to transform the current brain drain into a brain gain. Did you know that more than half of all high-tech start-ups in Silicon Valley were founded by a foreign-born entrepreneur or engineer— including such great companies (and huge employers) as Intel, Google, Yahoo!, eBay, PayPal, and many more? As chapter 4 demonstrates, these talented, educated immigrants don't take American jobs; they create them—by the millions! Yet our post-9/11 immigration policies are driving many of these people back to home countries like India and China, where they put their talents to work building those economies rather than ours. It's time to end immigration policies that only shoot ourselves in the foot.

Create smarter government programs to support basic science and research. Just as start-ups need a temperate regulatory climate in order to grow, so too do they need a soil that is richly fertilized with the nutrients of government-funded basic research. Chapter 5 introduces you to the man who led the Department of Defense research team that designed and built the early Internet. He reveals how the government-funded research programs that gave us the embryonic Internet, laser, GPS, magnetic resonance imaging, and DNA sequencing technologies later commercialized by start-ups are now threatened by myopic leadership and inadequate funding. Talk about cutting off our noses to spite our faces!

Our Saving Grace

The clock is ticking on America's future. The innovation underpinnings of our economic strength grow weaker by the month. Yet with all our problems, our nation still has something that is unique in all the world: a culture of enterprising inventiveness in which risk is rewarded and failure seen as just another learning experience on the road to eventual success.

Wherever I go in Europe and Asia, entrepreneurs and government officials alike tell me that this is without a doubt what they admire most about America. In their own countries, if an entrepreneur fails, usually he or she is finished. End of story. In some places, bankruptcy laws even prevent a failed entrepreneur from ever owning a business again.

Not so in the United States of America, the land of the second (and third) chance. That is our saving grace. That, and a remarkable ability to sooner or later pull our heads out of the sand and correct our mistakes that once led the great Winston Churchill to remark, "The American people always do the right thing—after they've tried every other alternative."

Well, America has tried the alternatives—both the "big government" approach and the "no government" approach. Neither succeeded in revitalizing the innovation engine that drives America's economic future because neither truly listened to the voice of the start-up entrepreneur who is the source of all breakthrough innovation and job growth.

Indeed, entrepreneurs are just about the only Americans *without* a voice in Washington. Big Business certainly has a voice. So does labor, as do teachers, retailers, bankers, insurers, doctors, and just about every social and economic interest group you can think of. Only entrepreneurs lack an organized voice. Yet ironically, entrepreneurs are "the vital few" upon whom all of society depends for economic progress, to quote the distinguished economist Jonathan Hughes.

It's time we tried a *smart government* approach—one that balances what Adam Smith called the "minimal but necessary" role of government with policies that effectively support the true engines of job creation and economic growth in America: entrepreneurial start-up businesses.

It's time we gave the leading role in the American economic drama to the start-up entrepreneur who creates wealth, not the Wall Street trader who merely manipulates it.

—Henry R. "Hank" Nothhaft
February 2011

Regulation

Liberating Entrepreneurs to Create Jobs

*T*he television reporter, wearing white laboratory coveralls and a hairnet, stands in the futuristic "clean room" of a Silicon Valley high-tech start-up company.

"It's the power behind more efficient, more profitable solar panels," he announces earnestly. "We'll take you inside the Silicon Valley start-up getting all sorts of ink . . . " he pauses, then looks at the bottle of dark liquid in his hands, "for its ink!"

Cut to images of a solar cell manufacturing line followed by shots of vast landscapes of solar panels deployed in various locations worldwide.

"The solar cell business is hot," explains the reporter. "They're being made by the billions, finding their way to rooftops all over the world. But as the solar cell business gets more competitive, it may be a jar of ink that separates the winners from the also-rans."

Close-up of a putty knife scooping out some inky-black goop from a jar.

"That ink is made here, inside the Silicon Valley headquarters of Innovalight, a start-up that's getting a lot of ink because of its latest deal—a three-year contract with Chinese solar giant JA Solar to sell its Silicon Ink to the panel maker. The patented ink, guarded as closely as the Coca-Cola formula, makes each cell and solar panel better."

Close-up on Innovalight's CEO Conrad Burke:

"It makes the solar cells way more efficient, and more importantly, it increases the bottom line of the solar cell manufacturing company."

Cut to various shots of technicians working in Innovalight's lab.

"That's good business for both sides," says the reporter.

Close-up on Conrad Burke again:

"Four billion solar cells will be produced worldwide this year. If we can have our technology put on a lot of those wafers that make those solar cells, we'll be pretty happy."

Cut to various scenes of solar panel arrays deployed around the world.

"Look at it this way," concludes the reporter. "If solar panel companies are at war, then these guys are the arms dealers."

Conrad Burke doesn't look like much of an arms dealer. Nor would most people peg him for a physicist, despite his easy familiarity with nanotechnology jargon and his advanced degree in physics from Trinity College in Dublin, Ireland, where he was born and raised. Instead, the forty-four-year-old Burke appears to be the classic Silicon Valley entrepreneur—intense, engaging if not charismatic, and wholly committed to the belief that his company's innovation will lead to a big leap forward for humanity and a very profitable business for himself and his investors.

Indeed, the only difference between Burke and most other entrepreneurs is that he has the rare good fortune of being able to live out the classic entrepreneurial dream scenario: getting in on a huge new gold rush—in this case, the $30 billion worldwide solar energy business—and, instead of having to compete with everyone else, simply selling the tools that everyone else needs to compete against each other. Imagine a pick and shovel merchant during the California gold rush of 1849 and you get the picture.

Yet as you'll shortly discover, despite his enviable position as an entrepreneur, Burke faces a funding, tax, and regulatory environment that makes it very difficult for any start-up to succeed anymore.

Described as a "maverick" in a 2009 Discovery Channel documentary, Burke left Ireland at twenty-one to pursue a high-tech career in Japan. After several years working for NEC, he came to the United States to become the youngest director ever at AT&T and Lucent. An entrepreneurial impulse led him to try his luck in a high-tech start-up in San Diego, but that business collapsed during the dot-com bust. After a brief stint as a venture capitalist, Burke decided that entrepreneurship was what he loved most and in 2005 took over the helm at Innovalight.

Burke has been in the spotlight ever since. Profiles on CNN and in *Time* magazine. Stories in the *Wall Street Journal, New York Times,* and *Greentech Media.* A ten-page portrait in the book *Earth: The Sequel.* Meetings with political leaders such as former Irish Prime Minister Brian Cowen, former presidential candidate John McCain, and ex–California governor Arnold Schwarzenegger. He has been invited to the White House twice and in 2006 received the prestigious Technology Pioneer Award from the World Economic Forum at Davos. In October 2010, Burke won Ernst & Young's coveted Emerging Entrepreneur of the Year award.

Burke understands, of course, that all this attention is really for his company's flagship Silicon Ink, a bottle of which he offers for inspection. Up close, it's a bit of a disappointment. Instead of the futuristic images of nanotechnology we've come to expect from movies like *Terminator 2,* with its shape-shifting liquid-metal cyborg, this stuff looks like an ink-colored cross between ordinary shoe polish and old-fashioned axle grease.

But there is nothing old-fashioned about Silicon Ink. This is tomorrow's physics applied to today's energy problems, nanotechnology to reshape the economics of an entire industry. Thanks to more than a hundred man-years of research and development, Burke and his team have succeeded in doing what no one else had done before: reengineering silicon crystals at the atomic scale in order to produce liquid silicon semiconductor material.

"The nanoparticles are about five nanometers in size," he explains. "That's five-*billionths* of a meter, smaller than a virus. I mean, if you were shaving in the morning, from the time you picked up the razor until you actually brought it to your face, your hair would have grown ten nanometers. So our particles are half the size of that one second's worth of hair growth."

Reducing silicon to nanoscale offers two key advantages for solar cell production. In the first place, it enables Innovalight to optimize the energy output of its liquefied solar cell material. The company does this by fine-tuning the size and concentration of silicon nanoparticles, called quantum dots, to take advantage of the sun's full spectrum of light. It also boosts the number of electrons that each nanoparticle throws off when struck by a photon of light.

In addition, because nanoscale silicon remains liquid at much lower temperatures than the 2,552 degrees Fahrenheit melting point of normal silicon, the ink can be printed or "painted" onto standard five- or six-inch semiconductor wafers using low-cost industrial screen printers. The result is a solar cell with a higher energy conversion rate and lower cost per watt—one that doesn't force manufacturers to use costly new materials or redesign their production process.

"It's a completely radical way to think about how semiconductor material can be deployed," Burke explains. "And it's all patented up the kazoo— patents and trade secrets. You have to buy the ink, and we're the only ones who know how to make it. But even if you had the ink somehow and tried to use it yourself, it wouldn't work. You need a process. We need to show you what to do, how to use it. And that process is also patented." Innovalight currently has sixty pending or issued patents in its competitive arsenal.

Innovalight's new technology is getting results. The firm made big news in September 2009 when its silicon ink achieved an unprecedented 18 percent conversion efficiency in tests conducted by the U.S. Department of Energy's National Renewable Energy Laboratory (NREL). Conversion efficiency refers to the percentage of sunlight that a solar cell can convert into usable energy. At the time, standard solar cells could only achieve a 15 to 16 percent conversion rate. By the middle of 2010, Innovalight had reached a 19 percent conversion rate—still a full percentage point above anyone else in the industry. By mid-2011, the company expects to achieve a 20 percent conversion rate—a full 2 percentage points better than other solar cells—and its target for the year 2012 is a 3-percentage-point advantage over traditional solar cells.

If you're wondering what's the big deal about an increase of 1 to 3 percentage points in solar efficiency, bear in mind that every 1 percent boost in the solar energy conversion rate yields $100 million in additional profit per year to a solar cell manufacturer with a gigawatt production line. No wonder JA Solar signed a three-year deal with Innovalight in July 2010 to supply the ink, or that another Chinese solar maker, Yingli Green Energy, did the same two weeks later. Three months after that, a third Chinese solar maker, Solarfun, signed on as well, followed soon after by JinkoSolar Holdings, one of China's largest solar manufacturers and a firm that is listed on the New York Stock Exchange.

Is Silicon Ink the Holy Grail of the solar industry? It's probably more accurate to say that the ink is a very important step on the road to making solar energy more cost-effective. As a July 14, 2010, report on JA Solar's deal with Innovalight by industry analyst Jesse Pichel of Jefferies & Company noted, "[Silicon Ink's] 1-point improvement in conversion efficiency will reduce per watt silicon and wafer costs by 6–7 percent." Reducing the cost of solar energy is one of the major challenges in transforming solar energy from a niche industry into a ubiquitous and economical power source for industry and consumers worldwide.

As for Innovalight itself, Burke said he expects that it'll be a $100 million company by the end of 2012, and "very, very profitable." With $50 million in venture funding from U.S., Norwegian, and Singaporean investors and growing success in the market, the company is "hopefully on a vector toward an IPO," says Burke, which would enable the firm to maintain its independence and obtain the growth capital it needs to scale up hiring and innovation.

For all of Innovalight's achievements, however, Burke concedes that, like all entrepreneurs today, he faces a whole new set of challenges that threaten even the brightest start-up's prospects for success and have already begun eroding the health of the innovation ecosystem itself.

"I'm passionate about this country," he insists. "There's nowhere else I would want to be. But I do worry, because it's getting a lot harder to succeed in this environment. Capital is much less available. It's probably harder for a start-up to raise money than it's ever been. Especially for any sort of manufacturing. Yes, Silicon Valley is still innovating. But it's mostly the Twitters and the Diggs and other software start-ups that don't need much capital. Which is a big part of why we're getting trumped by China in clean technologies like solar that do require capital."

Indeed, Innovalight itself originally had a very different business plan. "If we had had this conversation two years ago," Burke says, "I would have told you that I was planning to raise capital to build a 200-megawatt solar manufacturing plant. But pretty quickly I discovered that there's very little stomach in the venture capital community for that kind of $90 to $100 million capital-intensive commitment. I also realized that it would be very difficult to compete as a manufacturer in the U.S., given the incentives that China and other nations offer manufacturers but America doesn't. So in the end I decided it would be smarter to build the ink and license the technology to manufacturers than try to manufacture ourselves."

He pauses a moment. "I'm actually happy with my decision. I've got a lot less capital-intensive business. It's going to be a lot more profitable. It's very rich in IP [intellectual property]. True, I'm not going to employ as many people as I would have with a factory. But I can tell you if I had gone out and tried to raise triple-digit millions of dollars to build a factory in the U.S., I would have been kicked out of the boardroom and down the stairs."

As you'll soon see, most of Silicon Valley's movers and shakers openly acknowledge that it is almost impossible to obtain funding for any sort of capital-intensive start-up business. The problem is not simply the limitations on capital or on the types of innovation that can attract funding. It's also the increasingly burdensome business environment for start-ups.

"It's getting really stifling here," Burke explains. "The bureaucracy, the fire department and environmental permitting, it really slowed us down and cost us money. I'm all for doing things properly. We don't want to poison the environment. We're committed to that and it's one reason why I'm in the solar business. But for a little start-up like ours, the process of starting a business has gotten pretty painful. And the taxes here, I mean, they're ridiculous. We had to pay almost a million dollar tax on $10 million worth of manufacturing equipment that we bought from Germany. That's not a tax on our income; it's a tax on growing our business."

Burke here refers to the 2003 extension of the use tax, essentially a sales tax on tangible property bought outside the state or over the Internet. Such a tax is controversial enough when applied to consumer goods purchased by individuals—only nineteen states include a use tax line on state income tax returns. It's even more controversial when applied to businesses. Iowa, for example, offers an exemption for business purchases of certain machinery and equipment. California does not.

But perhaps the biggest long-term problem—not just for entrepreneurs and investors but, more important, for society as well—is what people here in Silicon Valley call "the lack of exits."

"The ability to go public, to do an IPO, has definitely dried up to a large extent over the last ten years," Burke points out. "And that's the last thing we need—to lose those IPOs for venture-backed start-ups."

Adds Pascal Levonsohn, a venture capitalist and author of a textbook on venture capital: "IPOs in the U.S. for small capitalization emerging growth companies, the core job creation engines for the U.S. economy, are disappearing. If we don't fix the IPO problem in America, we will not fix the job problem in America. I can't understand why our legislators and policy makers don't understand this. If they did, there would be no higher priority than promoting regulatory and tax reform to stimulate IPOs again."

If there's no way for a start-up to fund the scaling-up of its innovation efforts through the public capital markets, then the only other option (or "exit") is to be acquired by a large company. As we'll vividly demonstrate later in this chapter, that usually kills the innovation right in the cradle, before it can even begin to work its job-creating magic in society.

To be sure, entrepreneurs have always faced tough challenges, from lack of funding to burdensome regulation and taxes. What's different now is that in the last decade these problems have grown and hardened into embedded structural flaws that have now achieved enough critical mass to fracture the underlying architecture of entrepreneurial innovation in America.

That architecture, often called the "Silicon Valley model," is the envy of the world, and for good reason. Nourished by a delicate alchemy of entrepreneurialism, venture capital, government support for basic science research, and what used to be a relatively laissez-faire regulatory climate, risk takers with little more than a vision and new technology have for decades launched start-up ventures that have gone on to create whole new industries and millions of new jobs. These entrepreneurs have truly been "the vital few," in economic theorist Jonathan Hughes's famous phrase, upon whom the welfare of all of society has depended.

In 1957, a start-up called Fairchild Semiconductor was formed by Robert Noyce, Jean Hoerni, Eugene Kleiner, and several other engineers to exploit the economic potential of the newly invented semiconductor integrated circuit. That start-up fueled the emergence of a $300 billion global semiconductor industry that today employs close to a million people and serves as the guts of an even larger $1.2 *trillion* consumer electronics industry that employs many millions more. Out of Fairchild later grew industry powerhouses such as Intel and National Semiconductor, not to mention the most famous venture capital firm in the world, Kleiner Perkins Caufield & Byers, which helped launch AOL, Intuit, Google, Genentech, and three hundred other high-tech leaders.

Nineteen years later, Steve Wozniak and college dropout Steve Jobs started Apple out of the latter's garage, ignoring the sclerotic prognostications of tech giants such as Xerox and Hewlett-Packard that there would never be a mass market for personal computers. Today, one billion PCs are in use worldwide, and the industry, which employs millions worldwide and generates $300 billion in revenues, is expected to sell another billion PCs by 2014.

At around the same time, another college dropout named Bill Gates launched Microsoft, dedicated to the then-laughable proposition that software was not just the "mayonnaise on the sandwich" of hardware (to quote early employee and now billionaire Nathan Myhrvold) but something valuable in its own right for which people would pay. That tiny firm became a $60 billion a year global enterprise at the heart of a software industry that employs 21 million people worldwide and generates $330 billion in revenues—$1.2 trillion if you include all information technology products and services. The market research firm IDC estimates that companies just within Microsoft's ecosystem—that is, the five hundred thousand hardware, software, and services firms that use, sell, or service Microsoft software—earn more than $500 billion annually and pay more than $100 billion in taxes to their local economies around the world. All this from just one start-up!

What those start-ups did for the semiconductor, PC, and software industries, Genentech and FedEx did for the $100 billion biotech and the $180 billion air express industries. We can thank entrepreneurs Herbert Boyer and Fred Smith for that. (Fred was in Basic School at Quantico with me, and we served as young marine officers in Vietnam at around the same time.)

Then there's the Internet, first created by a 1967 Defense Department research project led by researcher-turned-entrepreneur Larry Roberts (profiled in chapter 5), who then founded the first public data network, Telenet. Start-ups such as UUNET and America Online offered early online access in the 1980s, but the commercialization of the Internet only really took off with start-up Netscape's 1994 release of the first mass-market Web browser, used to navigate the hypertext Web created by Tim Berners-Lee at the European Organization for Nuclear Research (CERN). The 1999 launch of search start-up Google then made the vast resources of the Internet far more accessible to hundreds of millions of people (and turned "google" into a verb in the dictionary).

Today, one-quarter of all humans on the planet use the Internet, and according to the U.S. Census Bureau, business and consumer e-commerce is now a $4 *trillion* a year business. Add in the value of the Internet as a communications medium and in reshaping the dynamics of industry itself, and we're probably looking at an industry with a $6 *trillion* impact on global society. That's one-tenth of the total gross domestic product (GDP) of all nations on earth combined—all thanks to a government research project and the Silicon Valley model of entrepreneurial innovation.

Today that model, and the whole innovation ecosystem built around it, is at risk. During the last decade, which many of us in the Valley call "the lost decade," much of the innovation activity and the wealth creation generated by the semiconductor, PC, and software industries has fled from our shores. In some of tomorrow's key technology sectors—alternative energy, next-generation LED illumination, advanced displays, and new materials—America has now been reduced to merely a bit player.

As the *New York Times* put it in an article about the 2010 Silicon Valley Index on the health of the region's innovation engine: "Silicon Valley's economy is sputtering and risks permanently stalling." And it's not just Silicon Valley that is at risk. As the entrepreneur and author Judy Estrin told the *Times*, "Silicon Valley is both a barometer and a spark for the rest of the country, and if we don't protect that innovation [environment] here, it's going to be hard to sustain [it elsewhere] in the country."

It's impossible to overstate the threat this poses to our nation. Don't forget, virtually all economic growth and increases in living standards come from breakthrough technological innovation, and almost all of that transformative innovation—the kind that creates new industries and millions of new jobs—is conducted by start-ups. Later in this chapter, we'll discuss some rather startling new research from multiple researchers on the sources of job creation, but suffice it to say that all net job growth in the U.S. over the last thirty years has also come from start-ups.

So when entrepreneurs such as Conrad Burke warn that start-up growth is being seriously undermined—and his comments were seconded by dozens of entrepreneurs, venture capitalists, economists, and Silicon Valley "tribal elders" interviewed for this book—we would do well to listen. They are talking about America's sole engine of job creation grinding to a halt.

These aren't the sort of people who usually cry wolf. Entrepreneurs are generally optimists by nature, and if anything, says Emmett Carson, author of the aforementioned Silicon Valley Index, "We're [used to] sitting on our laurels and singing 'We're Silicon Valley!'" Not any more. Today, says Carson, "We *are* at risk."

Different people, of course, point, *Rashomon*-like, to different aspects of the problem. Many talk about "the crisis in venture capital." Others bemoan "the demise of the IPO." Some condemn the rapid erosion of high-value manufacturing in the United States. But almost everyone, even in the liberal stronghold of Silicon Valley, expresses dismay at how decidedly challenging the tax and regulatory environment has become for start-ups over the last decade.

It is no easy task to offer a fully dimensionalized portrait of the erosion of America's innovation ecosystem during the "lost decade," nor to tease out its various elements and show their interconnections. But one way to try, perhaps, is to ask three simple questions:

- Could a great company like Apple *get funded,* were it just starting out today?

- Could Apple *be built* today?

- Could Apple *succeed* today?

Could Apple Get Funded Today?

The story of Apple's birth is old, but it still bears repeating—especially for those who don't understand how uniquely uncomplicated it used to be to start new ventures in America.

In 1976, Steve Jobs and Steve Wozniak, two old friends from high school, began building the world's first fully assembled personal computer in Jobs's bedroom, and then later his parents' garage. They convinced the owner of a local electronics shop to sell the finished computers—called the Apple 1—at $666.66 each ($2,500 in today's dollars), $500 of which the shop owner would give to them. Early results were good. But it soon became clear to Jobs and Wozniak that they were going to need financing to expand the business. They prevailed upon Mike Markkula, a former Intel executive who had put some of his own money into Apple, to pitch the legendary Arthur Rock, one of Silicon Valley's original venture capitalists, and a man who had previously backed Fairchild Semiconductor and Intel, among other high-tech successes.

Here's how Rock described his encounter with the Apple founders in a 2002 interview with the Silicon Genesis oral history project at Stanford University: "I met with Jobs and [co-founder Steve] Wozniak, and, gee, I really didn't think I wanted to be involved with them. Steve Jobs had just returned from six months in India with a guru or whatever. And they didn't appear very well." What Rock meant by that, as he explained in a separate interview, was that "they kind of turned me off as people. Steve had a beard and goatee, didn't wear shoes, wore terrible clothes, hair down to his collar."

What's more, says Rock, "they were bragging about the blue box they had invented to steal money from the telephone companies" (the device enabled them to make long distance calls for free), "and I didn't like that too much. But Markkula kept after me and said, 'You've got to come down to the Homebrew Computer Show in San Jose.' I decided I would go down. And there were all these booths at the show, [but] there's nobody at any of the booths. They were all at the Apple booth. And I could not get close to the Apple booth. I mean, here I came down to see Apple and I couldn't even get there. So I decided there must be something to this."

Did he really think many consumers would buy a personal computer? According to Rock, "Steve's rhetoric—and he had plenty of rhetoric—was that everybody would use a personal computer eventually. [But] the idea of a personal computer got pooh-poohed at first [by most experts] because the only application people could think of initially was putting menus on the computer and putting the computer in the kitchen so a housewife could pull up her menus from the computer. That seemed kind of hokey to me. But in any event, I thought maybe there would be a market, and it turned out to be that there was."

Who knew, right? Well, obviously Steve Jobs knew. And Arthur Rock knew enough to trust that the people crowding Apple's booth knew. But very few others did, that's for sure.

Could a similar venture get funded today? Could a twenty-year-old college dropout, just back from six months in an ashram somewhere, attract funding for a capital-intensive venture based on the manufacture (yes, the *manufacture*) and sale of a $2,500 consumer product unlike any that had ever been bought by consumers before? One whose potential uses were at best unknown, and possibly nonexistent? And one for which the total current market size was exactly zero?

When we asked Apple cofounder Wozniak that question, he agreed that Apple probably couldn't get funding were it just starting out today. "It would be much harder for that to happen today," Wozniak acknowledged. "It's a changed battlefield. There's so much money at stake now, and you're competing against the whole world. It's also harder to manufacture in the U.S. And the venture capital game is different, less willing to take [those risks]."

James Beldock, the president of start-up ShotSpotter, agrees. His firm develops gunshot and explosion location and detection systems for use in law enforcement, homeland security, and the military. Its unique technology is built around a wide-area acoustic surveillance system that can operate in diverse environments, from urban communities to critical infrastructure, airports, and military bases. ShotSpotter's geo-location systems enable police officials in a city to know the exact location of a gunshot within five seconds of its occurrence, compared with the average three and a half minutes required for a 911 call to come in to dispatchers. More than a dozen cities now employ ShotSpotter's system (as does the FBI and military), and many have reported 30 to 40 percent reductions in violent crime and homicide rates in the areas covered by the systems.

Beldock describes the current climate of venture capital investing. "There's very little capacity in the system for investing in the future any more," he explains, pointing to a whole confluence of factors, from the lack of exits (more on this shortly) to venture capital's lower returns and longer time requirements compared with the situation a decade or two ago.

"Suddenly the VCs [venture capitalists] are turning around and saying, 'Good God, it's going to take us eight to ten years to get out of this damn thing when it used to require four?'" he observes. "So that raises all of the stakes. You know, they have to put so much more in to make their economics work. And the reason they have to do that is because the market is requiring them to deliver much more fully baked companies than it used to require. Yet at the same time, the expected value of the exit—the IPO or acquisition—is lower. So the returns are going to be lower." He laughs. "You know, you can make the same amount of money in four years or ten years, and depending, you'll look like a genius or an idiot."

The end result of the scale of economics being so much bigger yet the returns so much lower, insists Beldock, is that "the tolerance for amateur hour is necessarily lower." He describes ShotSpotter's own experience seeking funding earlier in its history: "When I presented ShotSpotter on Sand Hill Road, I ended up running through this list of requirements with the venture firms that almost sound absurd. You know, does this have the capacity to be a global business? Is this a business that will have millions of customers? Is this a business where you already have three, four, or five generations of product laid out?"

He laughs ruefully. "Those were the first three questions out of their mouths. And I just sat there, you know, and I said to myself, 'Jesus Christ, what are they trying to do? Create General Electric here? Or Google?' Even Google couldn't have answered all those questions affirmatively when it was just starting out."

In the end, ShotSpotter did receive funding from Lauder Partners, City Light Capital, Claremont Creek Ventures, and other investors. But other promising ventures did not. The "homerun-ism" that Beldock talks about suggests that a risky hardware start-up such as Apple would probably not be funded in today's environment, and as a result, would not have been able to develop a new industry that changed society and materially raised the standard of living for all Americans.

The question is, How many of today's Apples are not getting a chance?

"You got it!" says Beldock.

ShotSpotter's new CEO, John Peters, confirms Beldock's view of venture capital today. (Peters was executive vice president of start-up Concentric Network, one of the first nationwide Internet service providers, when I was its CEO in the mid-1990s. We led it to a $70 million IPO in 1997, followed by a $2.5 billion acquisition by XO Communications in 1999. I negotiated the deal with Dan Akerson, the CEO of Nextlink, who is now the new CEO of General Motors.)

"It's much more difficult to get new ventures going these days than it used to be," Peters says. "The overarching theme today is that you've got to do more with less. You've got to have what they call a 'lean start-up,' and work out a lot more risk ahead of time on a lot less money than you used to have to do."

What a difference from the bubbly euphoria of the dot-com boom. "I remember back in 2001 when I started this company Sigma Networks," Peters recalls. "I had Benchmark Capital as the primary investor. Now, every year they would have their annual get-together for all the CEOs of their portfolio companies. They'd fly the CEOs and the families out to Santa Fe, New Mexico. And we'd have some seminars in the morning, you know, and maybe have some authors come in to talk about their new business books, that sort of thing. Then we'd play in the afternoon. And at night they'd throw a big party. One night they took all of us out to a dude ranch and flew Willie Nelson and his band in for a concert."

Peters laughs. "Can you imagine that? Today they'd take you out to McDonald's . . . and they'd make *you* pay!"

Why should we care about the state of the venture capital industry? Despite the fact that probably only one of every six hundred start-ups ever receives venture capital funding each year, this uniquely American form of risk capital has always had an outsized and positive influence on America's innovation and job-creating machinery.

A 2010 study by the highly-regarded academics Josh Lerner of Harvard and Steven N. Kaplan of the University of Chicago noted that over 60 percent of the start-ups that achieved enough success to undertake an IPO were venture-backed—even though, once again, only one-sixteenth of 1 percent of all start-ups ever receive venture funding.

Other research demonstrates that VC-backed start-ups produce, in the words of one study, "orders of magnitude" more employment and revenue growth than non-VC-backed firms. Exactly how much greater job growth occurs at VC-backed versus non-VC-backed firms is hard to pin down. The National Venture Capital Association (NVCA) itself says that job growth at VC-backed firms is 1.6 percent versus 0.2 percent at non-VC-backed firms, making VC-backed firms roughly 8 times more productive at creating jobs. Another source, however, estimated that "VC-backed firms are 150 times more likely than average start-ups to create jobs." We also know that VC-backed firms produce more patents, and more high-quality (i.e., more often cited) patents, than non-VC-backed firms. And although VC-backed firms conduct only 3 percent of industrial R&D in the U.S., they produce 15 percent of all industrial innovations in America.

Since 1970, VCs have invested roughly half a trillion dollars in more than twenty-seven thousand start-ups in the U.S. Those venture-backed start-ups that succeeded employ more than 12 million people today and contribute a staggering $3 trillion to the economy, according to the NVCA. That represents 21 percent of total U.S. GDP and 11 percent of our private sector employment.

Today, however, the job- and industry-creating magic of venture capital has eroded, and many entrepreneurs and VCs alike attribute this at least to some degree to the changing complexion of the venture capital community itself. They talk of the influx of investment bankers and "numbers guys," lured by the attraction of outsized returns during the height of the dot-com boom, and of an industry no longer as concerned with helping to build great companies and new industries.

Probably no one speaks more eloquently to this issue than Albert "Rocky" Pimentel. Rocky's thirty-year career in the wilds of Silicon Valley's entrepreneurial community follows a not-uncommon trajectory from entrepreneur to venture capitalist and back again. He was part of the founding management team of Conner Peripherals, later acquired by Seagate Technology. Later, he was senior vice president and chief financial officer at both LSI Logic and WebTV Networks, the latter of which was acquired by Microsoft. He also did CFO duty at start-ups Glu Mobile and Zone Labs, where he led the successful negotiation and merger with Check Point Software. But Rocky was for many years also a partner at the VC firm Redpoint Ventures, which invested in such high-profile start-ups as Netflix, MySpace, Fortinet, HomeAway, Juniper Networks, and my own company, Danger, where he served on our board of directors. Rocky then went back to the operational side of the street, as chief operating officer and CFO of antivirus and security software firm McAfee, acquired in mid-2010 by Intel.

"When you look at the characteristics of the original VC greats like Sequoia Capital or Kleiner Perkins," says Pimentel, "you see that the founders were business people, people who actually ran companies, who understood the risks, the rewards, the challenges, the need to be able to deal with people at all levels. I'm talking about people who spent, you know, fifteen years in sales management, or marketing management, or general management, learning how to run a company through successful and unsuccessful cycles. It was this street education and street smarts that made them better venture capital investors than many of the people doing it today. Today's venture capital has become more of a professional investors' discipline. And a lot of start-ups now are dealing with VCs who don't have any true, deep operating experience."

He thinks back over his long career. "I remember in the 1980s, it seemed like anybody who got to an IPO had almost gone out of business twelve months before. You know, it's not easy starting and building a new company. The vast majority fail. So it's always such a challenge, a test of fortitude, to push through to the goal line. And I think almost every company has to go through some sort of mortal inflection point in order to finally secure their existence as an independent public company."

And right there, Pimentel insists, "is where all the cookbooks on business success completely fail. It's because they never capture the importance of the human element. That's where I think the venture capital train has gotten off the track in the last ten years or so—neglecting the human element. I really do stand by that characterization."

He pauses a moment. "Every one of the companies I've been with or invested in is like a piece of art to me. Or like a sports team. People working in a start-up always create this unique chemistry with each other, and with their investors. And the ability to motivate, to lead, to execute a business plan effectively . . . it all depends on understanding that chemistry."

He points to the core of the problem. "What I think has happened here is we've gotten into a scenario where private equity has become just another investment, just a money-making machine, which really wasn't the nature of start-up funding in the past. In the old days, they were trying to build companies for the long term, and build new industries. Of course you always had the intent to make a lot of money. But there was also an emotional attachment to the idea that you were also building something new and meaningful for society."

He pauses again. "Today? People are impatient, you know. They want quick returns. Venture capital is just another investment vehicle now, nothing more."

Now, some might say that Rocky is naive, an idealist. But I can assure you that when he was on the board of my last company, Danger, he was as tough-minded and diligent a director as they come—and no more willing to throw his money away on Pollyanna dreams than any other bottom line–oriented investor. If someone with Rocky's experience in Silicon Valley warns that venture capitalists are losing their way—becoming mere extractors of profit rather than simultaneous builders of lasting businesses that benefit society—then he's probably not alone.

Indeed, the widely read *All Things Digital* blog reported that a recent survey of more than five hundred VCs and CEOs at venture-backed firms found that "a large share" of the respondents complained about "VCs without operational experience" and "investment banker types [who] add little value." Similarly, the *New York Times* quoted Marc Andreessen, the founder of start-up Netscape and now a high-profile angel investor, criticizing the newly minted "MBAs that have invaded the industry." The paper also quoted VC "tribal elder" Franklin "Pitch" Johnson urging would-be venture capitalists to "get a real job in an operating company, because what we back is operating companies—until you understand that, you can't be much of a venture capitalist."

The short-termism and numbers-only approach of much of the venture industry today means that "very little disruptive innovation is [being] born," says entrepreneur Georges van Hoegaerden. Adds one attorney, who asked to remain anonymous but has worked intimately with start-ups and venture capitalists for more than fifteen years: "VCs used to do God's work. I'm serious! Sure, they wanted to make a ton of money. But they also knew they were helping build something of real value for the nation. Now they're just flipping start-ups for a quick buck."

I am personally aware of venture investors who deliberately fund start-ups with very little capital and no long-term horizons for the express purpose of creating a product or a feature that will be attractive to potential acquirers. They can often make very good money by cheaply and quickly building what amounts to a faux company and then flipping it.

A similar point was made by Carl Schramm and Harold Bradley, the president and chief investment officer, respectively, of the Ewing Marion Kauffman Foundation, in a high-profile 2009 column in *BusinessWeek*. "Instead of working to make their best startups strong and independent, they're 'flipping' them, as private equity firms do with troubled companies they buy."

One VC who insisted on anonymity conceded that flipping does take place. "No question that this happens, although I would say it is a pretty marginal trend today compared to back in 2006 and 2007 when a lot of start-ups were launched with a so-called 'business plan' of being acquired by Google. The big acquirers—Google, Microsoft, Facebook, Cisco, etc.—have bought these companies at sometimes-ridiculous multiples of ten times revenue."

Why? Because for the acquiring firm, it's like outsourcing R&D at a lower cost. Google, for example, spent $1.1 billion to acquire twenty-two start-ups in the first half of 2010 alone. And for the VCs, it means a quick and easy return for their increasingly disgruntled investors.

Not exactly building companies to last, is it?

To be sure, venture practices like these that create neither jobs nor lasting economic value are more the fault of the venture industry's dismal returns than of any big change in personnel. And there's no doubt that venture capital is in crisis today. The total amount invested in the first half of 2010 was just north of $11 billion, compared with $18 billion for all of 2009. This uptick reflects the slightly improved economy—or at least the reduced sense of panic among VCs—compared with the worst of the recession in early 2009. But it's still way below the $51 billion invested in 1999, let alone the $100 billion invested in 2000. The shrinkage is certainly in part a rational retrenchment from the "irrational exuberance" of the dot-com boom days, but it is also suggestive of an industry unsure of itself and uncertain how to move forward. Overall, there are fewer funds today, fewer first-time funds, less capital in the biggest funds (with a few exceptions), and fewer people working in the venture business. Some analysts expect the venture industry to continue to shrink by another 30 percent to 50 percent.

Bottom line, VCs simply aren't getting the returns that they used to. In fact, the returns stink. Venture capital's ten-year returns over the last decade are –3.69 percent—that's a *negative* 3.69 percent. In the year 2000, by contrast, the ten-year returns for the 1990s were running around a positive 28 percent. During the "lost decade" of the 2000s, it seems, venture investors would have done better to park their money in a Bank of America savings account paying maybe 1 percent interest.

To be sure, investors in the Dow, S&P, and NASDAQ earned even worse returns during that ten-year period. But remember, VC investments are illiquid—you can't pull your money out like you can with equity investments—so the "risk-adjusted" returns are actually much worse than the numbers suggest. Besides, comparing VC returns with those of other investments is not an apples-to-apples affair. Venture capital investors expect much higher returns than those who invest in the stock markets, and if they don't get them, then at some point they will leave the venture asset class, making less capital available to invest in start-ups and breakthrough innovation.

If the venture capital system weakens, so will job creation. As a society, therefore, we need to either find some way to revive the venture industry or invent a new way to fund the start-ups that create jobs.

"Some VCs say, 'We'll get through this somehow like we always have,'" notes Curtis Carlson, CEO of SRI International (formerly the Stanford Research Institute), a prestigious research center that has been incubating new ideas and business for more than sixty years. "But others are terrified. I mean, Sequoia has been one of the few VC firms right now making money. They are really disciplined. I mean, they are brutal. They are absolutely going to make money, right? But I heard [venture partner and billionaire] Mike Moritz say that he thinks Silicon Valley only has fifteen or twenty years left. Sequoia has eight offices. Only one is left in America."

Indeed, the only bright spot for VCs (other than social media) is overseas investments in Chinese, Indian, and other start-ups, which now account for more than 40 percent of total venture investment. Good for VCs, perhaps, but is the offshoring of venture capital good for America?

One can appreciate the appeal of high-growth emerging markets overseas, but it also suggests that VCs are becoming less interested in the innovation opportunities here at home. Which, of course, only further constrains the kinds of innovation that can be successfully undertaken by entrepreneurs in the United States. VCs can talk all they want about how good companies can always attract funding—or about how committed they are to investing in cleantech—but once you drill down beneath the platitudes, the picture doesn't look so heartening.

Damon Matteo, for example, is a top executive at the famed Palo Alto Research Center (PARC, the inventor of laser printing, Ethernet networking, and the graphical user interface now used in all computers), where he is vice president of intellectual capital at this last of the great industrial laboratories in the U.S. PARC develops technology, usually in concert with private firms, and then helps to spin out new businesses built around those technologies.

"We've got materials, hardware, and science capability. And we've got natural language technology," Matteo explains. "But because of the investment required to make these into going concerns, it's hard to get any traction—any interest from the VCs—for anything that looks like a hardware or hard science or capital intensive play in cleantech."

Venture capitalist David Ladd, a former partner at the prestigious Mayfield Fund, agrees. "We would not fund a company that was building hardware or semiconductors," he concedes. "Nor any of the tough physical sciences. It's just too hard and expensive. We'll invest in China instead and let them do it. So what's left is all the Web 2.0 stuff, which I don't consider to be true innovation, to be honest with you. Just from the street level, I can tell you that we're seeing less and funding less true innovation these days."

As a December 16, 2010, article in *BusinessWeek* put it, "While venture capitalists are pouring money into social networking, e-commerce and online-game companies, investments in chipmakers are close to a 12-year low. And yet semiconductors—made from silicon wafers—provide the brains for everything from computers and mobile phones to nuclear missiles."

Jeff Brody is a founding partner with Redpoint Ventures and an early investor in my last company, Danger, who also served on its board of directors. He says that the venture industry is simply not prepared, given its current economics, to commit the scale of funds required to help an entrepreneur seize what he calls "an industry-changing opportunity" any more.

"The next big thing?" asks Brody. "I have no doubt it's coming. I just worry that it's not going to come here."

He has good reason to worry. Total VC and government investment in cleantech in the U.S. reached $4.9 billion in the second quarter of 2010. But in China that same quarter it topped $11.5 billion. As one headline in *BusinessWeek* put it: "America Sits Out the Race."

Dow Jones reported on August 10, 2010, that U.S. venture investors are now even seeking capital and deals from China in hopes of boosting the prospects of their own cleantech portfolio companies, which can't raise the capital they need in the United States. "Certainly [the Chinese] have beaten the U.S.," one analyst told the newswire. "But that's like beating the [slow] kid down the block in kickball." In other words, it's not even a contest any more.

Conrad Burke, whose Innovalight had to alter its business plan when it became clear that investors would not pony up for its original capital-intensive solar manufacturing plan, finds the whole situation rather ironic. "When I think of Silicon Valley—and I've wanted to come here since I was a teenager back in Ireland—I think of the semiconductor chip. I think of the computer. I think of communications, and telecom. None of which we really do any more."

Indeed, the constraints upon innovation have gotten so severe that, according to investment banker Richard Hart of Deutsche Bank in San Francisco, "We're on the tipping point of really losing our dominance in a number of different industries all at once."

None of this is meant to denigrate the remarkable achievements of Facebook, Twitter, and other social media innovations of the past decade, which have touched the lives of hundreds of millions of people worldwide. Facebook and similar companies have created enormous social value by serving as the platforms for new innovation, new productivity increases, and new businesses. Indeed, many new start-ups have been launched using the Facebook platform, and thousands of small firms use Facebook to market their business or products. But these low-cost social media start-ups appear to be producing a smaller impact on job creation and overall economic growth than has been true of start-ups historically.

"I was amazed when I visited Facebook's office in Palo Alto," recalls venture capitalist Dan Burstein of Millennium Technology Value Partners, whose fund invested in the company several years ago. "They had the majority of their worldwide employees there—about 900 people. And I thought to myself, here's a company with 500 million users that is worth maybe $35 billion. And yet it had less than a thousand employees?"

Employment at Facebook now tops 1,400, and its market value was estimated at $50 billion in January of 2011—and that could soar to $70 billion or even more by the time it goes public. By way of contrast, the $35 billion Sony Corporation employs more than 170,000 people, $50 billion Boeing employs 157,000 people, and the $70 billion Walt Disney Company employs 144,000.

To be sure, most job creation occurs *after* a start-up undertakes an IPO, and Facebook is not scheduled to do so until 2012. So it is difficult to say precisely how much of the problem here is due to the kinds of start-ups being funded today (i.e., low-cost Web 2.0 ventures rather than capital-intensive manufacturing or product start-ups) and how much is due to the fact that the IPO market itself is seriously constrained. Virtually everyone agrees, however, that venture investors' reluctance to fund the kind of start-ups that produce the greatest economic impact for America is a major piece of the puzzle behind our stalled engine of job creation.

"There are no lack of [semiconductor startup] ideas, but it's becoming harder and harder to find investors," venture capitalist Ken Lawler told *BusinessWeek*. "It takes too much money and too much time."

For the first time in our history, it seems, the historic connection between technological innovation and job creation has broken down. And for the first time as well, the wealth created by innovation is going mostly to a handful of founders and venture capitalists rather than to thousands of employees and the community at large.

"If you talk to any institutional investor," says Burstein, "they'll tell you that the top 10 percent to 20 percent of VCs make up nearly 100 percent of positive returns. That's why there continues to be huge pressure to get into the top funds—Sequoia, Kleiner Perkins, Benchmark, and the like. The great venture funds have no problem continuing to attract capital." Burstein's last fund, Millennium Technology Value Partners II, was heavily oversubscribed as well. The problem is that if present trends continue and hundreds of poor-performing funds dissolve, as is expected, there will be less total capital for new ventures. And the capital that remains, as we have already seen, will increasingly be deployed in low-cost social media start-ups or in emerging market opportunities in India, China, and Brazil.

Thus, the actual amount of venture capital left for big-vision start-ups capable of changing the employment picture in America will be diluted several times over. This is why federal, state, and local governments need to get more involved, and why tax laws need to change, so that investment in more capital-intensive, job-creating start-ups can be incentivized.

"The danger is not that risk-takers with capital will disappear," agrees Burstein. "It's that going forward, there will no longer be a close correlation between backing a successful business and the amount of U.S. economic growth and employment that this business will create."

Could Apple Be Built Today?

The first critical decade of Apple's existence was witness to a remarkable change in the tax and regulatory policies of the United States and the entire industrialized world. From 1981 to 1986, statutory corporate tax rates plummeted in the U.S. from 50 percent to 38 percent, and in the other, mostly European, countries that make up the Organisation for Economic Co-operation and Development (OECD), from even higher than 50 percent to roughly 40 percent.

It was an especially encouraging time for American start-ups. The Employee Retirement Income Security Act was changed to allow pensions to invest in venture capital. And the tax on capital gains was lowered from 35 percent to 20 percent. These two changes during Apple's first decade contributed to the explosive growth in venture capital funding for start-ups from $424 million to $4 billion a year. Compared with start-ups in other nations, U.S. start-ups also enjoyed more relaxed tax treatment of business outlays for plant and equipment, and the U.S. 22 percent marginal tax rate was much more start-up-friendly than the OECD's 34 percent marginal tax rate.

Economists consider marginal tax rates to be potent influencers of business investment, as this analysis published on the U.S. Treasury Department Web site suggests:

> The essential idea [behind the 1980s tax cuts] was that taxes have their first and primary effect on the economic incentives facing individuals and businesses. Thus, the tax rate on the last dollar earned, i.e. the marginal dollar, is much more important to economic activity than the tax rate facing the first dollar earned or than the average tax rate. By reducing marginal tax rates it was believed the natural forces of economic growth would be less restrained. The most productive individuals would then shift more of their energies to productive activities rather than leisure, and businesses would take advantage of many

more now-profitable opportunities. It was also thought that reducing marginal tax rates would significantly expand the tax base as individuals [and also businesses] shifted more of their income and activities into taxable forms and out of tax-exempt forms.

In other words, lower tax rates on the last dollar earned encourage individuals and businesses to work harder, take more entrepreneurial risks, and expand their operations because they can keep more of the fruits of that added labor or activity. A Small Business Administration study found that a reduction in the marginal tax rate of 1 percentage point increases the rate of start-up formation by 1.5 percent and reduces the chance of start-up failure by more than 8 percent.

Likewise, governments have found it far more valuable to lower marginal rates and claim a more modest share of a rapidly growing economy than to raise rates and try to extract a larger share of an economy constrained by the disincentives of high marginal rates.

Real-world results bear out the truth of that statement. Although statutory business tax rates plunged in both Europe and the United States after 1981, corporate tax revenues as a percentage of GDP have soared from a low of 2.3 percent in 1980 to 3.7 percent in 2005.

Tax rates don't just influence how much investment and growth a firm will choose to undertake. In an increasingly globalized economy, they also profoundly affect *where* a business will chose to invest or expand.

As University of Michigan economist James Hines wrote, "Taxation significantly influences the location of foreign direct investment, corporate borrowing [and] research and development performance." Added the University of Toronto's Jack Mintz, "Economic studies show conclusively that business taxes significantly affect investment in a country. High tax rates on capital result in less investment and less economic growth." A 2008 World Bank study, meanwhile, found that a 10 percent increase in the effective tax rate reduces the investment-to-GDP ratio by 2.2 percent and foreign direct investment by 2.3 percent.

This is where one has to question whether Apple, were it starting out today, could be successful—at least as an *American* firm. Because ever since the start of Apple's second decade of existence in 1986, the relative tax and regulatory burdens on U.S. start-ups have grown exponentially, whereas those on European and other foreign ventures have declined sharply.

Since 1986, all the countries of the OECD have continually lowered their statutory and marginal business tax rates while the United States has not. The year 2010 was the twentieth consecutive year, in fact, that the OECD nations reduced both taxes and regulation—cutting, for example, the regulatory cost of starting a new business by 32 percent—while the United States has done exactly the opposite. Indeed, since 2000, twenty-seven of the thirty nations in the OECD have reduced their corporate tax rates by an average of more than 7 percentage points each. In the European Union, the average reduction in tax rates since 2000 has been by 9.6 percent. Meanwhile, U.S. rates have remained unchanged.

As a result, America now has the highest corporate tax rate in the world (with the lone exception of Japan). At 39.2 percent, it's more than 50 percent higher than the OECD average of 25.5 percent. What's more, in half of our states, the combined federal and state tax is actually higher than Japan's. Silicon Valley start-ups, for example, incur a tax rate of 40.7 percent.

Interestingly, the tipping point at which it became more advantageous for tax and regulatory reasons to locate outside rather than inside the United States occurred around the year 2000, which, as we've noted earlier, marked the onset of a whole slew of "lost decade" problems. That's when the average statutory corporate tax rate in other OECD countries fell below ours (it has kept falling ever since), and that's when the effective marginal tax rate for the other G-8 nations fell below America's 23.6 percent rate to its current level of 19.5 percent.

It's as if, when no one was paying attention, an astonishing reversal took place. A supposedly stodgy "old Europe," home to what some have called "the bureaucratic nanny state and the cradle-to-grave tax-and-spend welfare system," suddenly transformed itself over the last decade into a more hospitable place to do business in many ways than good old laissez-faire America.

And lest anyone think I'm ignoring the credits and loopholes available to business, numerous studies show that the *effective* tax rates actually paid by U.S. businesses are far higher than those paid by their competitors in other countries. An October 2010 report by the Information Technology & Innovation Foundation (ITIF), for example, noted that "When it comes to corporate tax competition, Europe is more competitive than the United States, with most [European] nations having made a conscious choice to keep effective tax rates low in order to become a more attractive location for business investment. In 2008, the average effective corporate tax rate in EU-10 nations was 11.2 percent. The average effective rate for EU-15 countries, at 20.5 percent, was still one-third less than U.S. effective corporate tax rates, at 32 percent." That is a significant disparity.

To be sure, European nations have lowered their taxes not just to become more attractive for business investment and job creation. They have also done this to discourage tax avoidance and maximize the total revenues received. A number of empirical studies by OECD economists and others have discovered that the best "revenue-maximizing" tax rate—the rate that brings in more total revenues than either a lower or a higher tax rate—is around 25 percent.

(In chapter 3, you will see industry-by-industry comparisons of the effective corporate tax rates paid by U.S. companies compared with those paid by their foreign competitors. It shows that U.S. tax rates are way out of line with the norms in Europe and elsewhere in the world.)

This will surely come as a surprise to those who tend to regard complaints from start-up executives about taxes as simply the whining of corporate fat cats who don't want to pay their fair share. I won't deny that there has at times been some truth to this perception, especially as it involves the complaints made by Big Business. But even a cursory comparison of tax rates in the U.S. versus those in other nations today will show how uncompetitive we have become—and why so many businesses are now relocating jobs and operations offshore.

And not just offshore, either, but out of Silicon Valley to other states as well. Over the last ten years, thousands of businesses and at least 1.3 million jobs have moved out of California to other states, as have more than a million residents, making California the number one state in the union in the numbers of people fleeing it. The outmigration is not solely due to high taxes, of course, but California is rated the forty-eighth worst state in the nation for taxes by the Tax Foundation and now has the highest capital gains tax rate in the nation, with a combined federal and state rate of 25.3 percent. All this in the supposed home of entrepreneurial start-ups!

Start-ups in Silicon Valley also face the nation's highest cost of living and regulation, higher-than-average unemployment, the nation's worst educational system (despite once being the best), a paralyzed state government with half a trillion dollars in unfunded pension liabilities, a $25 billion state deficit larger than that of most nations, and a political climate that many say is hostile to businesses. All this explains why in 2010 *Forbes* and *Chief Executive* both ranked California as the *worst* state in the nation in which to do business. The highly regarded Milken Institute made no value judgment and simply called California the *most costly* state in which to do business.

This state of affairs is driving business away. Literally. On August 3, 2010, the cost of a one-way Budget moving truck from Los Angeles to Dallas was $1,582. The price to return to Los Angeles, however, was only $480—less than one-third the cost of leaving it. A Budget rental spokesman said rates are entirely determined by demand. More demand, higher rates.

That California may be transforming itself from entrepreneurialism's birthplace to its graveyard does not bode well for the nation as a whole. This state, after all, is home to one-quarter of all patents issued in the U.S. and a staggering 13 percent of America's total GDP. So why, then, are so many people and businesses moving out of the most beautiful and temperate climate in the nation—a state that once also boasted the world's most fertile soil for entrepreneurial start-ups—for the deserts of Nevada, Arizona, and Texas?

Just ask Tim Bacci, cofounder of the venture investment firm BlueLine Partners and a Silicon Valley veteran with more than fifteen years' experience building and running software start-ups, "It's just become too expensive, too burdensome, to stay here anymore," he told us. "I love California, but we're moving our operations out of state [in 2010]."

Or ask Alfred Lin, the former CFO and number two executive at Zappos who recently left the world's biggest online clothing retailer to join the VC firm Sequoia Capital. "There's no way we could have sustained a competitive operation [at Zappos] with the number of employees we were going to need to hire," he explained in an interview. "That why we moved to Nevada." Zappos today employs close to two thousand people—jobs that could have been California's to keep.

Meanwhile, Gary Shapiro, the CEO of the Consumer Electronics Association trade group, publicly called California "the Greece of the United States."

As the popular joke has it, California remains the best place in the world to build a successful small business. All you have to do is start with a successful large business.

"No state has suffered a greater reversal of fortune than California," notes *Forbes*. "While California's economy has come roaring back before, any resurgence this time will be [undermined by] an extremely complex regulatory regime that leads companies to shift much of their new production and staffing to other states [or countries]."

Just how bad is the regulatory burden on Silicon Valley start-ups? There is some dispute over the precise cost of regulation on California businesses. One study from the California State University at Sacramento put the cost of regulation at $134,000 per small business, with a statewide loss of 3.8 million jobs, but that study has been criticized. A study from the Small Business Administration (SBA) in 2006 that many consider more reliable put the cost of compliance with federal regulations alone at $7,647 per small firm. The SBA repeated its study in September 2010, and reported that the cost of regulation had increased to $8,086 per company by 2008. Those costs are not borne equally by all businesses, however. Lacking economies of scale, small businesses incur regulatory costs 42 percent greater than those of larger firms.

No one in his or her right mind denies the need for sensible regulation. We certainly don't want reckless Wall Street derivatives traders to hang the whole country out to dry again. Nor do we want to drive around in cars with exploding gas tanks or allow toxic dumping in the air we breathe and water we drink. But the operative word here is "sensible"—admittedly a subjective term, but one that by any reasonable measure ought to include *not* killing the start-up goose that lays the golden egg of job creation. Protracted unemployment isn't good for your health or the economy, either.

Here, one would have to say that the street-level view of regulation, even by the denizens of liberal Silicon Valley, is pretty damning. Consider Conrad Burke's description of what he had to go through to open Innovalight's facility in Sunnyvale.

"It was very, very hard to open up our facility here," Burke recalls. "We needed permitting—every kind of permitting you can imagine. Fire, safety, environmental. You can't be dumping chemicals, obviously. And we all want to have clean air here. But for the small start-up like ours, it was pretty painful. You need a permit for everything."

He described his interactions with the fire department. "Okay, so the fire department comes by and says, 'Well, you need more fire sprinklers there, you need to move that door there, you need an exhaust here, and on and on,'" Burke recalls. "So we said okay, okay, okay. And we're all running around like little mice, chasing after this fire department inspector and taking notes. But, hey, if that's what you've got to do, then that's what you've got to do."

Burke describes what happened a few weeks later. "He was supposed to come back and reinspect it, but we couldn't get him for weeks and weeks because they're so understaffed. Then he finally came and said, 'Okay, but you also need to do this, that, and the other thing.' And I'm kind of like, 'Man, you should have told me that four weeks ago.' So we start the whole cycle again—this slow, painful, and very expensive process. And that was just with the fire department. There were all sorts of other regulations we had to meet as well."

He shrugs. "All these issues with the permitting and regulation, I mean, it was really slowing us down. And costing us money. And the bureaucracy! But we did everything by the book, overly so. I mean, I'm not going to risk my reputation as CEO and have somebody get hurt or killed. Or cause some sort of environmental damage. I'm just not going to do that. But, you know, you've got to work with me here, right? I mean, I'm creating jobs in this community. Yet it's almost like they were pushing us as a business away, making it almost impossible for us."

Finally, Burke went to see the city manager. "I had to get pretty terse with him," he recalls. "I told him, look, we need your support here. We can't function. And I really kicked up a big tantrum and threatened to pack up our solar start-up and move elsewhere." He smiles ruefully. "Well, we finally got it all resolved. And now we're up and running fine. But it makes you wonder. I'm just a small start-up. What if I wanted to open a solar cell manufacturing plant and hire a thousand people? What would that be like?"

Burke contrasts his grueling experience in Silicon Valley, which other start-up executives say is typical, with the tax and regulatory requirements in other countries. "Taxes in California are really unbelievable. I mean, I get this bill from Sacramento for around $900,000 for that equipment I told you we bought. Meanwhile, I'm paying to the city, I'm paying for health care for my employees, and I'm not generating any revenue yet. So it was painful to send that check to Sacramento. These are precious dollars, and you're almost crying when you put it in the mailbox. And all you're thinking is, What did Sacramento do for me?"

Basically nothing, says Burke. In contrast, local, state, and national governments elsewhere in the world often go to great lengths to help start-ups.

"Back in Ireland, the corporate tax rate is 12.5 percent," says Burke. "Every nation is lowering tax rates to attract business—every nation except the U.S., that is. In Germany, they have very attractive incentives, particularly in the eastern states of Germany where, in the case of solar, you can actually get up to fifty cents on the euro back in your capital costs." In other words, instead of having to pay almost a million dollars in tax on the $10 million in equipment he bought, had Burke set up Innovalight in Germany he would have gotten a refund of up to $5 million on his equipment purchase in the form of capital grants.

Think about that for a minute.

"They also help you through the regulatory stuff," Burke adds, even though Germany is considered to be more environmentally strict than the United States. "And they have a feed-in tariff that pays citizens to use electricity from sources like solar. That's how they turned Germany into the largest solar market in the world, and created tens of thousands of cleantech jobs. And all that solar manufacturing equipment that we and the Chinese and everyone else uses? It's all coming out of Germany. Because the government cares about growing its economy and offers meaningful incentives to business."

Serial entrepreneur Gary Griffiths agrees. The founder and CEO of several companies in the past, Griffiths is today the CEO of a nine-person start-up called Trapit in Silicon Valley. He says the problem is not so much that the amount of regulation has dramatically increased all of a sudden. It's that the way that regulation is employed is causing the region to rapidly lose ground as an inviting place to start a new business and create jobs.

"Here in California," says Griffiths, "it's like the state is constantly playing 'Gotcha!' with you. You forgot to fill out this workman's comp form; you neglected to include the proper state agency code on that document. Meanwhile, if you go to another state or even to Europe, they ask you, 'How can we help? What do you need?'"

Regulation is a two-edged sword. Germany knows how to wield it to strengthen both environmental quality *and* job-creating businesses, which leads to greater prosperity and a better quality of life for all citizens. But in our hands, it's all too often a bludgeon that hits start-ups and small businesses especially hard.

Probably nothing illustrates that better than Sarbanes-Oxley, the biggest regulatory blunder of the "lost decade."

Could Apple Succeed Today?

It's difficult to imagine how a job- and industry-creating start-up like Apple could ever succeed in today's world. First and foremost, there would be almost no way for it to survive as an independent company and raise the capital needed to scale up innovation and hiring. That's because the IPO market, depending on your point of view, is either already dead, dying, or seriously crippled.

The years 2008 and 2009 represented the worst IPO market in forty years. In 2009, there were just twelve venture-backed IPOs raising $1.6 billion, versus two hundred seventy acquisitions totaling $14.1 billion. That was double the six IPOs that took place in 2008, but only one-fourteenth as many as took place in China that year.

As a 2009 white paper on the IPO crisis from the auditing and consulting firm Grant Thornton put it, "Given that the size of the U.S. economy, in real terms, is over 3 times what it was 40 years ago, this is a remarkable and frightening state of affairs." In contrast, the number of start-ups that went public before the start of this "lost decade" for entrepreneurialism averaged 176 per year during the 1990s. In 1999, there were 269 venture-backed start-ups that conducted IPOs.

There were signs of a modest IPO comeback in 2010. But as the *New York Times* noted, "Many of the largest IPOs are large established companies taken private during the buyout boom of 2005 to 2007—[including] Toys "R" Us, Nielsen, and the Hospital Corporation of America." Another exceptional case was General Motors.

To be sure, many analysts expect superstar social media firms such as Facebook, Zyngna, Groupon, and LinkedIn to hit the IPO trail late in 2011. But this is more a sign of a bubble in the investor mania for such firms than a return to health of the IPO market itself. For the vast majority of young start-ups—especially the all-important infrastructure, semiconductor, hardware, and cleantech start-ups that create large numbers of jobs—the chances of going public and surviving as an independent public company remain extremely limited.

In any event, IPO levels still remain well below their historic norms despite the fact that an increasing number of start-ups are maturing and desperately need the capital that an IPO would provide to finance their continued innovation and growth.

"And that, say analysts, has unsettling implications for American job growth," observes the *New York Times* in a November 18, 2010, article entitled, "Wall Street, the Home of the Vanishing IPO." Indeed, 92 percent of all hiring by venture-backed start-ups occurs *after* an IPO, according to data from the

NVCA as well as independent researchers. So start-ups, the only job-creating force in all of society, really need these IPOs. And so does America.

The IPO crisis has many causes, from structural changes in the market to what Grant Thornton called "a perfect storm of unintended consequences from uncoordinated regulatory changes." We focus on these regulatory changes here, if only because they are the factors most under our control. This whole book, after all, is about fixing the things that are within our power to fix. So let's look at the Sarbanes-Oxley financial reform.

Simply put, never has a regulatory reform meant to do so much good actually done so much harm. "Nobody who understood small companies would ever impose Sarbanes-Oxley on them," insists SRI's Carlson. "I mean, even under the best of circumstances, starting up a new business is a really hard and risky thing. Every little impediment you put in front of small start-ups is like a big boulder to them. Did Sarbanes-Oxley by itself kill the IPO exit for start-ups? No. But it sure made it much, much harder. People will look back at the effect of this law and say, 'Oh my God, in the whole last ten years, we didn't create any great new companies!'"

The *New York Times* concurs: "The incredible shrinking stock market is one of unexpected results of regulations like the Sarbanes-Oxley Act of 2002." Or, in the words of Redpoint Ventures' Brody, "Sarbanes-Oxley is a total nightmare."

The Sarbanes-Oxley Act (often called Sarbox) was enacted by Congress in 2002 following the Enron and WorldCom accounting frauds. The law's intent was certainly noble: to require higher standards of accounting, due diligence, and independent oversight of public companies in order to prevent fraud and to encourage greater investor confidence in the markets.

But, in actuality, the law has accomplished neither. No one can point to a single case in which Sarbox has either prevented or exposed a fraud, although it may have had a deterrent effect in some cases. Nor can anyone show how the law has buoyed investor confidence in the markets—especially after the financial meltdown of 2008. In fact, Goldman Sachs, AIG, and all the big banks whose irresponsible behavior led to this latest economic crisis were all Sarbox compliant!

Meanwhile, corporate fraud continues merrily along as always. The latest case: in July 2010, Dell Computer Corporation agreed to pay the Securities and Exchange Commission (SEC) a $100 million fine for hiding secret payments from Intel that inflated its earnings.

"Had Sarbanes-Oxley done the trick, corporate books from coast to coast would be ruler straight," the *Wall Street Journal*'s law blog observed. "But alas, that's not the world we live in."

No kidding. Meanwhile, the enormous accounting costs, diversion of resources, increased litigation risk, and bureaucratic dead weight associated with Sarbox compliance have hardly created healthier public markets. In fact, Sarbox has driven hundreds of firms to go private and quit the public markets altogether—or at least to go public on the London, Shanghai, or other foreign stock exchanges. The data firm Dealogic reported that in 2010, Chinese companies introduced 391 global IPOs worth $89.5 billion. American companies undertook about a hundred IPOs, most of them larger firms, but still worth only $15.69 billion.

In addition, during a two-month span alone in mid-2010, two huge German concerns—Daimler and Deutsche Telecom—delisted from the New York Stock Exchange. They joined ten other German firms, and hundreds of others worldwide, that have recently quit the U.S. stock market.

Notes the *New York Times*: "Scores of big-name public companies have passed into private hands. Others have been gobbled up by rivals. As a result the number of companies listed on the nation's major exchanges has plummeted, to 4,048 today from a peak of 7,459 in 1997."

But it's the disproportionately large burdens that Sarbox imposes on small public companies that pose the greatest danger to the future of the American economy. In the eyes of virtually everyone in the entrepreneurial innovation community—and most independent experts as well—Sarbox has seriously hurt the ability of start-ups to go public.

Consider, for example, that when first enacted into law in 2002, the SEC estimated that the cost of Sarbox compliance would average $91,000. But according to most estimates, the cost of compliance is actually a whopping $1 million to $3 million per year—and that's just for small firms!

Before my last firm, Danger, was acquired by Microsoft, we filed an S-1 with the SEC in 2007 registering our intent to go public. As part of our plan to become a public company, we spent $3 million and a year's worth of preparation to get ourselves in compliance with Sarbox.

For a typical small public start-up with, say, $10 million in net income, a $3 million charge against earnings for Sarbox compliance means a 30 percent reduction in profit and market capitalization, which inhibits the firm's ability to fund future innovation and growth. This forces firms to wait and grow their earnings before going public—an effort ironically undermined by the Catch-22 lack of IPOs to finance that growth. This, of course, reduces the returns to these start-ups' venture investors and leaves everyone twisting slowly, slowly in the wind.

"For most entrepreneurs, the initial public offering used to be the ultimate sign of success," noted *BusinessWeek*. Not any more. "The increased costs of being public are forcing more entrepreneurs to think at least twice before going that route."

John Berlau, director of the Center for Entrepreneurship at the Competitive Enterprise Institute, wrote that "the total annual costs for all public companies just to comply with the 'internal controls' section of Sarbanes-Oxley is $35 billion per year . . . And money isn't the only cost. A single average public company also devotes 30,700 man-hours to compliance each year."

Indeed, the *Sarbanes-Oxley Compliance Journal* reported in January 2007 that "the consensus is that it is roughly four times as expensive to go public today." The fact that there is a publication solely devoted to Sarbox compliance helps explain why the law is often referred to as the "Full Employment for Accountants Act."

In the 1990s, companies were going public with market caps of $30 million to $50 million. Nowadays, a firm must be several orders of magnitude bigger before it can even consider going to the public markets. Analysts say the big investment banks would be hesitant to take any firm public that is worth less than $100 million to $250 million.

"Small IPOs have gone the way of the dodo bird," David Weild, the ex–vice chair of NASDAQ, has stated. That might actually be a cute line were it not for the fact that small IPOs have been the eagle of American job and economic growth for generations.

The bottom line, according to Berlau, is that it is "highly unlikely" that a start-up the size Apple was when it went public in 1980 could ever go public today. And that's true not just for Apple. As Home Depot cofounder Bernie Marcus told *Investor's Business Daily,* "I honestly don't believe we could start the Home Depot in today's regulatory climate."

To be sure, Sarbox isn't the only culprit in the demise of start-up IPOs. As Grant Thornton noted in its white paper, structural changes in the market such as decimalization, which by pricing stocks in cents rather than fractions took some profits out of trading, reduced the incentives brokers had to list small companies. In addition, new regulatory rules such as Regulation Fair

Disclosure, NASD Rule 2711, and the Global Settlement—which were aimed at reducing conflicts of interest in analyst research at the major investment banks—all had the unintended consequence of eroding research and inhibiting the ability of small public companies to get analyst coverage.

But bottom line, noted a *Wall Street Journal* editorial, "[Sarbanes-Oxley] has neither prevented frauds nor instituted fairness. But it has managed to kill the creation of new public companies in the U.S., cripple the venture capital business, and damage entrepreneurship."

It has also damaged the democratic nature of wealth creation in America, since it helps to ensure that the ownership of the next crop of great start-ups will be held in the hands of professional and institutional investors—or large corporate acquirers—rather than the investing public for as long as possible, if not indefinitely.

Indeed, when a company like Facebook gets funding from elite Goldman Sachs investors rather than the millions of ordinary people who make up their user base and are the source of the company's success, it makes a statement, explained Lise Buyer of the IPO advisory firm Class V Group in a January 7, 2011, e-mail interview with Dawn Kawamoto of AOL's *Daily Finance* Web site. It says, in effect, "You, the little people, aren't entitled to buy this stock. This opportunity is only for the rich and famous."

And remember, it's not the superstar high-flying start-ups such as Facebook that we're most concerned with here. They will always be able to attract funding, public or private, whenever they want to. It's the rank-and-file start-ups—the companies that have always translated their innovation into the bulk of new jobs in America—that now find the door to the public capital market difficult if not impossible to pry open.

Looking back on it, ex–Republican congressman Michael Oxley, one of the sponsors of the bill (along with then Democratic Senator Paul Sarbanes), conceded in an interview with the *New York Times* that he hadn't understood the effect that Sarbox would have on small businesses. "Frankly, I would have written it differently," he lamented. "But at the time, everyone felt like Rome was burning."

As for the future, there is good news and bad news in the Dodd-Frank financial reform law passed in July 2010. The good news is that small companies worth less than $75 million will henceforth be exempt from some of the more draconian and expensive requirements of Sarbanes-Oxley. In addition, the law directs the SEC to study and report back by April 2011 on the advisability of exempting firms worth up to $250 million from compliance.

The bad news is that we probably need an exemption up to $500 million to make any real difference in the depressed IPO market. The other piece of bad news is that Sarbanes-Oxley was only 66 pages long, with 16 new regulations, and look at the damage it inadvertently wrought. The new Dodd-Frank bill is a staggering 2,319 pages long, with 243 new regulations.

Who knows what accidental Frankensteins may be lurking inside it, ready to come out and terrorize the entrepreneurial villagers?

What's So Bad About Mergers and Acquisitions?

Who cares if 96 percent of VC-backed exits in 2009 were by acquisition rather than IPO? The founders and investors got their return, right? And likely got rich. So what's the problem?

For the investors, none. For society, plenty.

That's because society generally loses when a start-up is acquired by a large enterprise. The start-up's innovation is used to support the acquirer's existing business, not disrupt it by creating a new business or new industry. And few if any new jobs are ever created.

Remember, virtually all of the major innovations that powered the U.S. economy to unrivaled prosperity over the last century—including the postwar invention of semiconductors, personal computers, software, the Internet, and biotechnology—were actually created by small start-ups.

With one possible exception, that is. Only the cellphone industry appears to have been midwifed by a large incumbent firm, Motorola. This exception to the usual rule that only start-ups create new industries may have been because of the government's gate-keeping role in parceling out the radio spectrum needed for cellphone communications. It may also be the result of the huge levels of investment required to get a Federal Communications Commission (FCC)-approved technology off the ground. Originally, the FCC allocated frequency only to AT&T and to its monopoly regional Bell companies. When the U.S. Justice Department broke up AT&T in its 1984 antitrust action, the local Bell companies retained their cellular licenses, and deep-pocketed entrepreneurs such as Craig McCaw bought up the remaining one in each market. Meanwhile, AT&T and its rival Motorola had each spent billions over the course of their twenty-five-year competition to develop cellular transmission technology and the mobile devices that could use it.

Motorola, with decades of experience in mobile communications, including everything from police car radios to moon landings, spent fifteen years and well over $500 million in today's dollars just to develop the first truly portable phone, the DynaTAC 800X, and then get it approved by the FCC. Only Motorola then had the market muscle to drive customer adoption nationwide.

Aside from this one case, we know of no new industry where the inciting breakthroughs were made by a large incumbent firm. Indeed, when it comes to the kinds of innovation that create new industries and millions of new jobs—and that raise the living standards of all of our citizens—the big incumbents are generally either irrelevant or actively stand in the way.

To be sure, big companies also innovate, mostly to improve existing products and services. On very rare occasions, they even come up with spectacular leaps forward in an existing industry, as Apple did for the music industry with its iPod and for the smartphone industry with its truly outstanding iPhone. Large firms also employ a major share of the workforce and contribute mightily to total economic output. So of course America needs strong leaders of existing industries as well as creators of new ones.

That said, it is undeniable that innovation at large firms generally tends not to be of the kind that historians of technology call "disruptive" or "transformative," meaning that it usually doesn't create whole new industries or lead to the development of millions of new jobs and higher living standards for all.

The reasons for this are twofold. First, the sheer scale of operations at large firms, the weight of entrenched bureaucracy, makes them less agile and imaginative than small firms in responding to new technology and market opportunities. But more important, large firms cannot help but be more concerned with maximizing the return on their *existing* businesses than in disrupting those businesses and risking the revenue streams that they depend upon by venturing into unproven products and markets.

That's why Hewlett-Packard rejected as "nonviable" the first prototype personal computer when it was developed by employee Wozniak in 1976, who later went on to found Apple Computer with Jobs using venture capital backing. "HP rejected five separate proposals of mine for a PC," Wozniak recalls. "To HP, the people who would buy a computer were the people already using computers—and they already had $10,000 machines for that corporate market. They couldn't see why consumers would ever want one."

That's also why, that same year, the giant Xerox corporation rejected multiple proposals from its own researchers to develop a personal computer—and then later also rejected laser printing, Ethernet networking technology, and the graphical user interface now used by all PCs that had been developed at its PARC laboratory. If it weren't for then-small start-ups like Apple and Microsoft, which developed the software that made the PC more usable, the PC industry and its millions of jobs might never have been created (or at least might have been substantially delayed).

This is not a new phenomenon. Earlier in the twentieth century, the Edison Company disparaged the notion of a gasoline-powered automobile, aircraft engine firms rejected proposals for a jet engine, and the Marconi Company refused to consider the idea of television. This sort of myopic rejection of radically new ideas is a common feature of large firms.

Indeed, innovation at large incumbent firms is primarily defensive in nature, meant to consolidate existing market share or strengthen oligopolistic contests with industry rivals. Innovation by small start-ups, however, is primarily offensive in nature, meant to open up and conquer heretofore-unexploited market opportunities or to disrupt and reorder existing industries.

Economists Thomas J. Prusa and James A. Schmitz Jr. found that even within an existing industry such as software, "new firms have a comparative advantage in developing new categories [of software], while established firms have a comparative advantage in developing subsequent improvements within existing categories."

Or, to put it in more human terms, innovation at large firms is run by managers, not entrepreneurs. As the economist William J. Baumol put it in his 2002 book *The Free-Market Innovation Machine*, "[Corporate R&D] is not the realm of the unexpected, of the unrestricted exercise of imagination and boldness that is the essence of entrepreneurship. It is, rather, the domain of memorandums, rigid cost controls, and standardized procedures, which are the hallmark of trained management." Innovation at large firms becomes a "bureaucratized activity," he wrote.

In contrast, the independent inventor, the upstart small firm that defies conventional wisdom and pioneers a whole new industry—these are not merely the clichéd icons of a bygone era but the motive force of all technological and economic progress in modern society. We have been fed the carefully cultivated myth that large organizations with their armies of scientists and engineers are needed to conquer the future. But that is only true in the case of a future already envisaged and in need simply of a means to get there—a Manhattan Project, for example, to work out the engineering required to unleash the power of the atom. For futures that are not already glimpsed or even imagined, for new technologies to feed and power the world, for the awesome new cures and breakthrough economic growth that will give our children a better life than we had—for all that, we need the entrepreneur.

Indeed, the late British economist John Jewkes said that when it comes to innovations that change the world, "organization man need not apply." In his seminal 1958 work *The Sources of Invention,* Jewkes reviewed the histories of sixty major inventions of the twentieth century and found, to everyone's great surprise, that they were all the work of entrepreneurs and small firms.

Rocketry, acrylics, the zipper, the aircraft industry, the jet engine, the radio industry, the television industry, power steering, the helicopter, cellophane, neoprene, air conditioning, the electron microscope, instant cameras, magnetic recording, fluorescent lighting, radar, safety razor, stainless steel, and the world's first cyclotron—these are just a few of the twentieth-century breakthroughs that came from small firms. To these we must add all the biomedical, computer, software, and other information technology breakthroughs that came after 1958.

The reasons why it's always the entrepreneur who makes the great leap forward for mankind can be found in basic human psychology. "The limitations of teamwork are obvious," Jewkes wrote. "Teamwork is always a second best. There is no kind of organized coordination which approaches in effectiveness the synthesizing which goes on in one human mind. A large team is essentially a committee and therefore suffers from the habit, common to all committees but especially harmful where research is concerned, of brushing aside hunches and intuitions in favor of ideas that can be more systematically articulated."

Or as Sir Alexander Fleming, the discoverer of penicillin, once put it, "[Corporate R&D] is a very good way of employing a certain number of people, paying salaries, and not getting very much in return."

In contrast, here's the entrepreneur:

Men with great powers of originality are in many ways a race apart. Their great gifts arise from the habit of calling everything, even the simplest assumptions, into question. They are in the grip of inner compulsions which lead them to assume the right of deciding how their special powers should be employed and how best a task should be approached. [They] resent interference. Many of them are, by temperament, wholly unsuitable for work in any research institution which is formally organized.

"I am a horse for single harness," said Einstein once, "and not cut out for team work."

Adds Wozniak: "Real inventors, they're a different kind of person. They like to think for themselves. They don't usually thrive in large companies, although they'll try to hold a job in one until they can realize their dreams of going off on their own."

Indeed, as the nineteenth-century British economist John Stuart Mill put it, to expect anyone but the entrepreneur to lead our march of progress is to raise the question "whether our march of intellect be not rather a march towards doing without intellect, and supplying our deficiency of giants by the united efforts of a constantly increasing multitude of dwarfs."

The Death of a Start-up

John Stuart Mill's warning has more than a little relevance to the ultimate fate of Danger, the company that I led as CEO for six years until its acquisition by Microsoft in 2008 for $500 million. For here is a classic case of a start-up being acquired by a big firm and, as a result, losing its innovation and job-creation potential.

Danger was cofounded in 2000 by Andy Rubin, Joe Britt, and Matt Hershenson. (Rubin went on to develop the Android operating system for Google's new smartphone platform.) The company developed a highly regarded smartphone, branded the T-Mobile Sidekick and the HipTop in different markets, that the press called "sexy" and "innovative" for its unusually close integration with social networking and its abundant apps. Plus, it was incredibly easy to use.

Our phone uniquely combined software as a service with online messaging and social networking services, and was especially popular among teens and young adults—a critical demographic in this market. Our integration of social networking with MySpace, the hot social network destination of the day, was market leading. The amount of text and Web traffic we generated was truly groundbreaking. In fact, when we mentioned our user statistics to others outside the company, we were often met with disbelief. Our average user generated 1,000 e-mails, 3,300 instant messages, 750 Web pages, and 120 SMS text messages each month. Though a bit pedestrian by today's standards, this was an amazing profile given that we only had second-generation cellular networks at the time. In this respect we paved the way for the revolution in mobile communications now taking place among young wireless users, in which voice calling over smartphones is dropping by 25 percent while text services are doubling each year.

Our early success was also fueled by nonpaid endorsements from a large array of sports and entertainment celebrities. These included Jessica Simpson, Eva Longoria, Tony Hawk, Snoop Dogg, Dwayne Wade, Derek Jeter, 50 Cent, Paris Hilton, Nicole Ritchie, Seal, Heidi Klum, and Demi Moore, who IM'ed Ashton Kutcher on *The David Letterman Show*. Designer versions by Juicy Couture, Dwayne Wade, and Mr. Cartoon and one-of-a-kind versions by the likes of Tommy Hilfiger, Diane von Furstenberg, and even JLo helped build the phone's profile and desirability.

In sum, Danger had a radically popular product that won numerous "product of the year" awards and at one point had 1.3 million paying subscribers. Our user base was just as committed to Danger's Sidekick as Apple's customers today are to the iPhone, and our revenues had reached a greater than $100 million per year run rate.

So we decided to go public and filed for an IPO in December 2007. But we remained open to other alternatives, especially given the feeble nature of the IPO market post-Sarbox. Microsoft, meanwhile, was looking for a way to improve its position in the fast-growing smartphone market and wanted to be able to compete with the likes of Apple's popular iPhone. We had several other interested suitors, but none so motivated as Microsoft. Because we were able to negotiate a price that provided a financial outcome at least as good if not better than an IPO, with dramatically less risk, we agreed to be acquired by Microsoft in April 2008.

I felt that given our alternatives, the Microsoft deal was the best outcome for all concerned. I made clear to Microsoft that I was not going to stay on when the acquisition was completed, but was available to assist it in any way possible to make sure that the transition was as frictionless as possible. Danger had a unique, entrepreneurial culture, so it was going to be a big shock for our employees to join a huge organization, no matter how much sense the deal made or how good the "golden handcuffs" were. Along with our revolutionary technology, supported by over a hundred patents and patent applications, Microsoft acquired virtually all of Danger's key engineers and technical staff, who joined Microsoft as a result of the generous offers it made.

I did, however, have one negative premonition before the deal closed. The executive staff of Danger, with the exception of the CFO and the founders, had all worked for me at my previous start-up, Concentric Network. That means that much of the Danger team had already worked together for thirteen years. So on several occasions, I offered to brief the incoming leadership from Microsoft about the key strengths of our executive team as well as critical aspects of our operations and customer base that only an insider like myself would be privy to. Microsoft never took me up on the offer, which I found surprising and not typical of most M&A deals.

In any event, I can say without hesitation that Microsoft acted with extraordinary professionalism and fairness throughout the complex negotiations as well as during the transition that Danger employees made into becoming Microsoft employees.

I left Danger the day the acquisition closed and immediately took a position with Tessera. Although I maintained personal contact with many of the Danger team, all of us respected Microsoft's strong confidentiality policy and resolutely adhered to it. About what happened *after* the acquisition, therefore, I only know what I read in the press.

According to numerous press accounts, postacquisition development on the Danger smartphone and platform technology was plagued from the beginning with problems, power struggles, and missteps. In the end, this resulted in the June 2010 release of Microsoft's renamed Kin phone to a less-than-tepid reception among consumers. It sold fewer than eight thousand units, and Microsoft pulled it off the market barely two months after it was released. Analysts estimate that the whole episode may have cost Microsoft close to a billion dollars, including the acquisition cost for Danger.

What happened? According to one autopsy written for *Computerworld*, "In a smartphone world dominated by phones that run apps, it ran no apps. It was a phone designed for those interested primarily in social networking, yet had poor Twitter support and no instant messaging client. It was as expensive as more powerful smartphones, and required a costly monthly service contract. In about the only smart move Microsoft made concerning the Kin, it killed the phone after less than two months."

Insiders have attempted to fill in some of the blanks about what went wrong. On a blog called *Mini Microsoft*—a Web forum for anonymous Microsoft insiders—former Danger-turned-Microsoft employees described what happened to the smartphone project.

"When we were first acquired, we were committed to help this project out and show our stuff," wrote one former Danger employee. "But when your best ideas get knocked down over and over, and it began to dawn on us that we were not going to have any real effect on the product, we gave up. We took long lunches and went on coffee breaks [where] the conversation always went something like this: 'Did you hear that IM [instant messaging] was cut? YouTube was cut? The App store was cut? We began counting down to the two-year point so we could get our retention bonuses and get out."

According to analysts, the most critical mistake that Microsoft made was to replace Danger's Java-based smartphone operating system with a Windows operating system—and not even the new Windows 7 at that, but the older Windows CE mobile operating system.

Here we see once again the irresistible drive within a large incumbent firm to maximize the return on its *existing* business, not disrupt it by creating a new business. For Microsoft, that existing business is built around Windows. The internal logic of a $60-billion-a-year Windows revenue stream inexorably drove Microsoft to expand the Windows franchise to one more device, even if it meant sacrificing the product features that led it to acquire Danger in the first place.

This is not a problem with Microsoft alone. It could have (and has) happened at many large acquiring firms. As Redpoint Ventures' Brody conceded, "We've got a bunch of companies in our portfolio that will never go public. So they're going to be sold. They're going to be sold into big, bureaucratic organizations that will squelch their innovation."

Adds Deutsche Bank's Hart: "If you look at the histories of once-great start-ups, you see that there's always a calcification of innovation after an acquisition."

Remember, VC-backed start-ups account for only 3 percent of total corporate R&D yet produce 15 percent of all industrial innovations. They are thirteen times more innovative per worker than large firms, creating more patents per employee, more patents in cutting-edge scientific and technical fields, and patents that are more revolutionary technologically than those of large firms. Indeed, start-ups produce patents that are twice as likely as those from large firms to be found among the ranks of the highest-impact patents. They also generally develop innovations that are of far greater social and economic value than those of big firms.

And when it comes to job growth, the contest isn't even close. Economists used to believe that small businesses created most jobs. But thanks to a new U.S. Census Bureau database called Business Dynamics Statistics (BDS) that tracks job creation with the annual number of new business starts, we now know that it's not so much small businesses that create jobs as it is *new* businesses that do so (although these are obviously mostly small). *All* net new job growth in the United States since 1977, in fact, is due to new start-up businesses. If you took them out of the picture and looked only at large or established firms, job growth in the U.S. over the last thirty-four years would actually be negative.

This new understanding among economists is based on research conducted independently in 2010 by researchers led by Tim Kane at the Kauffman Foundation as well as a team led by University of Maryland economist John Haltiwanger. Haltiwanger's study reported that although start-ups one year old or younger account for only 3 percent of employment, they are responsible for a whopping 20 percent of new job growth.

To be sure, only a very small percentage of these new start-ups—the really fast-growing "gazelles"—create the bulk of those new jobs, notes economist Scott Shane. For 77 percent of the six hundred thousand new businesses started each year, he says, "life is nasty, brutish and short." Indeed, the environment for start-ups has soured so dramatically that the *Wall Street Journal* reported on November 18, 2010, that a hundred thousand fewer start-ups with one or more employees were launched in the year ending March 2010.

"Historically, it's the young, small businesses that take off that add lots of jobs," economist Haltiwanger told the *Journal*. "That process isn't working very well now."

What Is to Be Done?

So why is America so paralyzed about how to deal with the recession and kick-start job creation again? Why have we allowed ourselves to fall so far behind that we now rank last in the world, according to the ITIF, in the innovation progress we have made over this last, lost decade? Why can't policy makers see the central role of start-ups in economic growth and do whatever it takes to promote them?

The answer is that Washington simply doesn't understand the needs of the entrepreneur. Indeed, start-up entrepreneurs are just about the only Americans *without* a voice in Washington. Big Business certainly has a voice. So do labor, teachers, retailers, insurers, bankers, doctors, and just about every social and economic grouping you can think of. Only entrepreneurs lack an organized voice. Yet ironically, they are "the vital few" upon whom all of society depends for economic progress, to quote the distinguished economist Jonathan Hughes.

So what is to be done?

First and foremost, let's end this mindless one-size-fits-all approach to regulatory policy. Who ever said that it was either smart or fair to impose on start-ups the same burdensome regulations meant to keep Big Business from sinking the whole economy? Entrepreneurs and venture capitalists don't leverage debt. They don't risk other people's money. They build and invest in productive businesses and new technologies, not arcane credit default swaps or other financial instruments. In other words, they create wealth, rather than simply manipulate it. And their operations pose absolutely zero risk to the overall economy. Indeed, the total amount of money invested in venture-backed start-ups this year wouldn't even pay for the 2010 bonuses received by executives at Goldman Sachs and the other big banks.

Let's look at this issue from the standpoint of what America needs. Granted, our citizens need the Goldman Sachs of the world to be regulated sensibly or they'll destroy the whole economy again. But we also need the Innovalights of the world to be liberated from their regulatory chains so they can grow, innovate, go public, and create jobs for all Americans again.

Our most urgent goal should be to restore the IPO market to health so that innovative start-ups can obtain the capital needed to create jobs and launch new industries. We must exempt firms under $500 million in market value from the costly audit and reporting requirements of Sarbanes-Oxley. This also means amending SEC rules on the separation of research and banking at the major investment banks in order to encourage analyst coverage of good-quality small firms. In addition, we should enable the formation of what the NVCA calls a VC-backed "Private Market Platform" that would enable prescreened investors to buy private shares of small firms that don't yet have the scale to go public directly on NASDAQ. We should also loosen strictures against investors of somewhat more modest means contributing to start-up funding.

President Obama himself understood this when he signed an unprecedented executive order on January 18, 2011, to "ensure that regulations protect our safety, health and environment while promoting economic growth." Never before has a Democratic Party leader taken such a high-profile stance on behalf of *sensible* regulation. As the president noted in an op-ed he wrote for the *Wall Street Journal* that day, "Sometimes, those rules have gotten out of balance, placing unreasonable burdens on business—burdens that have stifled innovation and have had a chilling effect on growth and jobs."

Our second priority must be to create special tax breaks, capital grants, and incentives for capital-intensive start-ups, especially manufacturing start-ups, as well as for the venture investors willing to risk the often-substantial funds these large-scale job creators need to succeed. State and local governments should participate in offering these incentives, for the simple reason that they will be the first beneficiaries of any jobs created by these "big vision" firms.

And speaking of the states, it is simply outrageous that the state of California—home to Silicon Valley, the start-up capital of the world—no longer offers capital gains treatment for long-term investments in new technology ventures. Capital gains tax rates should be restored so that the state once again encourages rather than hinders the growth of entrepreneurial start-ups.

We should also offer a one-time reduction in capital gains rates to 10 percent for purchasers of IPO stock that they hold for a three-year period. This will also help restore the critical IPO job-creating machinery.

In addition, we must either forgive or defer use taxes levied against start-ups for the purchase of new equipment to grow their businesses. In fact, in critical emerging fields such as cleantech, we should really be giving start-ups capital grants up to 50 percent of the cost of new plant and equipment, just like the very smart Germans do. We should also reduce or defer the statutory and marginal income taxes paid by start-ups in their first three years of existence.

As Donald Bruce and Tami Gurley-Calvez noted in their 2006 study on the impact of taxes on entrepreneurship: "Tax policies have important implications for entrepreneurial activity. The induced behavioral responses, often in the form of good business ideas that are either not pursued or that end prematurely, likely result in significant efficiency losses in the economy. Our empirical results suggest that entrepreneurial responses to tax rate changes can be rather large."

Hiring credits? Sure, but only to businesses five years old or younger—not to corporate giants. As for the new health reform mandate that businesses must file 1099 reporting forms for every supplier with whom they spend more than $600 starting in 2012, this needs to be scrapped immediately. Why anyone felt that small businesses should be the ones to shoulder the burden of health reform is beyond me.

R&D tax credits? Incredibly, the United States is the *only* major nation on earth that doesn't provide a permanent and predictable R&D credit to business. Let's create one, and then go even further. In an op-ed in the *New York Times,* I proposed an innovation tax credit that would give small start-ups half of the money back that they spend on getting a patent (see chapter 2 for the details on how many jobs this would create). This plan received wide support.

These modest proposals barely touch on the broad range of creative ideas that could be considered to encourage start-up growth and success. Once it is recognized that the secret of U.S. economic success has always been its start-ups, then I'm sure economists and policy makers can come up with a wide array of creative measures that can promote start-up growth and job creation.

All it takes is a willingness to distinguish between the big corporate giants that need to be regulated and the small entrepreneurial start-ups that need to be liberated.

If we do that, then we can get the engine of entrepreneurialism going again in this country, and get back to our habit of producing one new industry every decade or so that generates millions of new jobs. That will help revitalize the American Dream for tens of millions of middle-class citizens.

It's not too late for America to be great again, not by a long shot. Even with all our problems, we've got a powerful ace up our sleeve—the most powerful of them all, in fact. It's our culture of regeneration, our grassroots enterprise, and our belief in the second chance.

"In Europe, where I grew up, you know a lot of times failure means you're finished," says Conrad Burke. "Not in America. Here it's a badge of honor—assuming you can learn from your mistakes. Silicon Valley forgives failure if you get up and dust yourself off."

So does Redpoint's Brody: "We just don't have a huge fear of failure. We're not afraid to fund someone who has a few stains on their resume. As long as he's passionate about the technology, about the market opportunities, and wants to get rich, I love to get behind him."

As SRI's Carlson put it: "The real magic of America is the bottom-up way we build small companies. No other country has that, none—at least not like we do here. And these new, small companies . . . they're vulnerable—like little sprouts coming up. You have to water them, and weed them, and if somebody steps on them, that's the end of them."

Amen.

Meanwhile, just as we need a regulatory regime that nurtures start-ups, so too do we need a patent regime that gives start-ups the tools they need to attract venture funding and thus ramp up their innovation and hiring. That's the subject of our next chapter.

The Patent Office

Innovation Denied

On a blustery cold day in January 2010, an inventor and entrepreneur by the name of Mirk Buzdum sits in his office on the northeast edge of the abandoned A.O. Smith factory in Milwaukee, a city struggling to recover from the loss of 70 percent of its manufacturing jobs. Tall and casually well dressed in slacks, shirt, and tie, this thirty-nine-year-old son of Serbian immigrants has the earnest, no-nonsense manner of a middle manager at a Fortune 1000 corporation—which is what he used to be before he quit his fifteen-year corporate career five years ago to take up invention full time. But his fervent intensity reveals itself when he leans forward in his chair and holds up in a trembling hand what he says is the secret to a $40 million business opportunity.

It's a two-inch-diameter saw cup for a hole saw, a tool widely used by contractors to drill out large-diameter holes in doors, walls, metal pipe, and kitchen counter surfaces so that, respectively, lock sets, plumbing, conduit, and sink fixtures can be installed. To the untrained eye, there doesn't appear to be anything remarkable about the saw cup he's holding. But Buzdum, clearly excited, insists that it's what you don't see that matters.

"See? No burn marks! Our low-friction coating takes all the heat out of it."

This, as it turns out, is no small matter. Not only are traditional hole saws inefficient—a contractor might spend only a minute to drill out a two-by-four but then five minutes more trying to extract the plug of wood that gets wedged in the saw cup—they are often dangerous as well. "These things generate a lot of heat," Buzdum explains. "A hole saw can drill at three thousand revolutions per minute, so if you touch it, you're going to the hospital. Or it can chew your hand right off if you accidentally hit the trigger. We documented a lot of injuries in the industry from hole saws, and some of the big contractors won't even use them any more because of that."

The low-friction coating is only one of four novel technologies that Buzdum and his partner Dick "Cappy" Capstran developed for their new hole saw design. The other three involve modifications to the design of the saw teeth, the pilot bit, and the saw cup itself that all have the effect of reducing the amount of surface area of drilled-out material that comes into direct contact with the saw cup. The less surface area in contact with the saw cup, the less friction and heat generated, which makes for a safer, faster, and more effective hole saw.

"With our saw, as soon as you drill, the slug falls right out," Buzdum insists. "You do not have to touch it, so there's no chance of injury. Bottom line, our saw outperforms the standard saw by what I would guess is a factor of six or so. Yet it costs less to manufacture."

Speaking of cost, Buzdum is quick to dispel any notion that an inventor's chief expense lies merely in the brainpower and time invested as he gives a tour of his shop, located in the former product development lab of A.O. Smith's giant car and truck frame manufacturing plant. When the company shifted production to Mexico a decade ago and slated the one hundred-fifty-acre site for demolition, Building 83, as it was known, was taken over by the lab's former manager, Steve Yokosh, who retooled the site into a venture called B83 Testing and Engineering. The facility now sports millions of dollars of high-end machines that evaluate product designs from an international array of manufacturers for structural integrity and durability, shock and vibration resistance, and ability to withstand temperature and humidity stresses. Buzdum and his partner, along with two other entrepreneurs, lease space in B83 and share its facilities.

With the din of huge rotary actuators and electrodynamic shakers humming in the background, Buzdum describes some of the design, fabrication, materials, and other challenges that went into developing their new hole saw technologies. Each of their saw designs had to be fabricated and then stripped of factory-applied paint, blasted with an abrasive agent, baked to remove oils, in some cases heat-treated and tempered, and then sprayed and set to cure in an industrial oven. Much of this was done in equipment large enough to drive a car into—equipment that consumes large amounts of natural gas and electricity—and each step in the process had to be controlled by specialist engineers in each of the disciplines involved. Highly skilled metallurgist consultants were also hired to help them develop a coating— the coating alone cost "well into six figures," says Buzdum—that could withstand the heat and friction demands of a high-RPM saw. And throughout the development effort, Buzdum and his partner had to (literally) burn through dozens of teeth, pilot bit, and saw cup designs before they arrived at versions they considered market ready, with each iteration along the way having to go through all of the costly fabrication and metallurgical steps in the process.

"The truth is, we probably couldn't have done this work anywhere but Milwaukee," says Buzdum. "This city used to be called the 'machine shop to the world,' and even though most of the production has gone overseas now, the expertise that made it all possible is still right here. I could take you to a hundred machine shops in this city where people have all kinds of amazing skills, and we made use of that talent to help develop our saw."

The total cost to Buzdum and Capstran of all their research and development? Three-quarters of a million dollars. For one new and improved hole saw.

That's quite an investment for two independent inventors. But Buzdum and Capstran are in most respects quite typical of start-up entrepreneurs today. Social media and cleantech start-ups in Silicon Valley may get all the glory these days, but most of the six hundred thousand new businesses started in the U.S. each year aren't located in California and don't develop Web 2.0 or cleantech technology. Like Buzdum and Capstran's venture, many are developing new industrial products and services. But what all start-ups have in common, say Kauffman Foundation researchers, is that they are the sole source of net new job growth in the United States.

They can't create jobs, though, if they can't get financing. And they can't get financing unless they can get patents that offer investors at least the promise of market exclusivity and a return on their money. Unfortunately, the vital pipeline for patents is now blocked by the chronic underfunding and paralysis of the U.S. Patent and Trademark Office (USPTO). And just as burdensome taxes and regulation undercut start-up growth, so too the current dysfunction at the patent office is preventing many tens of thousands of promising start-ups from obtaining the funding they need to develop their innovative new products, services, and medical treatments for society.

Why would anyone choose the high-risk and often-difficult life of the inventor? For Buzdum, the impetus was a perfect storm of frustration with the cookie-cutter limits of corporate life, a challenging family crisis that made him question his life's goals, and a driving inner compulsion to reinvent the way things are done.

"I started with Tyco [a $40 billion diversified global manufacturing company before it was split up in 2007] when I was nineteen, right out of high school," Buzdum explains. "I was going to college, in civil engineering, when I began working in the warehouse of their flow control division, which makes valves and other products for water and gas distribution. But pretty soon after starting there, one of the managers asked me what my career path was and I said, 'Well, what do you have in mind?' And he said they wanted to bring me into the office, for inside sales. But after a short while they decided they wanted me to get a degree in marketing. So fine, I thought. I switched gears in college and they gave me a full scholarship."

By the age of twenty-one, Buzdum had been promoted to regional sales manager at Tyco—the youngest person ever to hold such a position in the company. Over the next thirteen years, as a member of Tyco's accelerated management program, he gained managerial experience in a variety of operating divisions. He also developed several new and enhanced flow control products that were patented by the company, although he never actually considered himself an "inventor" and always felt that he was simply doing his job. He was a perfect corporate manager.

"I always thought I'd spend my whole life there," he muses. "Funny, huh?"

Then a strange series of events happened, he says. "My wife and I were building a house. And one morning I drove by the job site in my truck and I happened to notice all the contractors sitting around reconfiguring the connections to their air tools—you know, nail guns, impact wrenches, air drills, and so on. They're a big deal in construction, and I realized that they didn't have any standardized connections. They kept having to swap them out depending on which tool they were using. So I watched them setting up like this for something like forty-five minutes and I just thought it was ridiculous.

We've standardized on everything else in this country, like electrical connections. Didn't anybody think to do it with air tool connections?"

Buzdum laughs. "Hell, all I could think about as I watched them was how this inefficiency was costing me an arm and a leg. There had to be a better way to do it. " So he invented one: an adaptor that provides a universal air tool connection. He built a few prototypes in his garage and gave them to the contractors to use.

"They loved it," says Buzdum. "One of the guys even said to me, 'Hey, you've got to patent this thing.' But I didn't know anything about that aspect of it. Anyway, a short time later a friend of mine saw it, and he told me I really needed to meet this guy he knew named Cappy. Dick Capstran. So I said sure. So my friend called Cappy and Cappy said, 'Send him right over.' So I went right over to his house—this was a Friday afternoon—and showed him my adaptor."

Even five years later, Buzdum seems incredulous when he describes what happened next.

"Well, here's this guy Cappy, who's already like eighty-seven years old at the time, you know, but a successful inventor who had built and sold three companies and had some financial ability. And he takes one look at my adaptor and on the spot says to me: 'Quit your job. You're going to start working with me on Monday!'"

Buzdum rolls his eyes. "Jeez, this guy is asking me to throw a fifteen-year career down the drain? With no guarantee of security or success or anything? Whoa!"

Dazed, Buzdum went home to have what must have been one of the most anxiety-ridden talks of his life with his wife Sally. It wasn't simply about chucking the security of a six-figure-income job with Tyco. It was also about survival, because Sally had just been diagnosed with stage four breast cancer. Luckily, she had health insurance through her own employer. But when a couple faces a health crisis of this sort, you can understand why they might want to have a second health insurance policy as backup—especially one as generous as Tyco's.

"It was scary," Buzdum recalls, "real scary. I was starting to have panic attacks as I realized, 'Holy crap! Am I going to walk away from a guaranteed secure life in the middle of all this?' But, you know, Sally and I really tried to be analytical about it. Weighed all the options, the pros and cons. But in the end it really came down to something, you know, deeper."

He pauses, shrugs. "We asked each other, 'What if this is your last day on earth? What if this really is your one and only life? Would you live it differently?' Despite the cancer and everything else we were going through, we just looked at each other and decided that if we didn't go for this opportunity we were going to spend the rest of our lives pissed off that we didn't."

So Mirk and Sally Buzdum decided to sell their house and put everything they had into a new joint venture with Dick Capstran.

Who was this octogenarian—now, nonagenarian—who could lure a solid corporate type into burning his ships and joining him on the uncharted shores of entrepreneurial innovation?

Cappy, as his friends call him, grew up on the south side of Chicago during the Great Depression. He was bored with high school, so he transferred to a technical school across town. The only problem was that he couldn't pay the fare for the streetcar he needed to get there.

"A bunch of us kids would just hang on to the back of the electric streetcar and try to ride for free," he remembers, "but the conductor would come around and whap you on the face with his stick and knock you off. So then you'd try the same thing with the next one that came by, and if you were lucky, you'd maybe eventually get to school."

In time, Cappy decided to quit trying and just learn technical skills on the job instead—assuming he could find a job. So he went to see the father of a friend who ran the Chicago branch of Lincoln Engineering (now Lincoln Industrial Corporation). But the man, Jack LeVally, refused to give Cappy a job because he didn't want to be responsible for him quitting school. A week later, Cappy came back and said he'd already quit school and wasn't going back. So LeVally hired him, and right away Cappy showed a knack for fixing things.

"They had these grease guns that were always jamming up and had to be sent back to the St. Louis headquarters for repair," he recalls. "And I just took them apart and fixed them all. And that saved the company enough in shipping costs to more than pay for my salary."

How much was he making each week?

"A lot," smiles Cappy. "A lot compared to nothing. This was the Depression."

Cappy also displayed a flair for experimentation and invention. "I figured out that if you took a high-pressure grease gun and built a new kind of nozzle for it, you'd get a spray instead of a stream. Then I modified it to handle glue and other heavy fluids, like forge lubricants and road paint with glass reflective beads held in suspension, which hadn't been possible before."

Which is how the first pressurized die forge lubricant sprayer in America was probably invented—by young Cappy Capstran, aged fifteen, in 1933. His method of atomizing and spraying hot die forge lubricant under pressure was a major advance over the old hand-mopping and swabbing procedure that resulted in much of the lubricant settling out into a solid and being wasted. Cappy's invention not only kept the lubricant in suspension, which greatly improved the metal forging process and reduced scrap wastage from 50 percent to 2 percent, but also eliminated the many serious injuries that resulted from the hand-swabbing process.

"We sold those systems like gravy," he recalls, "and my boss treated me real well as a result, pay-wise. He was real fair to me."

Indeed, when Cappy volunteered for the Navy during World War II, LeVally not only promised him a job when he returned, but also sent checks to Cappy's wife and child totaling $2,000 over the course of his two years of service. That was real money in those days.

When Cappy returned home from the war, LeVally sent him to Milwaukee to run the Lincoln Engineering operation there. He did that for several years, but eventually parted on good terms with LeVally and struck out on his own. He built several businesses; one of them, Garage Products, Inc., invented and licensed new technology to the automotive service trade. He obtained a number of patents, did well financially, and finally retired and sold his businesses.

By the time Buzdum came to see him in early 2006, Cappy, despite his retirement, still hadn't kicked the invention habit—it was he who designed the first tooth structure for the new hole saw. And he saw in Buzdum's restless and resourceful energy a way to get back in the game.

In a joint interview for this book, Cappy and Buzdum described their first meeting. "When Mirk came to see me," Cappy recalls slyly, "first thing I thought was, 'Well, here's a guy who pulled himself up by his bootstraps and finally stopped drinking.'"

"You were just jealous because I was better looking," Buzdum retorts.

"No, no," Cappy demurs, waving Buzdum quiet. "I have to admit, thanks to Mirk I'm a millionaire today. Of course, I was a multimillionaire before I met him."

"Don't listen to him," Buzdum insists. "It's just the senility talking."

"Senility? Hell, I'm ninety-one years of age and . . . " Cappy suddenly stops mid-sentence and stares off blankly into space. They both crack up again.

"No, really," says Cappy, "the first time I met Mirk, it just clicked. I thought to myself, 'Here's a young, smart me.'"

"Only much better looking, don't forget," adds Buzdum.

The camaraderie between the two men may seem surprising at first, given the more than fifty-year separation in age between them. But their bond makes more sense when you realize that as inventors they both share a rare quality: most people look at the tools and trappings of daily life and accept these as givens; Buzdum and Cappy look at them and see opportunities. Even more important, they share the bond of all those who defy conventional wisdom, forsake security, and risk everything on their entrepreneurial instincts.

Hitting the Big Time

Since the February 2006 inception of Cappy's Concepts LLC, their invention partnership, Buzdum and Capstran have invented and licensed a number of new tools and technologies for the construction trades and automotive service industry, including, for the latter industry, the Blazing Fast Saddle, the In-Floor exhaust removal system, and the Positive ID tailpipe adaptor, all sold through the large trade distributor SVI International. The pair say their annual revenues have averaged half a million dollars, which has usually been enough to cover the costs of R&D and of obtaining patents while leaving a little left over. Yet despite all the stresses and the cut in pay, Buzdum says he enjoys his new life as an entrepreneur and inventor. He feels he is creating things of real value, things that will last. Best of all, Sally Buzdum's cancer has gone into remission and she is now doing fine.

"I knew the instant I met Cappy that joining up with him was the right thing to do," says Buzdum. "I knew because it was exactly the way I felt when I met my wife for the first time. Met her on a blind date, and as soon as she said 'hello,' I knew I was going to marry her. I proposed on the second date. That was fourteen years ago and I couldn't imagine life any other way."

In the fall of 2006, the two prepared to launch their new hole saw (with Cappy's design by then improved upon by Buzdum) as their first multimillion-dollar breakout invention. With one patent already issued and applications on two of their other three hole saw technologies filed and presumably being processed by the patent office—the fourth wasn't filed until 2009—Cappy and Buzdum needed to find a large manufacturing and distribution partner. They commissioned a market research report (at a cost of $10,000) that pegged the global market for hole saws at $200 million, half of that in the U.S. It also broke out hole saw manufacturers by market share. From that, the inventors identified a multibillion-dollar tool manufacturer that they believed could access a $40 million market for their new saw.

Buzdum explains what he did next: "I called them up—a cold call, mind you—and said to the receptionist, 'Hello, I'm Mirk Buzdum and I've got patents and technologies for a hole saw. May I speak with someone please?'" He shakes his head and laughs. "I felt like a Kirby vacuum cleaner salesman. But hey, that's what you have to do to get your foot in the door."

He spoke with a product development representative, who asked him to sign a nondisclosure agreement and submit the issued as well as pending patents describing the invention. Sooner than he expected, he got a call from an engineer at the company, who asked him to come out to the company's headquarters and demonstrate his new hole saw. (Buzdum has requested that the firm be identified only as BigCo owing to the possibility of future litigation.)

Buzdum recalls what happened when he arrived for the demonstration. "I'm standing there in this company's lab in front of twenty engineers and managers, and they're all looking at me like, 'Who the hell is this guy?' And I'm nervous as hell, just shaking. Because right away I see that they've laid out a block of hardwood for me to drill instead of the usual soft yellow pine typical in the industry. Obviously, they wanted to really test me. But okay, I go ahead and drill a two-inch-diameter hole in it. And the slug just flies out and falls on the floor all by itself."

Silence. All the engineers just stare at the slug on the floor. "Then all of a sudden," he says, "this one engineer comes up and puts his arm around me. And he says, 'Okay, let's talk.'"

And thus began what promised to be a mutually beneficial relationship between the two inventors and BigCo, the manufacturer. Over the next eighteen months, Buzdum worked with the company to develop a marketing plan to commercialize the invention and made further modifications in the saw designs to better suit the firm's manufacturing requirements. Meanwhile, he and Cappy waited for their patent applications to be approved by a clearly overburdened and underfunded USPTO in Washington.

And waited . . . and waited. Eighteen months went by and still they heard nothing.

"It was nerve-wracking," says Buzdum, "because a patent is the only thing that gives our invention economic value and keeps us in business. Without a patent, a billion-dollar corporation wouldn't think twice about just taking it and never paying you a dime for it."

But wait, you ask: How did Buzdum and Capstran really know that their new hole saw was truly worth anything, with or without a patent? The proof came as a surprise—a rather demoralizing one. One day in the spring of 2008, Buzdum was walking the aisles at one of the world's largest home improvement retailers when he spotted his new hole saw on the shelf.

He was stunned. "I mean, it wasn't just similar to my saw. It *was* my saw! And it was manufactured by this company we were supposed to be partnering with."

Thus began eighteen more months of legal back-and-forth between the inventors and BigCo's heavy-hitter legal department. Knowing they needed expert help of their own, Buzdum and Capstran retained a well-known intellectual property law firm. They wanted to show BigCo that they weren't dealing with a couple of amateurs.

In November 2009, however, the dispute took an unexpected and dramatic turn. BigCo's attorneys sent Buzdum and Capstran's attorney documentation that they claimed was "proof" that they couldn't have stolen the two men's technology. It was a copy of one of the firm's patent applications with a filing date of March 2006, six months before Buzdum met with the company's engineers. And sure enough, right on the first page of the application there appeared a drawing of exactly the same tapered spade pilot bit the two men say that they invented. The inventors named in the patent application were the BigCo engineer Buzdum first met with in the fall of 2006, as well as an engineer at the firm's Chinese manufacturing facility.

Buzdum was floored. "I thought, holy crap! Did I somehow see their technology and unconsciously think it was mine? But how could that be? I filed our patent application for it on July 28, 2006, before I'd ever met with them. Could it be, then, that we had somehow both invented similar technology at around the same time, with them inventing theirs a few months before we developed ours? I mean, this sort of thing has happened before, you know."

Indeed it has. Alexander Graham Bell's 1876 race against Elisha Gray to the patent office, and their subsequent bitter legal battle over the rights to the telephone, was perhaps the most famous example of this sort of simultaneous invention.

"But I had trouble believing that," says Buzdum. "It's not just similar technology. It's exactly the same pilot bit design as ours. I mean, you could place the drawing of it from their application right over ours and it's a perfect overlay. So I didn't know what the hell to think."

BigCo's supposed proof gnawed at him. "I took a copy of their application home and read it over dinner with my wife. We were both totally bummed, because this was our financial future at stake here. But as I kept reading it over, it dawned on me that the text and the drawing didn't quite match up. I mean, sure, they had a drawing of the pilot bit. But they didn't refer to that pilot bit either in the description of the invention or in the claims language. Then I noticed something else strange: the drawing they used was labeled 'Figure 19.' Now, usually a published patent application will use 'Figure 1' on the first page. Why were they using 'Figure 19' for it?"

Buzdum's anger rises as he recalls what happened. "And then it hit me. Damn! I jumped up from the dinner table and ran to the office to check all the patent office documentation on their patent. And sure enough, their original patent application—filed in March 2006—didn't say or show anything about the pilot bit. Nothing at all. Only their *amended* application—which they filed in 2008 almost two years *after* I met with them—mentioned the technology.

"In other words," says Buzdum, practically spitting out the words, "it looked like a kind of fraud! We now had proof that we invented it first. Not only that, we had proof that eighteen months after I showed them the invention—probably around the time they decided to go to market with it and cut us out of the deal—they went and basically 'backdated' their application to claim it as theirs!"

As Buzdum and Capstran's attorney noted in a December 23, 2009, letter to BigCo: "It appears that your company added the subject matter of my clients' invention to your [amended] patent application *after* it was disclosed in confidence by my clients to [BigCo]. By putting my clients' confidential information into [your] published patent application, [BigCo] has destroyed my clients' ability to maintain this information in confidence until their patent issues."

As of late January 2011, it was still unclear how the dispute would be resolved. All four of Buzdum and Capstran's patent applications had finally been granted—some of them four years after being filed—but already they had spent more than $200,000 in legal fees, with the money coming from Cappy's savings and investments. BigCo probably assumed the two wouldn't have the financial resources to challenge them. And had they been any other small business inventors, BigCo might have been right. But Buzdum and Capstran are not giving up. If BigCo refuses to compensate them for using their invention, the two inventors could be looking at $5 million or more to litigate the matter. But a group of investors, impressed by the strength of their case, has agreed to finance any litigation against BigCo that may be necessary to secure justice.

"If the patent office had processed our application in eighteen months like they're supposed to, we wouldn't be in this situation," Buzdum insists. "Our technology would never have been stolen. The fact is, USPTO delays have jeopardized our business, maybe even killed it. And there are many, many other small business innovators in the same boat."

A National Problem

Indeed there are, as the award-winning *Milwaukee Journal Sentinel* reporter John Schmid revealed in his remarkable 2009 series of investigative reports about the effects of patent office delays on entrepreneurial innovators like Buzdum and Capstran. Their "David and Goliath" story, Schmid wrote, illustrates how the dysfunction at the USPTO is imperiling not only entrepreneurial inventors but the economic recovery as a whole and even America's global innovation leadership.

That a plucky reporter for a smaller city newspaper broke this story rather than the *New York Times* or *Wall Street Journal* is a testament not only to Schmid's and the *Milwaukee Journal Sentinel*'s enterprising journalism. It also demonstrates just how obscure the patent office really is, and how little the media, the policy community, or the public at large understands the USPTO's critical role in job creation, economic progress, and the quality of life of all Americans. As you will shortly discover, the stakes in patent office performance are just about as high as they get.

Here's the problem. Since 1992, Congress has diverted nearly $1 billion in applicant-paid fees already earned by the USPTO to other uses (such as to help pay for the 2010 census), leaving the patent office understaffed, under-resourced, and wholly unable to deal with the threefold increase in patent applications over the last twenty years.

As a result, the patent office now takes an average of 3.7 years to rule on a patent—and many applications take 6, 7, or even more years. As of January 2011, the total number of patent applications waiting for approval was a staggering 1.2 million—triple the number just ten years ago. More than half of these applications had never even had an initial review.

Simply put, this threatens America's future. According to the 2008 Berkeley Patent Survey, 76 percent of venture-backed start-up entrepreneurs and 67 percent of *all* start-up entrepreneurs say patents are vital to obtaining financing from venture capitalists and other investors. Similarly, Jerry Cao of Singapore Management University and Po-Hsuan Hsu of the University of Connecticut found that start-ups with patents attract larger and more experienced venture capital investors and "significantly larger amounts" of investment. A third recent study conducted by the consulting firm IPVision in association with the MIT Sloan School of Management found that strong patents were closely associated with start-up success.

"It is the intellectual property that [provides] the basis for investors to place their resources at risk," wrote Mario Cardullo, counselor for technology and entrepreneurship within the International Trade Administration of the U.S. Department of Commerce.

In other words, no patent often means no venture financing—and no way for start-ups to create the new products, new jobs, and new industries of tomorrow. Even Gary Locke, President Obama's Secretary of Commerce, who oversees the USPTO, concedes that this situation is untenable. "This delay causes uncertainty for inventors and entrepreneurs and impedes our economic recovery," he told one newspaper.

No kidding. By eroding the certainty of patent protection, it also undermines the economic incentives for innovation itself, if for no other reason than that it reduces the likelihood that entrepreneurs and investors can realize a return on all their hard work and investment.

Starved for funds and resources, and hamstrung by a nearly 50 percent turnover rate among its underpaid examiners, the USPTO in previous years tried to deal with this backlog through policies that can only be described as Kafkaesque. First, it suddenly cut its allowance rate on patents from the 65 percent rate that had prevailed during the previous three decades to barely 40 percent in 2007–2008. In other words, some experts say, the agency arbitrarily denied patents to deserving innovators just to reduce the backlog of waiting applications.

Interestingly, the surprisingly effective new director of the USPTO, David Kappos, has promised to change that practice. Already there are signs that the allowance rate is beginning to inch back up to historic levels.

The patent office also tried to clear the logjam by "accelerating" the examination of a small business's patent—but only if that business agreed to abandon another application it filed.

Says Buzdum: "For small entrepreneurs like us, this is like burning the furniture to keep warm. We're not a big company. We don't have a lot of extra money to file trivial or frivolous patent applications the way giant patent factories like Microsoft and IBM do. If we're going to spend thousands of dollars to apply for a patent, it's because it's vital for our business."

Starting from Schmid's original reporting, our own investigation confirmed that the dysfunction at the patent office has hamstrung entrepreneurs across a wide range of industries.

Consider the case of the biotech start-up MatriLab, which had developed a wound-healing gel based on technology licensed from the University of Wisconsin in 2002. The company won the Wisconsin Governor's Business Plan Contest and was led by Kathleen Kelleher, an entrepreneur with twenty-five years' experience in the biotech industry, including stints as chief operating officer for Amarillo Biosciences, senior director of corporate licensing at Searle Pharmaceuticals, and vice president of planning and business development at Curative Technologies.

"The technology was originally developed by Dr. John Kao, a brilliant and highly respected professor of pharmacy and biomaterials at the University of Wisconsin," Kelleher explains. "We felt our product had real potential in the $100 million market for the treatment of burns as well as diabetic ulcers, and in joint repair and regenerative medicine."

But there was a problem. Because the company couldn't get its patent approved or even examined, it was unable to attract the new investment it needed to commercialize the product. Potential investors, after all, wanted to be assured that this start-up had some degree of exclusivity for its product before putting money into the company. So in 2007, five years after it filed its patent application for the wound-healing gel, MatriLab went belly up.

In the end, the USPTO did eventually issue the patent—but only seven years after MatriLab's application was filed, two years after the company went bankrupt, and too late to save a promising new health innovation that might have done the public some good.

"I'll be the first to admit that getting a new company and new product off the ground is challenging in the best of circumstances," concedes Kelleher. "But because the patent office works like molasses, it made a challenging situation totally impossible. It's a shame, too, and not just for MatriLab. Our new treatment might have helped a lot of people."

Says Kao, the inventor of MatriLab's wound-healing technology, "The fact that we were engaged in meaningful discussions with venture investors and industry partners shows that our technology had real value. But without a patent, they could not move forward with us."

In other words, in many cases even the most innovative medical discovery in the world and a dollar will barely get you on the bus if you don't have a patent that can attract the funding you need to commercialize that discovery and get it into the hands of patients who need it.

The impairment of the patent office affects innovators not only in Wisconsin, of course, but all over the nation as well, including in the heart of Silicon Valley itself. Just ask Vern Norviel, a partner in the highly regarded Silicon Valley law firm of Wilson Sonsini Goodrich & Rosati, where he leads the patents and innovation counseling practice. The former general counsel at Perlegen Sciences, a biotech start-up that scans the human genome for new therapies, as well as at the publicly traded biotech firm Affymetrix, which pioneered the use of DNA chip technology, Norviel is intimately involved with some of the most exciting innovations in life sciences today. And to say he is frustrated with the impact that USPTO dysfunction is having on the development of new medical treatments is an understatement.

"Over the last few years, all my life sciences companies have either been slowed down or stopped by problems with the patent office," Norviel declares. "And I mean *all* of them. That's because in this field it's absolutely necessary to have a bulletproof patent. It can cost a billion dollars to bring a new drug to market, and no one is going to invest that kind of money unless they know they've got exclusive rights to it and can get a return on their investment."

He mentions one company in particular that he's working with, Innate Immune, whose experience, he said, "just makes me mad at a very visceral level."

In the first place, says Norviel, "They have a new treatment for lupus that is clearly patentable—I mean, if anything is patentable, this is it. It was invented by a world-famous immunologist at Stanford named Sam Strober. But it's also personal for me. I have a former girlfriend from many years ago and she got lupus. It's very tragic, because this a horrible disease. For some people it's deadly. And there's no treatment for it, just steroids, which only treat some of the symptoms and can be very damaging to the body."

He pauses a moment. "So here this company has the first drug that might really treat this disease, and they can't get a patent. They've been waiting seven years for it! They had venture investors ready to give them $30 million to move the drug toward clinical trials. But without a patent, they backed out. So now the company survives on little bits of friend and family money."

Innate Immune's CEO is Dr. Andrew Perlman (Strober serves on the board), a man who has helped lead several successful biotech companies in the past, including as senior director of clinical research at Genentech. According to Perlman, Innate Immune also had a corporate partnership in the works with a large drug manufacturer, but as he puts it, "their attorneys were alarmed that we did not have the patent, so the deal fell through."

Again, no patent means no business—and no help for suffering patients. "With some people, the only manifestation of their lupus is a characteristic skin rash," Perlman explains. "But many other patients manifest their lupus with kidney failure that ultimately requires them to go on dialysis or need a transplant. It can also cause cardiac disease or central nervous system disease. So it can definitely be life threatening."

Recently, one of Innate Immune's patents finally issued. But what if the firm had gotten its patent in reasonable time? "Had the patent office worked like it's supposed to, our drug would be in clinical testing by now. How great would that be for people? But now? Well, I can't say how many more years it will be before we can get this treatment out to people."

Meanwhile, three thousand miles away in Florida, Roger Hoffman, with thirty-six patents to his credit, is probably America's most prolific inventor of environmental technologies for the paper and water treatment industries. Like the other innovators profiled here, Hoffman is not just some crackpot inventing a new method for exercising a cat (yes, there really is a patent for that). As chief operating officer of a paper mill in the 1970s, he invented technology that enabled his firm to become the first in the world to discharge absolutely no contaminated waste—technology that is now widely used throughout the industry. He was a founder of the National Office Paper Recycling Project involving firms such as IBM, Xerox, and Eastman Kodak, and he also put his expertise to work helping companies as diverse as Walmart and McDonald's change their environmental practices. He has received numerous awards, including one from the Environmental Protection Agency, and was honored in 1991 by the first President Bush in a Rose Garden ceremony for his outstanding innovations in the environmental field.

When he became an entrepreneur and founded Hoffman Environmental Systems in 1993, Hoffman says, the patent office worked efficiently on behalf of innovators. "One of my water management patents issued in eleven months," he recalls, "which was important in enabling us to generate earnings from our discoveries and keep inventing."

But over the past decade, the system has gotten jammed up, with some of Hoffman's patents taking up to eight years to issue. He describes one particularly galling experience:

> We had one patent that, even after several years, was just going nowhere at the USPTO. We finally called up the examiner who was reviewing it, and he gave us verbal notice of allowance that it was going to issue. Well, months go by, and we still hadn't gotten the official notice. So we called the examiner back—and kept calling every few weeks—leaving voice mail for him each time. Still we heard nothing. Finally, we called his supervisor to find out what was going on. And the guy says, "Oh, sorry, but that examiner no longer works here. I guess we should have turned off his voice mail." Gee, you think? Anyway, the kicker was that the supervisor then says, "Well, unfortunately, we have to start all over with the examination." Unbelievable. So that was three more years wasted until it issued.

What makes the whole process worse, Hoffman insists, is that the patent office now publishes two-thirds of all patent applications for all the world to see eighteen months after they are filed. Because of this, he claims, his discoveries have been stolen by large companies. Hoffman says he has been involved in litigation with two of the biggest paper manufacturers in the world for infringing his patents. One of them, Georgia Pacific, settled a few years ago. But he remains embroiled in an extended legal battle with International Paper, which has used its immense financial resources to attempt to drown him in litigation costs, hoping he'll give up the fight.

As economist and 1996 Ross Perot vice presidential running mate Pat Choate wrote in the *Huffington Post,* "America's largest corporations are using a business technique called 'efficient infringement' [whereby] they calculate the benefits of stealing someone else's patented technology against the possibility of being forced to pay damages."

And they can't be forced to pay, of course, if the victim can't get his patent issued.

For his part, Hoffman says he never wanted to be a litigator. He just wanted to be an inventor, which he considers a noble profession. "I'm sixty-five years old now," he says. "Do I really want to spend the last years of my life and all my resources fighting the bastards who are stealing my inventions? The whole situation just breaks my heart."

And what of the tens of thousands of small business entrepreneurs who don't have the resources to commercialize their own inventions without investor financing, or to wage a multimillion-dollar legal fight against a multinational corporate infringer? As former patent examiner John White, now a patent attorney representing small businesses, told the *Milwaukee Journal Sentinel*: "This story is repeated thousands of times. Many entrepreneurs have no choice but to give up on their dreams."

The Biggest Job Creator You Never Heard Of

Why should anyone spend a lot of time worrying about the problems of a hundred thousand or so entrepreneurs harmed by patent office dysfunction? After all, the so-called recovery has evaporated in front of our eyes and close to 30 million Americans are unable to find full-time jobs. The second wave of foreclosures has already begun with a vengeance—this time affecting people who did *not* buy too much house but instead simply had too little savings left to pay for a mortgage that would have been perfectly affordable if only they still had a job. Across the country, teachers are being laid off, fire and police services are being cut back, and many cities and even a few states are on the brink of financial collapse. So against all this, in the middle of the worse recession in eighty years, why concentrate our worried attention on the logjam at one of the most obscure agencies in federal government?

Because for all its obscurity, the patent office is still the single-greatest facilitator of private-sector job creation in the nation. There can be no recovery until we once again start creating the new jobs and new industries of tomorrow. And as we demonstrated in chapter 1, job creation depends upon start-ups, the vast majority of which—at least in the high-tech field—need patents to secure the financing that enables them to hire and grow their business.

"Hundreds of thousands of groundbreaking innovations are sitting on the shelf literally waiting to be examined," noted USPTO director Kappos in a May 2010 speech to a biotechnology conference. "[This results in] jobs not being created, life-saving drugs not going to the marketplace, companies not being funded, businesses not being formed."

How many jobs are not being created because of the patent backlog?

"Millions," said Kappos. "Millions of jobs."

I first met Kappos soon after he was appointed by President Obama. Then, in February 2010, I helped organize a meeting in Silicon Valley between Kappos and a number of small business entrepreneurs during which the USPTO director listened intently to their stories of woe caused by the patent office backlog. Kappos showed no defensiveness at these meetings. He seemed completely sincere in his stated intention to solve the problem.

In the months that followed, we kept up a steady communication. I shared with him more stories about entrepreneurs we had interviewed for this book who had been harmed by USPTO dysfunction (including the case of Innate Immune). In return, Kappos and his staff were extremely helpful in finding the data we needed on small business patenting trends that were buried deep in the byzantine bowels of the USPTO's outmoded information systems.

Meanwhile, it had become clear that the only way to focus Congress's and the American people's attention on "America's innovation agency," as Kappos calls the patent office, was to vividly demonstrate the USPTO's role in job creation. In today's dire economy, after all, job creation is the Holy Grail. If a strong case could be made that a well-functioning patent office means more jobs, Congress might act—or so we and thousands of entrepreneurs hoped.

Kappos testified before Congress. He issued a white paper—the first in USPTO history—outlining the cost to the nation in lost job creation from the patent office backlog. He traveled around the country holding "innovation forums" to lobby for more funding and support for the patent office. And he went out of his way to hear the concerns of small business.

"Everyone knows that small businesses create jobs," says Kappos. "They create jobs quickly and they create more jobs by far than large businesses do." He laughs. "And I'm a guy who came out of big business—twenty-six years at IBM. But we all know that the most disruptive innovation—the kind that creates jobs—comes from small businesses. I truly believe that restoring this agency to health will have a disproportionately positive impact on small business, and therefore on the country."

Knowing that Kappos had taken a huge pay cut (as had all his top staff) to come to work in Washington, I couldn't help but be impressed with the dedication he showed as a public servant. I remember thinking to myself, "So *this* is what good government looks like."

Meanwhile, as Kappos worked the halls of Congress, my coauthor David Kline and I tried to generate public awareness of the issue by writing an article for the prestigious *Harvard Business Review* that called the patent office "the biggest job creator you never heard of." It generated a number of comments in the magazine, the interest of several news organizations, and interestingly enough, even sparked a call from the White House's National Economic Council.

Then we teamed up with Judge Paul Michel, the newly retired chief judge of the U.S. Court of Appeals for the Federal Circuit, which handles the nation's patent appeals. Judge Michel is widely respected for his integrity and exceptional record on the court. Together we presented a two-pronged jobs plan in an August 5, 2010, guest editorial (or "op-ed") in the *New York Times,* headlined "Inventing Our Way Out of Joblessness."

In that op-ed, Judge Michel and I urged Congress to provide the patent office with a $1 billion surge of capital to restore it to proper functioning. "This," we wrote, "would enable the agency to upgrade its outmoded computer systems and hire and train additional examiners to deal with the threefold increase in patent applications over the past 20 years. Congress should also pass pending legislation that would prohibit any more diverting of patent fees and give the office the authority to set its own fees.

"Once the patent office is back to operating effectively," we argued, "the backlog of 1.2 million applications should yield, judging from history, roughly 780,000 issued patents, about 137,000 of which would go to small businesses." Going forward, then, the agency would likely grant an additional 88,000 or so patents over the next three years. All told, by 2014 small businesses would have received a total of approximately 225,000 patents that they could use to secure financing to build their businesses and hire more workers.

To be sure, not every patent creates a job or generates economic value. But some, we wrote, "are worth thousands of jobs—Jack Kilby's 1959 patent for a semiconductor, for example, or Steve Wozniak's 1979 patent for a personal computer. It's impossible to predict how many new jobs or even new industries may lie buried within the patent office's backlog. But according to our analysis of the data in the 2008 Berkeley Patent Survey, each issued patent is associated with somewhere between 3 and 10 new jobs."

Therefore, we argued, "restoring the patent office to full functionality would create, over the next three years, at least 675,000 and as many as 2.25 million jobs. Assuming a mid-range figure of 1.5 million, the price would be roughly $660 per job—[which is] 525 times more cost effective than the 2.5 million jobs created by the government's $787 billion stimulus plan." Even if you assume that only 10 percent of the money allocated under the stimulus plan has actually been spent, our plan would still be nearly fifty times more cost effective per job created.

The second prong of our plan involved a novel "innovation tax credit" to incentivize job-creating innovation. The core concept was first suggested by Ted Sichelman, a professor at San Diego Law School, University of California, and one of the authors of the Berkeley Patent Survey. But in our conception, as outlined in our *New York Times* op-ed, "Congress should also offer small businesses a tax credit of up to $19,000 for every patent they receive, enabling them to recoup half of the average $38,000 in patent office and lawyers' fees spent to obtain a patent. Cost, after all, is the No. 1 deterrent to patent-seeking, as the patent survey found.

"For the average 30,000 patents issued to small businesses each year, a $19,000 innovation tax credit would mean a loss of about $570 million in tax revenue in a year. But if it led to the issuance of even one additional patent per small business, it would create 90,000 to 300,000 jobs."

Ultimately, we contended, "Fully financing the patent office and creating an innovation tax credit could mean as many as 2.5 million new jobs over three years, and add up to 600,000 more jobs every year thereafter."

Schmid's articles in the *Milwaukee Journal Sentinel*, our articles, and those of other journalists and business leaders, and especially Kappos's forceful leadership all contributed to the president finally issuing a public appeal on July 12, 2010, to Speaker of the House Nancy Pelosi for $129 million in immediate supplemental funding for the USPTO. That, in turn, led to congressional passage of the USPTO Supplemental Appropriations Act (H.R.5874) and its signing by the president on August 10, 2010.

A good start, to be sure. But then on September 30, 2010, as part of a stopgap budget measure, Congress froze any further funding for the patent office. The net effect is that the USPTO is on track to collect $365 million in user fees in 2011 that it will not be allowed to spend unless Congress specifically authorizes it.

As the patent lawyer and insightful policy critic Gene Quinn noted on his widely read *IP Watchdog* blog, "That means there is a $1 million per day national innovation tax being imposed because Congress refuses to let the Patent Office keep the money it collects."

Remember, the patent office costs the American taxpayer not one single dime. Not one. It is entirely funded through patent applicant fees. Indeed, it is the only arm of the entire federal government that is wholly self-supporting.

What the Founding Fathers Knew

For most citizens, the patent office really is the biggest job creator they never heard of. But America's Founding Fathers knew very well its extraordinary value to the nation.

At the time of our nation's birth, after all, the men who had led the revolution and were tasked with writing the Constitution struggled not just with the challenge of creating lasting political structures that could defend the hard-won freedom and sovereignty of the newly liberated colonies. They were equally concerned with finding some way of stimulating the rapid growth of industry and commerce to ensure the new nation's economic survival.

And make no mistake: the survival of the United States was far from certain in those days. Ours was a backward agrarian economy, dependent on imports and lacking significant domestic industry, with a population of barely 3 million inhabitants. Britain, meanwhile, with whom we had just fought a war and would soon fight another, had three times our population, boasted the most powerful economy on earth, and was the leader of the emerging industrial revolution. Therefore the design of institutions that could encourage economic activities and investments that spurred the rapid growth of America's primitive economy was a matter of prime importance at the Constitutional Convention of 1787.

The founders, of course, had studied European institutions, including their patent systems, and noted their tendency to reinforce the wealth and prerogatives of elites rather than the welfare and productive capacity of the whole of society. In Britain, for instance, patents were favors granted "by grace of the Crown" and were often only secured through court connections. What's more, according to economic historians B. Zorina Khan and the late Kenneth Sokoloff, patents "were subject to any restrictions the government cared to impose, including the expropriation of the patent without compensation." Patent application fees were ludicrously high—ten times the per capita income of the average citizen—which put the system out of reach of all but the wealthy. And contemporary writing, including an 1830 book entitled *A Practical Treatise on the Law of Patents for Inventions,* noted that British patent law severely limited the ability of inventors to sell or license the rights to their discoveries, which further restricted innovation to the wealthy few who had the capital to commercialize their own inventions. The fact is that Britain's leadership of the industrial revolution had much more to do with its extensive commercial holdings, large manufacturing base, and vast stores of amassed capital than to any systemic encouragement of innovation in British society.

America had no such capital or commercial assets. All we had were abundant—but still untapped—natural resources, and a population unique in the world for its prolific, enterprising, and independent character. Ours was the world's fastest-growing population, doubling in size every twenty years. We were also widely literate (albeit most lacked higher education) and informed by what Washington Irving called "the general diffusion of knowledge." Most important, unlike the tenant farmers and laborers who made up the bulk of England's rigid class society, the vast majority of Americans were free-holding small farmers, merchants, shopkeepers, artisans, and mechanics—the forerunners of what we today call the middle class—who were possessed of what publisher Hezekiah Niles called "a universal ambition to go forward."

This was our only asset, our ace in the hole. And men such as George Washington, Thomas Jefferson, and James Madison knew they had to find a way to unleash the creative and productive potential of this mass of independent citizens if the country was to industrialize and survive.

As Jefferson wrote to his daughter Martha in 1787, it was precisely because America was bereft of Europe's vast resources and left to its own devices that "we are obliged to invent and execute; to find means within ourselves, and not to lean on others."

But how to do that? From the historical record, it appears that the founders very deliberately (Khan and Sokoloff say "quite self-consciously") sought to construct a patent system that would do what no other patent system in the world had ever done before—namely, stimulate the inventive genius and entrepreneurial energy of the masses of ordinary people.

They did this first of all by introducing for the first time in any nation's constitution an intellectual property clause. Section 8 of Article 1 of the U.S. Constitution, which was adopted on September 5, 1787, by unanimous consent of the delegates, obligated the new national government to "promote the progress of science and useful arts, by securing for limited times to authors and inventors the exclusive right to their respective writings and discoveries."

This first-ever intellectual property clause was the subject of more than a little debate. Jefferson, like some other delegates, was uncertain about the wisdom of granting "temporary monopolies" (i.e., patent rights). America, after all, had just waged a bloody war of independence to overthrow the British monopoly of trade and political power. As other delegates noted, however, a monopoly of trade contributes nothing to the output of a nation and is a far cry from the temporary incentives granted to inventors that actually do stimulate economic growth. It's only the poverty of our language that makes us apply the same word "monopoly" to describe these two very different things.

In the end, the delegates agreed with Madison when he warned that the wellsprings of creation—whether of literary works or of inventions—would dry up unless authors and inventors could make a living from and profit by their efforts. In Madison's view, "The public good *fully coincides* with the [patent rights] of individuals." Jefferson himself would later fully agree with Madison, after he had seen the practical results of the first patent law.

The real genius of the founders in creating the conditions for future American prosperity, however, lay in the way they enabled the rights of inventors to manifest themselves in everyday life. The first patent law passed by Congress on April 10, 1790, deliberately set patent fees to a level any ordinary citizen could afford—initially $3.70, but three years later raised to $30. This was still less than 5 percent of the rate in Britain. Patent fees remained $30 for the next seventy years, ensuring that the patent system would remain open to all citizens during the industrial revolution.

They also restricted patents to only the "first and true inventor" rather than a corporate entity, and later adopted the world's first examination system for patents that ensured their novelty and validity (and therefore their commercial value). By other means as well—including greatly simplifying administrative procedures for applying for a patent as well as allowing anyone applying for a patent by mail to do so postage-free—they created a patent system that encouraged invention and innovation on a truly mass and unprecedented scale.

The results were dramatic. Whereas most of Britain's handful of inventors came from privilege—who else could afford to dabble in inventive activity?—the vast majority of America's many thousands of inventors came from humble beginnings. They were farmers, factory workers, merchants, mechanics, and carpenters and other artisans for the most part.

Indeed, of the four hundred so-called great inventors of the nineteenth century in America, over 70 percent had only a primary or secondary school education. Half had little or no formal schooling at all. And many of the most famous names in American invention—men such as Matthias Baldwin (locomotive), George Eastman (roll film), Elias Howe (sewing machine), and Thomas Edison (electric light and phonograph)—had to leave school early to support their families.

What's more, the majority of these inventors had no special scientific or technical expertise. Like our own Buzdum, Capstran, and Hoffman, they had only the general knowledge common to most citizens of their day. What distinguished them was their ingenuity in using that general knowledge to solve the practical problems of daily existence and exploit the commercial opportunities that arose as a result. In short, they were *entrepreneurial*.

But perhaps the most crucial element of the American patent system was that it did not simply encourage ordinary people to participate in inventive activity. It made it *economically feasible* for them to do so. By creating a means for inventors with little or no capital to license their discoveries to companies and enterprises that could then commercialize them, the patent system enabled relatively large numbers of ordinary people to generate income from invention and even make it their full-time career. Which naturally generated even more innovation.

And in those days, before the emergence of in-house corporate R&D departments in the early twentieth century, patent licensing was the principal means by which new discoveries were commercialized. Announcements of new patented discoveries were placed in publications such as *Scientific American* that were expressly founded for the purpose of disseminating information about patents. Commercial enterprises would then license or purchase these patented inventions and use them in their product development.

American Bell Telephone's new product pipeline, for example, operated like most others at the time. In 1894, its R&D department licensed seventy-three patents from outside inventors, while developing only twelve inventions from its own employees.

Thomas Blanchard was a typical inventor-licensor. He was the son of a small farmer who invented and patented a mechanical tack-maker in 1806 that could fabricate five hundred tacks per minute, each superior to tacks made by hand. He sold the rights to his machine for $5,000, quite a sum in those days. He then invented a lathe to produce uniform gun stocks, and the patent he received for it enabled him to attract investors for the production of those gun stocks for the local Boston market. But Blanchard also leased the rights to this invention to gun producers nationwide, as well as to manufacturers of tool handles and wheel spokes. The income he generated from patent licensing enabled him to make inventing his full-time career, and he went on to invent a wood-bending machine, an upriver steamboat, and a steam wagon that was used until the introduction of railroads in the U.S. He received a total of twenty-five patents during his career.

That patents could be used as *tradable assets* was a wholly unique feature of the American patent system, and it led to a dramatic rise in the per capita patenting rate as large numbers of people without wealth started inventing and licensing their discoveries to firms that commercialized these inventions. By 1865, the U.S. per capita patenting rate was triple that of Britain's, according to that year's annual reports from the commissioners of patents in both countries. These same annual reports for 1880 indicate that 85 percent of all patents in the U.S. were licensed by their inventors, compared with only 30 percent of patents issued in Britain.

"The ability to trade patent rights also supported specialization by providing a means for the technologically creative to mobilize capital to support the development of their ideas," observed Naomi Lamoreaux and Sokoloff in *Financing Innovation in the United States: 1870 to Present*. "By mid century, inventors were increasingly operating as independent entrepreneurs who specialized at invention and extracted the returns from their discoveries by selling off or licensing the patent rights to a variety of different firms."

Today these inventor-licensors would be called "non-practicing entities" (NPEs) or, as some today call them, "patent trolls." But this confuses the harm sometimes caused by real patent trolls with the beneficial effect that invention labs, universities, patent licensing firms, and other inventors without the wealth or scale to commercialize their own discoveries actually had upon U.S. technology development and economic growth. For it turns out that it was precisely the ability of American innovators to specialize in invention while leaving commercialization and sales to others that enabled the United States to develop the most innovative and successful economy in the history of the world.

As Jefferson himself noted, the distinctive American patent system had "given a spring to invention beyond my conception." Only thirteen years after the first patent law was enacted by Congress, the United States had already surpassed Britain—until then the unrivaled leader of the industrial revolution—in the number of new inventions patented, even though Britain still had more than twice America's population. By 1860, the number of new inventions patented in the United States was several times the number patented in Britain, although our populations were by then approximately equal in size.

According to Lamoreaux and Sokoloff:

> [Foreign] observers attributed much of the country's rapid technological progress to its distinctive patent system. Quite revolutionary in design at inception, the U.S. patent system came to be much admired for providing broad access to property rights in new technological knowledge and for facilitating trade in patented technologies. These features attracted the technologically creative, even those who lacked the capital to directly exploit their inventions . . . and also fostered a division of labor between the conduct of inventive activity and the application of technical discoveries to actual production. It is no coincidence that Britain and many other European countries [later] began to modify their patent institutions to make them more like those of the Americans.

All of this makes the opprobrium heaped upon licensing firms by some big tech companies today rather ironic. They can talk all they want about NPE-initiated patent litigation being out of control, but the fact is that the patent litigation rate was actually far higher in the nineteenth century than it is today. Yet this did not seem to slow the industrial revolution any.

In fact, the industrial revolution never would have happened had it not been for NPE inventors like Blanchard and Thomas Edison who licensed most of their technology rather than commercializing it themselves. Patent assignment records show that an astonishing *two-thirds* of all of America's "great inventors" in the nineteenth century were actually NPEs.

Does it really make sense to consider Edison a "patent troll" just because he licensed most of his inventions rather than commercializing them himself?

As the inventor of electric light and power, the phonograph, and many other world-changing new technologies, his contributions to America's economic progress are beyond dispute. For Edison no less than for most other U.S. inventors of the time, licensing was the ticket to the American Dream.

Even today, most NPEs are not trolls but inventors and R&D firms that operate on the Edison model and specialize in invention. My own company, Tessera, for example, conducts very expensive cutting-edge research to develop new miniaturization technologies, which we then license to semiconductor and camera manufacturers worldwide. Of our 415 employees, 270 work full-time in our R&D labs, and 20 percent of those hold PhDs in various engineering disciplines.

In the words of Damon Matteo, chief of intellectual capital at the world-famous Palo Alto Research Center (PARC), "The breadth with which you define the term 'patent troll' is directly proportional to your likelihood of infringing a small company's patents."

In any event, the wisdom of the founders in creating a democratized patent system open to the masses of citizens, regardless of whether or not they had the capital to commercialize their own discoveries, had a profound effect not only on America's economy but on its culture as well.

"By the early nineteenth century," writes the eminent historian Gordon S. Wood in his 2010 book *Empire of Liberty,* "technology and prosperity were assuming for Americans the same sublime and moral significance that the enlightenment had reserved for the classical state and the Newtonian universe. Eli Whitney, inventor of the cotton gin, and Robert Fulton, creator of the steamboat, became national heroes."

And for the first time in human history, a nation had come to see its greatness not in empire or military might or royal lineage, but in its capacity for technological progress.

There was nothing preordained about our economic success, no special "Yankee ingenuity" gene in our hereditary stock. It was a patent system that, in the words of Abraham Lincoln (America's only presidential patentee), "added the fuel of interest to the fire of genius" in generation after generation of innovative small business entrepreneurs that sparked the creation of the American Dream.

That dream remains alive today, manifested in the roughly two hundred twenty thousand patents (half issued to U.S. residents) that the USPTO, despite its problems, still manages to issue every year. Certainly, some of these patents are for trivial inventions that won't appreciably benefit society. But many others are job-creating patents that enable start-ups to attract investors, hire employees, and develop the new products, services, and medical treatments that will benefit all society in the future.

New Risks, New Threats

Ironically, the more that the USPTO patent backlog threatens the intrinsic value of new invention today, the more such patents are needed by firms to protect the value of their inventions. Put another way, if patents have always been enablers of new business formation and job creation, today they have become often indispensable to start-up business survival.

Take Silicon Valley start-up ShotSpotter, profiled in chapter 1 of this book. Its former CEO and current president James Beldock believes that the backlog at the patent office is making innovation riskier than ever for start-ups like his. "The current climate, where it takes five years or more to get a patent, means that you've got to do everything you possibly can to protect the value of your technology," he explains. "So if you can't get your patent from the patent office in a timely way, then you've got to buy it from other companies. Of our fourteen issued patents, we had to purchase six from another company in the GPS field. And we've still got twenty-odd more pending at the patent office."

The irony, says Beldock, is that "the whole purpose of patents is to mitigate the risk of R&D, both to inventors and to the entrepreneurs and investors who back them. But in reality, what the USPTO has done, albeit inadvertently, is create a whole new genre of risk."

And not simply because of the backlog. The obsolete and woefully inadequate search and examination systems at the USPTO also carry very large risks for entrepreneurs, as I can personally attest. When I was CEO of Danger, a mobile Internet company that we later sold to Microsoft for $500 million (see chapter 1), investors refused to commit the $36 million we needed for our Series D round until we got an independent opinion from a top Silicon Valley law firm that our patents really were valid and that none appeared to infringe the intellectual property of competitors. That opinion cost us $100,000 and significant engineering resources, both of which could have been put to use hiring more employees or intensifying our R&D efforts.

Even that was not enough to mitigate all our risk. One of Danger's key patents related to the swivel hinge of our iconic T-Mobile Sidekick cellphone. We applied for that patent in 2000 right after the company was founded and finally won approval from the USPTO nearly seven years later. During that time, meanwhile, a very similar patent covering much the same sort of technology was issued to another company; this other patent was eventually acquired by Wireless Agents, a patent holding company, which then sued us for infringement.

Suffice it to say that the whole situation was a mess that ended up costing the company $3 million in legal and settlement costs. The irony is that, in my opinion, neither Danger nor the other company should have ever received their patents, because it later turned out that a major Japanese consumer electronics firm had filed for, and then abandoned, a patent on similar technology before either of us did. The patent office, however, lacked the sophisticated searching tools and human resources needed to uncover the Japanese prior art.

Despite all these problems at the USPTO, I believe that the greatest threat to our uniquely productive patent system comes from the large corporations who want to "reform" it.

For more than six years now, a handful of giant technology companies and their allies have been pushing various "patent reform" bills through Congress. Previous efforts failed in the face of opposition from small businesses, universities, and their allies. The latest version, the Patent Reform Act of 2011 (S.23), was approved by the U.S. Senate Judiciary Committee on February 3 and, as this book was going to press, was awaiting a vote by the full Senate. Even if it is approved by both houses of Congress and signed into law by the president, start-ups and their allies will keep fighting until the law is finally reversed or overturned.

To understand why, consider the two principal features of "patent reform." One calls for ending the historic practice in the United States of giving priority to the first to invent a new technology and instead giving it to the *first to file* a patent application for that new technology. Proponents of this move say implementing a first-to-file priority system would be less costly and more efficient. They also say that such a change would put the United States in harmony with other countries' patent systems and help to streamline patent application and examination globally.

It is certainly reasonable to assume, as proponents of first-to-file do, that implementing a first-to-file system might reduce the number of interference

proceedings used to determine the earliest true inventor of a new technology or process. These proceedings can cost hundreds of thousands of dollars and take an average of two and a half years to resolve.

However, as even first-to-file proponent Ryan K. Dickey acknowledged in an article in the *Boston University International Law Journal,* "The problem with the cost savings argument is that there are simply not many interference proceedings—less than two in one thousand patents enter into interferences." Put another way, only about a hundred fifty U.S. patentees every year ever have the need to resolve a conflict over who is the first inventor, and most of these are large corporations that can afford the cost of doing so. This hardly represents an economic or social burden great enough to warrant changing a patent system that has worked extraordinarily well to promote economic growth and national prosperity for two hundred twenty years.

Opponents of first-to-file, on the other hand, note that if such a system were implemented, it would shift the advantage decisively to large, deep-pocketed companies. With their legions of lawyers and many millions of dollars in resources, large corporations would be able to swamp the USPTO's inboxes with a tsunami of applications, shutting out independent inventors and small start-ups who do not have the equivalent legal and financial resources to compete.

Think about it: Would Buzdum, Capstran, and Hoffman, who can't afford to race to the patent office and spend $38,000 every time they have some vague idea for an invention, benefit from first-to-file? Or would BigCo, International Paper, and Microsoft (the latter of which received 3,094 patents in 2010 alone) be the winners in a system that privileges those with the swiftest legal resources rather than the most inventive minds?

As the Small Business Coalition on Patent Legislation noted, "Small firms are less likely to have funds to flood the PTO with patent applications. [This change] will inflict unprecedented harm on small firms that rely on patented innovations [and] will impede new investments and job creation in the very segment of the economy that is responsible for most of America's new jobs."

Don't just take it from them, however. A study conducted by McGill University on the results of Canada's change to a first-to-file system in 1989 found that "the switch failed to stimulate Canadian R&D efforts . . . and skewed the ownership structure of patented inventions towards large corporations, away from independent inventors and small businesses."

Proponents of first-to-file counter that since most patents are eventually assigned to large corporations anyway, doing away with the current first-to-invent system would not shut out small firms any more than they already have been. However, this ignores the unique character of U.S. innovation that we discussed in chapter 1, in which start-ups alone create the break-through innovations that lead to the development of new industries and millions of new jobs. Putting those who create the most jobs at the back of the line, and giving priority instead to the large corporate concerns that create the fewest new jobs, would be economically unwise, to say the least.

In the view of proponent Dickey, the stronger argument for first-to-file is that it would finally harmonize the U.S. patent system with those of Europe and Japan, where priority is given to the first to file rather than the first to invent. This, in turn, might help pave the way for a more efficient and less costly global patent system, and perhaps even to the creation one day of a single patent application good in all the major jurisdictions of the world.

As a slogan, "harmonization" has a certain utopian appeal. But there is lit-tle reason to believe it would (a) benefit the nation in any concrete way, or (b) even be possible to implement.

As for first-to-file benefits, proponent Dickey concedes that the "empirical evidence is unsettled" and "adopting first-to-file may not provide as many benefits as proponents claim."

Nor is there any reason to believe that harmonization on a single patent for the whole world is even possible. On November 10, 2010, after all, the European Union once again failed to reach agreement on the creation of a single patent good just throughout Europe. As the Belgian representative to the talks conceded, "There will never be unanimity on an EU patent."

So with what, pray tell, is the United States supposed to "harmonize"?

In the end, the first-to-file issue must be decided primarily on the basis of the best interests of the United States of America. And those interests argue against first-to-file.

First, the U.S. would pay a price in shifting to a new system. As Brad Pedersen and Vadim Braginsky observed in the *Minnesota Journal of Law, Science & Technology*, "Any time there is a fundamental upheaval in the basic rules govern-ing a legal system, there is a transition cost incurred. The costs of patent litiga-tion in the short term will certainly increase."

But even more important is the fact that if there was ever an issue on which the United States *should* go its own way—despite the fact that I do favor harmonization on many other legal and economic issues—it's in the field of patent law.

America became the most productive nation in the world, after all, precisely because we went our own way in 1790 and created the world's first and only democratized patent system designed to enable large numbers of ordinary people without wealth to become inventors. We were utterly alone in the world in doing this, and the result was the most successful economy on the face of the earth. Indeed, the benefits of our unique approach were so clear that eventually the rest of the world adopted most of the elements of our patent system.

However, some differences with other nations' patent regimes remain— such as our first-to-invent versus their first-to-file approach. This difference is merely a reflection of the continuing differences in the innovation process here in the United States versus the rest of the world.

As Pedersen and Braginsky note, "The U.S. patent system, with its first-to-invent standard and lower costs, can be considered primarily a distributed innovation reward system [designed to] encourage as much innovation as possible by as many different players[.] [It] enables and encourages participation at the grassroots level by players who do not necessarily have any significant market presence or financial resources."

"In contrast," the authors note, "the European Union patent system with its first-to-file system and its higher costs primarily exhibits characteristics of a centralized innovation reward system. [Its aim] is to lower the adoption costs for new innovation by facilitating and encouraging the [incumbent] players to improve and expand their technologies."

In other words, invention in Europe and Japan is still largely the province of large incumbent companies, whereas in the United States, innovation—at least the breakthrough kind—is the domain primarily of small start-ups and independent inventors.

I submit that we can live with the minor inefficiency of two different invention priority systems in the world. What we cannot live with is any change that might effectively undermine the proven wellsprings of American job creation and prosperity—small start-ups and independent inventors.

The second main feature of "patent reform" involves something called "enhanced post-grant review," which would enable any firm with sufficient financial resources to serially and continuously challenge the validity of a rival's patent after it was granted. Proponents say this would weed out the numerous poor-quality patents that are not truly novel and should not have been granted, thereby boosting patent quality overall. Given that as many as 40 percent of all adjudicated patents have at least some of their claims invalidated upon judicial review, the post-grant review proposal has had a certain appeal, which explains why a handful of respected organizations, including the National Academy of Sciences, previously endorsed it.

Leave aside for a moment the pot-calling-the-kettle-black irony of giant technology firms that each file thousands of patents every year complaining about "too many patents that shouldn't have been granted." Will post-grant review truly improve the quality of patents?

Perhaps of *some* patents—the 28 percent of patents issued to U.S. firms that go to small businesses, that is. Because only their Big Business rivals will have the full-time legal posses and financial wherewithal to pursue post-grant challenges against their smaller rivals.

As for the 72 percent of all U.S. patents that go to big corporations with more than five hundred employees, nothing about post-grant review is likely to challenge the much-larger number of bad patents from this group because small businesses simply don't have the resources to even try.

And make no mistake about the stakes here. Any erosion of patent certainty for entrepreneurs could have catastrophic results for start-up formation, growth, and funding.

"One of the first questions our firm considers in deciding whether to invest in a company is whether its business plan is backed by valid, enforceable patent rights," wrote venture capitalist John Neis in an article in *Medical Innovation & Business*. "Strong, reliable patents are what enable a nascent innovative company to create meaningful value by competing in large markets that would otherwise be inaccessible because of the existence of established companies with far greater resources. If the prognosis for [their patents'] validity is weak or highly unpredictable, the risks associated with that investment skyrocket, no matter how attractive [their business] idea."

Aside from financing, patents are sometimes also crucial in competition. The entrepreneur's one and only weapon in a contest with market-dominating incumbents, after all, is the patent protecting his or her new technology. Patents are the great equalizers, the six-guns of today's wild high-tech frontier. Allowing today's corporate giants to continuously challenge the validity of their upstart rivals' patents is akin to forcing the entrepreneur to carry a gun that only shoots blanks. Indeed, in the no-quarter-given world of business competition, it would mean the unilateral disarmament of the entrepreneur, who would have very little left to stop powerful market incumbents from crushing his or her business because the deed to his or her patents was forever up for challenge.

To be sure, not every start-up needs patents, nor are patents the only keys to a sustainable competitive advantage. Many times a first-mover advantage is more valuable, as is the case with many Web 2.0 social media start-ups today, many of which eschew patents. Other times, the advantage will lie in the superior cost-effectiveness, user friendliness, or practical use-value of a new product or service.

In most real-life business situations, however—at least as I have experienced them—a sustainable advantage comes from a combination of factors, including an early-to-market lead, best-of-breed implementation and execution, and strong patenting and trade secrets practices.

I am willing to concede that post-grant review could well offer some relief to companies such as Microsoft that spend upward of $75 million a year defending themselves against patent suits—and I am not unsympathetic to their desire for such relief. As the former CEO of Danger, I have had my own costly experience with patents that should never have been issued. So I am willing to stipulate that poor-quality patents can raise the cost of business in some industry sectors to some degree.

But let's put the so-called patent troll problem in perspective. In the first place, any free and open legal system like ours is necessarily going to be subject to a small number of abusive "strike suits" or "holdup suits" designed to secure settlements from deep-pocketed defendants eager to avoid the greater cost of going to trial. This occasional bad behavior by litigants is the price that we as a nation pay for allowing everyone to have unfettered access to the courts. Indeed, we fought a revolutionary war to obtain precisely that right for all citizens.

But even aside from that fact, the patent troll problem has been blown way out of proportion, as the retired chief judge of the nation's court for patent appeals, Judge Michel, can attest. The number of patent suits filed each year has remained constant over the last decade at less than three thousand. Of these suits, 90 percent are abandoned or settled each year. Of the three hundred or so suits that remain, two-thirds never go to trial but are adjudicated on summary judgment (of noninfringement in most cases). The nation is thus left with, at most, a hundred patent infringement trials per year—this in a nation of 300 million people, with over 1 million patents in force and more than a hundred thousand companies with a hundred or more employees competing against each other on a daily basis.

"This is not excessive," says Judge Michel, "especially in a technology-based economy."

In any event, there are much better ways to boost patent quality and reduce the minor economic burden of spurious patent suits than to undermine the ability of small businesses to use patents for funding and job creation, which would only harm the whole nation.

In fact, according to a study conducted by Case Western Reserve University economics professor Scott Shane, the proposed post-grant review process would increase patent pendency waiting periods by more than 25 percent and add an additional $2.2 billion to the current cost of patent litigation in the United States. What's more, reducing the certainty and value of issued patents would lead to a $4.4 billion reduction in total industrial R&D, the study found.

Ultimately, the best way to improve patent quality is to restore the patent office to proper functioning and give it modern examination tools so it can properly vet patent applications.

Here's how post-grant review is viewed by Dean Kamen, one of the nation's foremost independent inventors and a National Medal of Technology winner who developed the world's first insulin pump, home dialysis machine, cheap portable water purification system, and most famously, the world's first self-balancing people mover, popularly known as the Segway:

A patent is like a deed to real property. Imagine that instead of investing in R&D, you invest in a plot of land. But when you go to City Hall to get the deed so you can take out a loan to build a house on it, they tell you that you're going to have to wait five years to see if you can defeat any challenges to your deed that may come up before you get it. And that's assuming you even have the money to resist those challenges. I mean, that's insane. Who is going to invest all the money it takes to bring a new medical treatment to market if all the inventor can say is, "Well, I think I've got a patent for it, maybe, but I'm not really sure?"

But aren't there really some bad patents out there that shouldn't have been issued? "Sure, and we have counterfeiters, too," Kamen retorts. "Does that mean we should shut down the U.S. Treasury? Because that's what'll happen if you try to sell bonds with fine print at the bottom that says the bond is only *maybe* worth money, sometimes, if no one challenges it."

Besides, Kamen adds, "If you really wanted to improve the patent system, you'd give the USPTO more money—the money it needs to do its job properly—so it can raise the bar on quality, make the examinations happen faster, and hire more people with better education and give them better tools so they can do the work we ask them and need them to do. That's how you improve patent quality—by improving the value and certainty of patents, not destroying it."

Which Side Are You On?

Amidst all the posturing in the "patent reform" debate, nothing so succinctly expressed its fundamental character better than this November 4, 2009, headline in the *Wall Street Journal*: "Proposed Change in Patent Policy Pits Big Firms vs. Small."

Big firms versus small firms—that's really what it's all about.

It's about Mirk Buzdum and Cappy Capstran versus BigCo, and Roger Hoffman versus International Paper and Georgia Pacific. It's about the Innovalights and other cleantech start-ups of this world, along with the MatriLabs and the Innate Immunes, and whether or not they'll be able to secure the investment needed to bring us the new products and services, the new medical treatments, and the new energy sources we need to live healthier and more prosperous lives.

So make a choice: Which side are you on?

Don't side with the underdog for emotional reasons, or out of some romantic notion of David versus Goliath. Make a decision that's in the best and most pragmatic interests of the nation as a whole. Strengthen, not weaken, whoever is most likely to create the new jobs and new industries we need and grow the economy.

If you do that, then you must stand with small start-ups. For it is an indisputable fact that small entrepreneurial businesses, not large multinational companies, have always been the primary source of breakthrough innovation, new job growth, and higher living standards in America. Indeed, as we noted in chapter 1, all the major innovations that powered the American economy to unrivaled prosperity over the last fifty years—from semiconductors and personal computers to software, biotech, and the Internet—were all created by small start-ups. So were *all* of the 40 million new jobs created in this country since 1977, according to the latest research.

America cannot afford any more delays. Living standards are falling. The once-great American middle class is being systematically eviscerated due to short-sighted policies that have de-industrialized the nation and offshored not only our high-value manufacturing but also increasingly our high-tech R&D as well (see chapter 3). In the last decade, once-poor nations such as China and India have followed America's lead and built strong middle classes. If we don't want to show the world how a once-prosperous nation like ours can destroy its middle class, then we must get our innovation engine moving again.

A critical first step in doing so is to fix the patent office. Director Kappos has already made some important changes at the agency. He seems genuinely committed to helping the patent office meet its historic mission—the mission set by the Founding Fathers two hundred twenty years ago—of serving the needs of small entrepreneurial innovators and thereby growing the economy. But Kappos won't succeed unless Congress gives him the tools and resources to do the job.

Congress needs to provide a $1 billion surge of capital to help the USPTO get its house in order.

It needs to restore independent fee-setting authority to the agency, and end the disruptive practice of diverting USPTO fees to other uses, such as the 2010 census.

Congress should also support the establishment of regional offices of the USPTO (most especially in Silicon Valley, home to 12 percent of all U.S. patents issued each year). Doing so would facilitate better collaboration with stakeholders and enable the recruitment of more and better-qualified examiners to meet the growing workload and technology challenges.

Ultimately, Congress must recognize that the patent office—the only arm of government that takes not a single penny from taxpayers—is truly the nation's vital "innovation agency." It costs us nothing, and gives us back far, far more than most of us will ever realize.

Mirk Buzdum and Cappy Capstran are certainly rooting for Kappos to succeed, as are Roger Hoffman and Innate Immune's CEO Dr. Andrew Perlman. They have a huge stake in the patent system, just as all Americans have in them.

Manufacturing

The Banana Republic of Silicon Valley

Have you ever seen one of those dioramas in a natural history museum—the ones that feature a lifelike three-dimensional re-creation of a lost world or culture? I remember vividly the first time I saw one of the Native American dioramas at the Smithsonian in Washington. As I stood there and stared at the figures behind the glass—a woman holding an infant as she tended a fire, a man skinning a deer after returning from the hunt—I tried to imagine what the native people of early eighteenth century America were thinking. Did they know they were doomed?

I mention this because I've been pondering the fate of my old home town of Sharon, Pennsylvania, lately, wondering if something similar may be in store for my adopted community of Silicon Valley, where I've lived for the last twenty years. And I have to confess that although I've never been the pessimistic sort—you can't be an entrepreneur without a fierce optimism about the future—I do wonder if one day in the future, people will visit a museum and look through glass at a diorama labeled "The Lost World of Silicon Valley's Middle Class."

"See all the people—some in suits, some in jeans—going off to their jobs in the morning," the plaque in front of the diorama would read. "Note the well-tended yards of the owner-occupied homes, and over in the commercial districts, the enormous variety and vibrancy of businesses serving industry and consumers alike." Of course, the diorama would need to portray something of the social lives of these vanished people. So it might depict a park adjacent to a high school. "Back then," the plaque would note, "white- and blue-collar families would mingle together at public parks. Their children even attended the same schools—and these were public schools, no less, when cities could still afford to adequately fund such things."

In the previous two chapters, we showed how start-up businesses and innovators were being severely hamstrung by burdensome regulation, the crisis in venture funding, and the paralysis at the patent office. Now we will demonstrate how the offshoring of manufacturing over the last thirty years has not only damaged the nation's foundations of prosperity, but also now threatens the survival of Silicon Valley itself and the middle-class entrepreneurs who made it the nation's paramount innovation hub.

In the pages that follow, we will explode the myth that America can simply "specialize in innovation and research" while letting other nations do the manufacturing. You will discover precisely why, when manufacturing is offshored, innovation and the social wealth it creates inevitably follow. Hopefully you will see that if we want a strong and prosperous nation in which *all* can thrive, not just a tiny elite, then we must rebuild the connection between high-tech innovation and high-value production and rebuild a healthy manufacturing sector.

For now, however, allow me first to paint you a picture of one world that has already been lost. And another that may soon be.

I grew up in Sharon, Pennsylvania, a thriving, middle-class city of some twenty-five thousand souls when I lived there. It got its name (if you trust local lore) from an early eighteenth century settler who was so enamored of its fertile location on a broad plain along the Shenango River that he named it after the biblical Plain of Sharon in Israel. For its first hundred years or so, Sharon's main industry was agriculture and later coal-mining. By the early twentieth century, though, steel had come to dominate the local economy. In the 1960s, steel was still a growth industry.

My father, who like my mother had never finished high school, worked at U.S. Steel Products as a lithographer, supervising the printing of labels and logos on cans and other steel products. Many people think of manufacturing jobs as wretched and poorly paid, but the truth is that in those days production workers actually enjoyed a middle-class or even upper-middle-class lifestyle. We owned our own home, for example—a nice three-bedroom, two-bath dwelling at 433 South Oakland Avenue in Sharon—and most of the people with whom my father worked at the plant owned their own homes as well. My dad was into photography, so we had a dark room in the basement. We also had a garden in the backyard where we grew a lot of our own vegetables. I didn't realize it back then, but my dad was actually ahead of his time in some ways. He was an organic gardener who made all his own compost and didn't believe in commercial fertilizers. I remember we subscribed to both *Reader's Digest* and *Organic Gardening*.

Our family's standard of living was good enough, in fact, that when I was ten years old, my dad bought an acre of land up near Pymatuning Lake, about twenty-five miles from Sharon, and built a little year-round vacation cottage on it. It wasn't anything fancy—just a couple of bedrooms, a living room, and a screened-in porch—but I loved it. I was into fishing quite a bit back then, so I'd go up there with my dad and some of his friends and go fishing. I helped him plant some pine trees on the property, which I imagine are still there.

For a kid growing up in Sharon, life was good. There were public baseball fields all over town, and a very active Little League and Babe Ruth League, both of which I participated in. The town had a number of outdoor public swimming pools as well as an indoor one at the Buhl Club, which also had a gymnasium. Next to the Sharon Country Club was Buhl Park, which offered the only free public golf course in America at the time, as well as a large pond where little kids liked to fish. In the winter, that pond became our ice skating rink. In the summer, community picnics of one sort or another took place almost every weekend, usually sponsored by one of the local employers or one of the church or ethnic clubs, such as the German Home to which my father belonged.

When I turned sixteen in 1960, of course, life became even more fun. I had bought my first car, a 1954 Ford two-door, with money I had earned working after school and on Saturdays at State Street Bakery, where one of my duties was to scrape embedded dough off the butcher-block floor—an experience, incidentally, that cured me of any further interest in pastries or donuts. I customized my car at Mike's Auto Body, where we lowered the suspension, painted it metallic green, and installed a beautiful chrome tube grill on it with chrome lake pipes. In that extremely cool car, I would take dates to the drive-in movies and restaurants, or cruise with my friends up and down State Street (or drive over the state line to play euchre at bars in Ohio, where the drinking age was lower and the chances of getting served with a fake ID much better).

Looking back on it, Sharon actually presented fewer class barriers between people than one finds in most communities today. Indeed, what's interesting to me now, as I witness the growing divide here in Silicon Valley between those who are extremely wealthy and, well, everyone else, is how little we actually thought about wealth or class when I was growing up in Sharon. All of us—or at least all of my friends and I—simply thought of ourselves as middle class. This was true whether our parents worked in one of the factories, as mine did, or were teachers, lawyers, accountants, doctors, or even bankers.

One of my best friends, for example, was George S. Warren III. His parents owned the biggest bank in town and were members of the country club, and they had a year-round pool in their back yard with a bubble over it. Obviously, their house was bigger and nicer than ours. But it wasn't orders of magnitude bigger or nicer than ours. So although there were differences of wealth among us—some of my friends had more money than I, some had less—none of us felt it represented any sort of major divide between us.

Nor did we have what I call the "Titanic culture" that we see today, with people desperately scrambling to secure a precious spot for themselves on the life raft to the future while they watch everyone else sink slowly under the waves. Back then, we all felt like we were in the same boat—kept afloat by the same economic bulwarks—even if some folks had nicer berths on that boat than others. Back then, too, people didn't feel the need to display their wealth through their homes or lifestyles the way so many people do today. I remember, in fact, that at one point my dad was earning enough for us to afford a bigger home in a more upscale neighborhood, but he and my mom decided we were happy enough where we were, so why move?

This is not to say that there was no striving for upward mobility in Sharon. There was, and the town offered plenty of opportunities to achieve it. My own parents, like immigrants throughout American history, constantly stressed to my brother Carl and me the value of hard work and education. I was a pretty ambitious fellow in that regard, taking summer school classes—I remember one summer taking shorthand to boost my note-taking abilities—and earning a 3.3 grade point average. So although I had held manufacturing jobs for two summers, I chose not to follow my father into the mill but to go to college instead at the U.S. Naval Academy at Annapolis, Maryland, where I could receive a world-class education tuition free in exchange for serving my country—which I later did as a U.S. Marine officer in Vietnam. I suspect I won the appointment to Annapolis because of my grades, my performance as an Eagle Scout, and also my letters of recommendation—one of which was written by Henry A. Roemer, the long-time CEO of Sharon Steel, which was the town's only New York Stock Exchange–listed company. It is hard to imagine any wealthy industrialist today taking such an interest in the son of an immigrant factory worker, and for that I remain grateful to him.

Interestingly—and this is a crucial point—probably only 10 percent of my friends ended up going to college, yet this fact did not consign them to a dead-end future. In those days, there seemed to be a productive job and decent income for almost anyone who wanted it, college degree or no college degree. Some of my friends went to college, including George Warren, who, after getting a degree in restaurant and hospitality management, started the successful restaurant chain Quaker Steak & Lube in an abandoned gas station in downtown Sharon. But many others went to work at Sharon Steel or at other manufacturing plants in the area.

And in those days, manufacturing jobs were highly prized not only because the salaries and benefits were quite good by middle-class standards—often providing 100 percent employer-paid pension plans, which rarely exist anymore—but also because they offered real opportunities for advancement. If you showed some leadership and initiative, you could move into management. Or if you got into an apprenticeship program, then as a young man starting a family, you could enjoy an exceptional income—better even than that earned by many lawyers and other professionals at the time.

In fact, in an article in the Sharon *Herald* a few years ago, retired sports columnist Lynn Saternow recalled just how well manufacturing workers were paid: "In 1965, when I graduated from [high school], some of us went on to colleges, but a lot of kids opted for jobs in the local mills, which were booming. Westinghouse, Sharon Steel, General American and others provided thousands of jobs that paid very well. Even after college, when I took a job at the *Herald*, millworkers were making more money than many college graduates—including me!"

Not only was manufacturing most definitely *not* a dead-end career, it was actually the beating heart of Sharon's prosperous middle-class economy and democratized social scene. The manufacturing ecosystem, which economists say creates as many as fifteen additional jobs for every position on the factory floor, nourished a huge variety of businesses that served the plants and mills in the area. Just walking downtown, for example, you'd pass by printers and small lithographic shops that did specialty work for the mills, machine shops that fabricated prototypes for the plants and repaired their equipment, and vendors of all sorts of production, janitorial, and office supplies, not to mention a host of independent transport firms that brought these supplies to the mills. A number of industrial design and consulting businesses served the mills as well.

With manufacturing constantly pumping dollars into Sharon's economic bloodstream, a wide array of retail, professional, and service businesses were also able to grow and sustain themselves, creating even more jobs for area residents. We had doctors and lawyers and accountants, auto dealerships and repair shops and small shopping centers, painters and electricians and plumbers, restaurants and movie theaters and bowling alleys, and a nursing school, a major hospital, and several local colleges, including a branch of Penn State right in town. Sharon also sported a small Coca-Cola bottling plant in town, where you could go look in the window and watch the Coca-Cola bottles being filled, as well as a local ice cream manufacturing company. We even had a fair amount of family farming in the area as well, for I recall that we had a large farmer's market with its own permanent location downtown where the local farmers came in and sold their goods once or twice a week.

The Plague Strikes

Then, in the 1980s, a plague struck Sharon and the Shenango Valley—the plague of deindustrialization. Corporate mythology to the contrary, it was not caused by the sort of evolutionary modernization and productivity improvements that earlier in the century had led to a decline in agricultural employment. This disaster was caused by U.S. industry's wholesale refusal to invest in new technology in order to remain competitive with Japan and other lower-cost producers. To conflate the two would be analogous to claiming that because everyone must die eventually, death by suicide is a natural process.

And the truth is, basic industry's demise in the United States was self-inflicted. As the *American Decades* history series noted, "The largest and most integrated of the steel companies lost their technological lead. [They] failed to adopt such innovations as the basic oxygen furnace, continuous casting, and computer controls as these became available, even when the advantages of the new technologies became apparent in other countries. The ranks of upper management were characterized by inertia, the lack of an international perspective [and] an inflexible organizational structure." In a penny-wise-but-pound-foolish effort to maintain earnings, American auto, steel, and textile mills simply fired their workers and moved offshore.

Two decades later, long after I left Sharon to make my way as an entrepreneur, the Sharon *Herald* published a retrospective of the damage wrought by this deindustrialization.

"At one time you could buy everything you needed downtown," Mercer County Historical Society executive director Bill Philson told the *Herald*. "The sidewalks were crowded and the bustling downtown [was] full of activity."

Then came "the collapse of industries," as the *Herald* put it. "Midland Ross Corp. abandoned its National Castings foundry in Sharon in 1982. Chicago Bridge & Iron in Greenville and Greenville Steel Car closed around the same time. Westinghouse Corp. shuttered its Sharon Transformer Division in 1985." In the 1980s alone, the Sharon area lost half of its manufacturing jobs.

Then, in 1992, "Sharon Steel gasped its last breath [and] an additional 3,000 jobs expired."

The city's annual loss in wages and salaries was in the hundreds of millions of dollars. Home values plummeted; people began to leave the area in search of work. Yet still the deindustrialization process continued—and continued to produce new casualties, as a 2005 *Herald* interview with newly laid-off workers in Sharon illustrates. "Even with [unemployment] benefits," said the *Herald*, "they face overwhelming odds against finding another local job that can provide family-sustaining wages. Since other major local plants have closed over the years, there're few good job opportunities."

"It doesn't look good," Wally Felner, then experiencing his third layoff since the closing of Sharon Steel in 1992, told the newspaper. Added Justice Culp, then just twenty-five years old, "There's no jobs anywhere. There's nothing here that can pay you enough to support a family. I'm single and I can barely support myself."

Looking back on the loss of jobs, the collapse of property values, and the out-migration of young families in search of work, it's remarkable that Sharon even survived. But survive it did, albeit in weakened form. The grit and resourcefulness that Sharon's earliest settlers bequeathed to the local gene pool enabled the city to build a measure of shelter for itself from the storms of deindustrialization by becoming a center for health care and senior services. So in one sense, I suppose, the Wikipedia article on Sharon is correct when it says that "following the extensive national deindustrialization of the 1970s and 1980s, the city's economy diversified." But let's not kid ourselves about a euphemism like *diversified*. To judge from the concrete, measurable, real-life effects of deindustrialization on Sharon's quality of life, a more accurate word might be *crucified*.

According to the U.S. census, for example, the population of Sharon stood at 25,267 in 1960—the same as it had for the previous thirty years. By the year 2000, however, deindustrialization had reduced Sharon's population by an astonishing 35 percent to only 16,328. By 2008, it had fallen again to 14,869 (which is too low for separate data reporting in the 2010 census).

In 1960, the unemployment rate in Sharon was 5 percent—roughly the same as the national unemployment rate. By 2000, which was a time of great prosperity for the rest of the nation, Sharon's unemployment rate had shot up to 8 percent—double that for the country as a whole. Recently, it was still more than 4 points above the national unemployment rate.

In 1960, the rate of home ownership in Sharon was 16 percent higher than for the country as a whole. By 2000, home ownership had plummeted to 5 percent *below* the national rate.

In 1960, median family income in Sharon was an impressive 13 percent higher than median family income nationwide. By the year 2000, Sharon's median family income had fallen a crushing 30 percent *below* the national median. And it's still falling. In 2008, median household income in Sharon was 38 percent below that of the rest of the state.

In 1960, the government had not yet established an official "poverty line." But in the 1970 census, the first in which such numbers were recorded, only about 8 percent of Sharon's families lived below the poverty line. By 2000, however, 14 percent of Sharon's families were living below the poverty line— 5 percent more than the national average. In 2008, nearly 18 percent of all Sharon residents—and a heartbreaking one of every four children—were living below the poverty line. The 2010 census is unlikely to yield any better numbers.

This is what happens to a community when we allow a once-robust manufacturing ecosystem to die. And I say we "allowed" it to die because that's exactly what happened.

Many people, of course, assume that we are merely passive spectators to the process of technological change—that technology is something that *happens* to us. The prevailing view in America seems to be that technology is some sort of autonomous, mythic force beyond the reach of human control. It's like the weather or God's will, and there's nothing we can do about it.

But that's not true. Human beings have always intervened in the spontaneous forces of the marketplace and of technological change to shape these in ways we consider most beneficial. Put another way, economic and technological change always involves contests over political and economic power—over competing visions of what *kind of future* should be built.

As John Michael Staudenmaier, one of America's leading historians of technology, once wrote: "Why did the highway engineers who designed the U.S. interstate highway system in the fifties and sixties run the system through major cities rather than only up to their outer circumference? Who decided that those freeways were more important, as civic assets, than the neighborhoods they sliced through?"

Obviously, it was the auto, trucking, and oil industries that decided that. We might make a different choice today if given the chance. But back then, this decision reflected the prevailing (or at least the politically dominant) view of issues as varied as the role of cities and the nature of American individualism. Bottom line, it was cars versus public transit. Cars won.

So let's be honest about what happened to Sharon. It wasn't that manufacturing had all of a sudden become obsolete, like buggy whips in the era of automobiles. We still live in a world of things, after all—from cars and cutlery to computers and cellphones—and somebody still has to make those things. Nor was it the inevitable pain of progress that economist Joseph Schumpeter referred to when he coined the term "creative destruction," because nothing new ever replaced manufacturing to create a strong Sharon economy. And it certainly wasn't God's will that the town should suffer. Human beings did this: corporate executives who chose cost cutting and offshoring rather than innovation as their earnings strategy, and public officials who chose to believe misguided theories that America didn't need a vibrant manufacturing sector so long as it had a strong R&D and service sector. We the people killed the golden goose of Shenango Valley.

A National Catastrophe

And it's not just Shenango Valley that got its goose cooked. Like Sherman marching through Georgia, we have let our fetish for downsizing and off-shoring—and for manipulating wealth through financial innovation rather than creating wealth through technological innovation—lay waste to vast sections of the country. From the steel mills of Youngstown and Gary to the automobile plants of Detroit and Lordstown, and from the textile industries of the mid-Atlantic states to the machine tool producers of the Midwest, we have transformed the most powerful economic force multiplier in history—manufacturing, with its fifteen-to-one job creation potential—into the most potent job killer since the Great Depression. And the slaughter continues to this day. In the last ten years alone, more than one-third of America's largest factories shut down. That's 42,400 factories that have closed their doors, and 12 million Americans who have lost their jobs.

And don't kid yourselves that it's just the supposedly "outmoded" industries of yesterday, such as steel, autos, or textiles, that have been eviscerated. We have also systematically gutted our ability to produce the most advanced high-tech products and energy systems of tomorrow—from electric cars and solar cells to cellphones, computers, and next-generation LED lighting. If we're not making the advanced technology products we need, of course, then obviously we are buying them from countries that do. Which explains why the $30 billion trade surplus in high-tech products that our country enjoyed just ten years ago has today become a $56 billion *deficit*.

Those aren't just statistics. Those are real jobs lost, real communities destroyed, and real threats created not just to our economic future but to our national security as well. As a report from the National Defense University in Washington noted, "Manufacturing is critical to U.S. national power and its vital interests [and] particularly beneficial to the communities in which [it] is located." Yet today, notes the report, the nation's manufacturing sector "is on the wrong side of an inflexion point from which it may not be able to recover."

How bad is it? America now lags behind every other advanced nation on earth except France in the percentage of overall economic activity devoted to manufacturing.

To be sure, the United States remains the largest manufacturing economy in the world, producing as much as 21 percent of the world's manufactured goods. But the positive numbers on total output and productivity mask the worrying trend lines of ever-greater job losses and trade deficits, especially in high-value technology sectors, and ever-deeper cuts in the living standards of average citizens. This is not the inevitable result of technology change, which over time leads to greater output from fewer workers. Nor is it due to the supposedly excessive demands of labor or even the burden of recession. Manufacturing employment has declined 1,600 percent more than it has in all other industries over the last decade. This is the result not of evolutionary change but rather the wholesale transfer of jobs and industry offshore. For thirty years we have been sliding down a slippery slope of offshoring that has already destroyed the upward mobility of the middle class. Unless stopped, it will soon destroy the middle class itself.

To see the human cost of our willing emasculation of manufacturing, go to Detroit, which once had the highest median family income in the nation. Today, over forty square miles of that city's landscape—an area larger than Miami—now lies literally abandoned save for a few remaining residents who cultivate small food gardens in the patchwork of empty lots or hunt the raccoons that scurry about the seventy-eight thousand abandoned "feral houses" now being reclaimed by nature.

Notes the *Detroit News*: "A city the size of San Francisco could fit easily just within [our] empty lots. As nature abhors a vacuum, wildlife has moved in."

And people have moved out. The 2010 census is expected to show that Detroit, which once boasted a population of more than two million residents, has now been reduced to fewer than seven hundred thousand citizens, with a drop of more than a hundred fifty thousand people in just the last ten years. The last time Detroit held a population less than one million was almost a century ago, in 1920.

Indeed, according to Hunter Morrison, director of Youngstown State University's Office of Campus Planning and Community Partnerships, "dozens of American cities throughout the industrial Great Lakes states and the Midwest have lost half of their population or more over the course of one generation," reports Richard McCormack of *Manufacturing & Technology News*.

The last time this many cities anywhere in the world lost half of their populations in so short a time was during the Black Plague in Europe—in the year 1348!

McCormack took his readers on a Google Maps tour of Detroit's 48212 zip code, using the yellow "Google Man" tool to provide a street-level view, and reported his findings:

"Travel around Detroit's empty warehouses and bombed out industrial zones and you'll see telephone poles leaning sideways, boarded up storefronts, liquor stores, desperate churches standing sentry over barren wasteland, lone walkers, for-sale signs, dilapidated fencing, graffiti, weeds growing in parking lots—the urban prairie—discarded pallets, plywood and mattresses. And always there is a translucent sky beyond the lamp-posts and hodgepodge of wires."

He described some especially eerie sights. "I 'drove' on my computer past hundreds of places like 1136 Puritan Street. Neighborhoods that are gone; blocks with nary a house left on them. Overgrown lots. Burned out homes. You can put the Google Man icon in the middle of an intersection, rotate 360 degrees, and there's not a car in sight . . . If you zoom out a click or two, looking down at the neighborhood from 400 feet up, you will see serpentine furrows on the vacant lots. They are bulldozer tracks. Sidewalks and curbs are disappearing under weeds. There are empty playgrounds; dead trees and piles of debris."

But wait. "I find a house for sale on 8034 Georgia Street that is going for $11,900," he writes. "It's huge. I take the virtual tour: eight bedrooms and four baths. Cheaper than a new car. Check it out. It's on a corner lot. It's got a nice tub. It's abandoned."

This is not a diorama. This is real. "These neighborhoods were populated in the 1960s," McCormack reminds us. "Socially conservative, middle-class families kept tidy homes and manicured lawns." In fact, Detroit once had the highest concentration of single-family homes of any city in the United States.

"Tens of thousands of people have lost all they invested in homes and businesses," says McCormack. "I want to ask the few who remain, What do you do for a living? What are your plans? What happened to government? Does anyone care?"

If Detroit was ground zero of the deindustrialization bomb, then Sharon lay just outside the total destruction kill zone, in the area merely of "heavy casualties and major structural damage." In both cases, however, and in hundreds of other communities, a way of life has been lost—needlessly and unwisely. These cities and towns were once populated by middle-class families living the American Dream. Now they're hollowed out, struggling to find some mix of service and other employment that can suffice for residents in a world where genuine upward mobility is a thing of the past.

If this sort of deindustrialization continues unchecked, we'll eventually turn vast sections of the country into a kind of banana republic (only without the tin-pot dictators, one hopes). There will be a few wealthy people at the top, a huge mass of low-paid service workers at the bottom, and not a lot of people in between—the people we used to call the "middle class."

Silicon Valley at Risk

Think it can't happen to Silicon Valley? Think again, because the distance between the Shenango Valley and Silicon Valley is a lot shorter than you think.

To be sure, Silicon Valley has resources that Sharon and the Shenango Valley never had. It has a first-class university system that includes Stanford and the University of California at Berkeley, a globally oriented labor force, an abundance of entrepreneurs, and the world's most experienced venture capitalists. So Saratoga, California, will never become *exactly* like Sharon, Pennsylvania.

But with all due respect for those differences, the "hollowing out" of Silicon Valley has already begun. The University of California system, once among the finest in the world, is now being systematically gutted by state budget cutbacks. And according to the 2010 Silicon Valley Index, an annual report that examines forty different indicators of economic strength and community health, there are "clear warning signs" that Silicon Valley has entered "a new phase of uncertainty" in which its middle class is eroding and its standing as a high-tech innovation center is being put "at risk."

More than a million jobs have fled California in the last decade (see chapter 1). Per capita income is down 5 percent from 2007, and the number of people working without job security as independent or part-time contractors rather than full-time employees is rising. Office vacancy rates in 2010 were up 33 percent just over the previous year and had reached their highest levels in more than twelve years. Roughly 21 percent of prime Silicon Valley office space stood vacant, and one local Chamber of Commerce reported that "small and medium-sized businesses are disappearing weekly." In some Valley communities, more than one-third of all home sales are foreclosures.

As *Forbes* put it: "The likes of Apple's Steve Jobs and Google's Eric Schmidt may be minting money, but the region, as measured by declines in construction, manufacturing and business services, now has 130,000 *fewer* jobs than it did a decade ago."

But the most worrisome development, according to the Silicon Valley Index report, is that the percentage of middle-income households in Silicon Valley has fallen by 6 percent since 2002—a trend it ominously described as a "hollowing out of the middle."

"It's not a given that we will continue to be the epicenter of innovation," says Russell Hancock, CEO of Joint Venture: Silicon Valley Network, one of the report's two sponsors. And a major reason why the Valley's role as a nexus of high-tech innovation and a mecca of middle-class opportunity is now threatened is the loss of high-tech manufacturing in the region.

Take the semiconductor industry, the fountainhead of Silicon Valley's very existence. Semiconductors are the tiny electronic brains of nearly all electronic devices in the world today. No other product, in fact, exerts such an outsized influence on the performance of other industries and economic sectors—most especially the $1.1 trillion global electronics industry. Without them, there would be no cellphones, computers, printers, TVs, radios, video games, automobiles, passenger jets, or modern medical equipment. They make modern life possible, no less than hoes enabled our agrarian ancestors to build stable civilizations and spears kept our even more distant hunter and gatherer forefathers from starvation.

The semiconductor integrated circuit was invented by Jack Kilby, a young engineer at Texas Instruments research lab in Dallas, Texas, on September 12, 1958. In the half century that has passed since that day, the semiconductor has proven to be "the single most important driver of increased productivity and economic growth in history," according to George Scalise, the past president of the Semiconductor Industry Association (SIA). Here is one case, at least, in which the leader of a trade association was *not* engaging in hype.

The U.S. semiconductor industry employs a hundred eighty-five thousand people and is still the world market leader, with a 48 percent share of the $226 billion in global semiconductor wafer sales. During the last decade, semiconductors have either been the first or second top U.S. export category.

The problem, however, is that America also leads the world in one other semiconductor category: the number of semiconductor plant closings. In

2009 alone, fifteen semiconductor plants (known as fabs) shut down in the U.S. That's up from four plant closings in 2008.

This is a problem because semiconductor manufacturing in particular has long provided Silicon Valley with economic benefits that far transcend simply the high-paying jobs it provides or the massive investments in research, equipment, and materials it makes. Semiconductors sit at the top of the electronics industry pyramid, and the "knowledge spillovers" that semiconductor manufacturing generates lead to much higher rates of innovation and economic growth in related industries in Silicon Valley, including wireless, cameras, cellphones, and solar cells.

The flip side of semiconductor plant closings, of course, is new plant openings. Of the sixteen fabs worldwide that began construction in 2009 (six of them in China), however, only one is being built in the United States. That lone fab is not even in Silicon Valley but rather in upstate New York.

Bear in mind that a state-of-the-art wafer semiconductor fab plant now costs upward of $6 billion to build. To make such a massive undertaking more attractive to manufacturers, therefore, governments all over the world offer tax breaks and other incentives to defray some of those costs, hoping thereby to get those fabs located in their countries to the benefit of their economy and their people. All governments except ours, that is, but we'll come back to this in a minute.

The trends are clear. In 1980, American fabs produced 42 percent of the world's semiconductors. By 2005, that figure had fallen to 25 percent. And just in the last five years, we have lost nearly half of that remaining semiconductor manufacturing capacity, producing today only 14 percent of the world's supply of a device that America invented fifty-two years ago.

You don't need a weatherman to know which way the semiconductor trade winds are blowing—or that the industry's employment is blowing away with it.

And it's not just semiconductor manufacturing that we're losing. In the burgeoning wind energy sector, for example, the number of U.S. wind turbine manufacturing plants actually fell by a third last year, flushing fifteen hundred high-tech manufacturing jobs down the drain, even as the installed base of turbines in the United States increased by 40 percent.

Where did we get all those new turbines? That's where insult is added to injury, for it turns out that as much as $850 million, or 84 percent, of the $1 billion-plus in U.S. government stimulus funds used to buy all those turbines was actually given to foreign wind turbine producers. Those funds might be better used to stimulate domestic turbine production.

A similar story applies in virtually every advanced or strategic technology of the future. Next-generation LED illumination? Electric and hybrid car batteries? Electronic displays for tomorrow's gadgets? Advanced materials?

In each sector, America has now become a bit player.

Nowhere is the contrast between foreign and domestic high-tech manufacturing more apparent than in the solar energy industry. China dominates production today, while the U.S. produces only 5 percent of all solar cells—a device that we invented right here in the USA.

Just ask Conrad Burke, the forty-four-year-old Irish physicist and CEO of high-profile Silicon Valley solar energy start-up Innovalight profiled in chapter 1. Because Burke was unable to obtain financing for a solar cell manufacturing facility in the U.S., he changed Innovalight's business plan to license the ink to manufacturers instead. Most of Innovalight's customer base of manufacturers, of course, is located outside the United States—in Taiwan, Europe, and especially in China. A few still remain in the U.S.—at least for now.

"There are only three or four companies still making solar panels here," says Burke. "One is SunPower, which is here in Silicon Valley, although most of their manufacturing, quite frankly, is moving to Malaysia and the Philippines. Then there's SolarWorld, which is German-based, which has manufacturing in Portland, Oregon. Evergreen Solar is based in Marlborough, Massachusetts, but they're also moving offshore. And finally, there's another one . . . a German company named Schott Solar that is manufacturing solar cells near Albuquerque, New Mexico."

He laughs ruefully. "But ask me to list all the companies making solar in China and I could spend the next fifteen minutes rattling off names."

The reasons for this are not hard to understand. "The availability of capital in China is just so great," explains Burke. "I go to China every six weeks or so, and it's extraordinary to see the amount of infrastructure being built around solar manufacturing. It seems like every entrepreneur is building a gigawatt solar cell factory. Partly it's because labor costs are lower, and environmental regulations are not nearly as strict. But more than that, it's because they have a whole ecosystem in place whereby the government will provide you with land and buildings and incentives of every kind. And the reason they do that is because they really get it. They understand the benefits that manufacturing brings to an economy."

Why Manufacturing Matters

What are those benefits? A remarkable study published in June 2009 by the Milken Institute, an independent nonpolitical economic think tank, actually calculated the dollars-and-cents benefits of manufacturing to the Silicon Valley and California economy. The report, entitled *Manufacturing 2.0: A More Prosperous California,* concluded that "[m]ore so than any other industry, manufacturing has a multiplier effect, spawning job creation, investment and ancillary business activity."

Indeed, the study found that in some sectors, such as electronic computer manufacturing, 15 additional jobs are created outside the manufacturing sector for every job in manufacturing. The multiplier varied depending on the sector studied, so the institute chose a conservative average of 2.5 additional jobs created outside manufacturing for every factory position. In other words, California's 1.46 million manufacturing jobs also created jobs for an additional 3.64 million nonmanufacturing workers.

Unfortunately, noted the report, "California has been losing manufacturing jobs at a faster pace than the nation as a whole [and] progressively losing more of its manufacturing employment, particularly high-value-added manufacturing, to other states such as Oregon, Texas, Minnesota, and Washington." The trend is particularly pronounced in high-tech manufacturing. And the loss of this high-tech manufacturing has created "a wide gap between its capacity for ingenuity and entrepreneurship and its ability to efficiently commercialize innovation in manufacturing," the study found. "This gap continues to widen in part due to the burden of an onerous regulatory climate and some of the highest taxes in the United States."

Total taxes per capita in California, for example, were $4,993 in 2007. In contrast, the average per capita taxes paid in the states now wooing high-tech manufacturing away from California were 31 percent *lower*—only $3,803. When you add in the fact that California businesses pay the second-highest corporate income tax rate of all those states competing with it for high-tech manufacturing—and the highest corporate tax rate of any nation on earth when you combine federal with state taxes—it's hardly surprising that many Silicon Valley businesses are relocating to states such as Texas, Oregon, and Washington, or even moving overseas.

As the Milken study noted, "Losing manufacturing jobs has adverse effects on economic vitality, and the losses go deeper than employment, wages, and output. The presence of a single large firm requires the support of several smaller firms and contractors inside and outside the immediate sector. As a result, if a large firm leaves the state, the indirect impacts can be severe."

But what if California had not shed hundreds of thousands of manufacturing jobs over the last decade? What if it still maintained the same level of manufacturing it had in 2000?

The Milken Institute study concluded that the 476,000 manufacturing jobs that would have been preserved would have added $27.3 billion more in wages and $46.9 billion in economic output to the state. These are precisely the sort of jobs, the report noted, "that drive broad upward social mobility," which is the principal barometer of a healthy middle class. Manufacturing jobs in California, for example, pay on average 30 percent *more* than replacement jobs in the health and social services sector: $66,200 versus $51,700 per year.

The real pot of gold at the end of the rainbow, however, was the study's conclusion that keeping those 476,000 manufacturing jobs would have also created *an additional 1.17 million jobs* outside manufacturing that would have paid $47.8 billion in new wages and created $54.3 billion in additional economic output for the state economy.

To put it in terms any number-crunching state bureaucrat could understand, the state's economy—at $1.9 trillion, already the eighth largest in the world—would have benefited from the addition of $75 billion in new wages and $101 billion in additional economic output. Which means that California's economy would be more than 5 percent larger than it is today, surpassing Italy's to become the world's seventh-largest economy.

The benefits would go beyond wages and output, of course, to include the purchasing of additional goods and services and the generation of new tax revenues—an extra $5 billion in new state tax revenues, in fact, which would by itself cut California's deficit by 20 percent.

Put another way, had California stemmed the recent decline in manufacturing, it would be a very different state today. It would not be on the verge of bankruptcy, forced to pay state employees in IOUs, or beg (unsuccessfully) for federal loans to cover its bills. State offices would not have had to be shuttered two days every month—in Los Angeles, the mayor ordered city agencies to close two days *each week*—and spending on education would be stable or perhaps even growing rather than suffering from 2010's staggering 17 percent reduction in funding.

But the loss of those manufacturing jobs was *not* prevented, and as a result, the "hollowing out" of Silicon Valley and the state is now under way.

It's Happened Before

A certain self-satisfied complacency however, continues to blind many in Silicon Valley to the danger. This is hardly surprising, for when other nations keep sending delegations to study you in hopes of recreating some of your "Silicon Valley magic" for their own people, it's only natural to start thinking of your success as not only deserved but irreversible. Just as my own father found it difficult to imagine those giant mills ever closing down, many of the Valley's leading movers and shakers likewise find it impossible to imagine that their star, which has shone so brightly in the innovation heavens for fifty years, could ever fade.

But they would do well to brush up on their history, for they would find that there have been other Silicon Valleys in the past—other innovation hubs—that have risen and then fallen.

Take Cleveland, which like Detroit is today a poster child for the erosion of the Manufacturing Belt into the Rust Belt. Although this city made a bit of a comeback in the 1990s, it has long been the butt of jokes about the "mistake on the lake," a river that "oozes rather than flows," and about "spending a year in Cleveland one weekend."

One hundred years ago, however, Cleveland was probably the wealthiest and most exciting center of innovation in the nation, and the midwife of major technology breakthroughs in steel, electric light and power, machine tools, and automobiles. Indeed, it was the Silicon Valley of the late nineteenth and early twentieth centuries, and exhibited many of the same attributes of its modern-day successor. It nurtured overlapping networks of inventors, entrepreneurs, and venture capitalists, for example, and was a hotbed of patenting activity, just as Silicon Valley is today. And like Hewlett-Packard, Apple, and Google more recently, each of Cleveland's pioneering firms back then "spawned a whole host of spin-off and startup enterprises," wrote economists Naomi Lamoreaux and the late Kenneth Sokoloff in *Financing Innovation in the United States: 1870 to Present*.

The Brush Electric Company, for example, was founded by Charles F. Brush, the inventor of electric arc lighting, which was the dominant lighting technology until Thomas Edison's less costly and more appealing incandescent bulbs came into favor. In the early 1880s, in fact, Brush Electric installed about 80 percent of the nation's arc-lighting systems, including San Francisco's. But perhaps its greatest legacy lay in the inventors and start-ups it nurtured.

"From early on, the Brush factory was a magnet for ambitious young men who came to work in its shops, network with other technologically creative people, and catch the eye of investors eager to finance the next Charles Brush," noted *Financing Innovation*. Substitute the name Steve Jobs or Sergey Brin for Brush, of course, and you have a pretty accurate description of the cultural ethos of modern-day Silicon Valley. Only one hundred years ago in Cleveland, the "next Charles Brushes" were men like Alfred Cowles, the inventor of a process for smelting ore electrically whose technology eventually gave rise to Alcoa aluminum. Another Brush company alumnus was Thomas Willson, whose start-up grew into Union Carbide. Then there was Sidney H. Short, an early inventor of electric streetcars, as well as John C. Lincoln, inventor of the arc welder. Last but certainly not least among the brilliant inventor-entrepreneurs nurtured at Brush Electric was Elmer Sperry, founder of the Sperry Electric Company, whose most famous invention was the gyroscope that helped pilot ships and planes until the 1940s.

Why did Cleveland, this hotbed of entrepreneurial and inventive activity in the first quarter of the twentieth century, lose its drive and energy in the century's last quarter? One could say simply that the deindustrialization wave of the 1980s was responsible for Cleveland's demise, and leave it at that. After all, just by itself the loss of nearly half of the city's population, economic base, and corporate and personal wealth could not help but drive away the critical mass of inventors, entrepreneurs, and investors needed to sustain the city as an innovation hub.

But perhaps there is a more pertinent lesson for Silicon Valley in Cleveland's demise. As professors Michael Fogarty, Gasper Garofalo, and David Hammack note in their 2002 study *Cleveland from Startup to the Present*, Cleveland once had the highest patenting rate in the country, just as Silicon Valley now does, and this patenting was "[closely tied] to the manufacture of complex industrial equipment and consumer goods." When high-value manufacturing declined, however, the authors found that the existence of strong patenting activity by itself "[could not] guarantee development of a new industry or survival of an existing industry." This holds true whether we are talking about the Cleveland of old or the Silicon Valley of today.

Bottom line, unless high-tech innovation is linked in some measure to high-value manufacturing, no nation (or region) can capture the full economic benefits of new technology.

Modern-day proof of this axiom is not hard to find. As a September 13, 2010, article in the *Los Angeles Times* acknowledged, "Over the last two decades, U.S. scientists and engineers have discovered or pioneered the science behind one blockbuster product after another—from flat-panel screens and robotics to the lithium batteries [in] next-generation power tools and electric cars. Yet in almost every case, production, jobs and most of the economic benefits that sprang from those breakthroughs have ended up overseas."

The article went on to note that "America's innovative spirit may still be the envy of the world, but without more effective policies to translate those achievements into gains at home, the fruits of America's creative genius will probably continue to be reaped by others."

The Journalist, the Professor, and the Union Chief

Few voices in media, academia, and political circles have dared to offer a concerted challenge to the high-level indifference toward manufacturing's erosion in this country—at least not since Stephen Cohen and John Zysman's 1988 book, *Manufacturing Matters: The Myth of the Post-Industrial Economy,* failed to get much traction with policy makers. One voice that has is Richard McCormack, the editor of *Manufacturing & Technology News.*

A crusading editor of a type rarely seen these days, McCormack improbably fits the *New York Times*'s 1952 description of Humphrey Bogart's character Ed Hutcheson in the movie *Deadline, U.S.A.* as "an outraged and unrelenting man who fights on all fronts for the perpetuation of an institution in which he believes." If he is sometimes accused of being an alarmist, it's only because the conventional wisdom on manufacturing holds that anyone who warns against its loss is considered, by definition, to be an "alarmist." As for his pugnacious nature, McCormack admits to coming by this honestly, on his own.

"I've always been an aggressive kind of journalist," McCormack concedes. "I'm Irish, and I had a dad who was a very dominant guy, so I learned how to keep asking questions just to keep him from, you know, going into a rage. He was also a CEO of a company, so I learned to be comfortable around important people, senators and congressmen, whoever."

He also learned to dig below the surface of things. "I've always felt like I had to do the important stories and not just bullshit around. When I was editor of *New Technology Week* I was always telling my reporters to stop reading PR Newswire and Business Wire and instead go out and pursue the truth. Be aggressive. And keep asking questions."

It bothers him, though, that few seem to be very interested in asking questions about the loss of manufacturing and its effects upon the middle class. "I'm sort of this lonely voice in Washington. I went to this press conference [in February of 2010] put on by the Middle Class Task Force and I was the only reporter there." He corrects himself. "Actually, there were a few pool reporters there in the very beginning, when [Vice President] Biden spoke for fifteen minutes. But as soon as he left and they took down the teleprompters, everybody left. I was the only one there for the next two hours."

McCormack criticizes the politicians and trade groups that are supposed to advocate for U.S. manufacturing jobs. Some of his strongest fire, however, is reserved for economists, many of whom are "unbelievably backward on manufacturing," he says, yet "totally dominate the national debate."

That may be changing however. Willy Shih is a professor of management practice at Harvard Business School, where he teaches operations management and the challenges of building and sustaining a successful enterprise. His understanding of business does not come solely from books, however. Prior to joining the Harvard faculty, he worked for twenty-six years in the computer and electronics industries, most recently as president of Kodak's consumer digital camera business, which he established and grew to its first $1 billion in revenue. Thus his perspective on manufacturing is informed by the real-world dynamics of business competition.

"Like most business schools," says Shih, "Harvard has for years been advocating that businesses focus on their core competencies and outsource everything else. That's the majority view among economists as well, and it's been the dominant opinion for some time now. And at the level of the individual firm, outsourcing does often make sense. Sometimes the outsourcer can do a better job than you can. Or do it cheaper. But the problem is—and I've watched this happen in a number of industries like disk drives, precision bearings, semiconductors, and solar—it can have knock-on effects that damage the industry and the economy as a whole."

He offers up the example of Intel building a new chip manufacturing plant in China. "Intel will profit by having a plant there instead of in California. But how will the U.S. do when the benefits from manufacturing and the rest of the value chain no longer go to *our* economy?"

That question lay at the heart of a controversial article he wrote with colleague Gary P. Pisano, the Harry E. Figgie, Jr., Professor of Business Administration at Harvard Business School, for the prestigious *Harvard Business Review*. In it, Shih and Pisano argued that the "industrial commons"—which includes the R&D know-how, advanced process engineering skills, and manufacturing competencies of major technology firms as well as their suppliers—can be damaged and eventually destroyed by unchecked outsourcing.

Shih and Pisano agreed that executives who chose to outsource were merely "heeding the advice du jour of business gurus and Wall Street: Focus on your core competencies, off-load your low-value-added activities, and redeploy the savings to innovation, the true source of your competitive advantage." In fact, however, "the outsourcing has not stopped with low-value tasks like simple assembly or circuit-board stuffing. Sophisticated engineering and manufacturing capabilities that underpin innovation in a wide range of products have been rapidly leaving too. As a result, the U.S. has lost or is in the process of losing the knowledge, skilled people, and supplier infrastructure needed to manufacture many of the cutting-edge products it invented."

Most worrisome of all, say Shih and Pisano, is the fact that "decades of outsourcing manufacturing has left U.S. industry without the means to invent the next generation of high-tech products that are key to rebuilding its economy."

Their article sparked a flurry of debate on the HBR Web site, with arguments such as "Why the U.S. Tech Sector Doesn't Need Domestic Manufacturing" being posted in opposition to Shih's "The U.S. Can't Manufacture the Kindle and That's a Problem." Shih believes that the article and resulting controversy legitimized the debate within academia over manufacturing's role in society—and for that alone it represented a breakthrough.

Interestingly, the corporate executives who would normally have been expected to chime in with their views on the HBR Web site remained surprisingly silent on this issue. "I invited a lot of people I know who are senior executives at major American corporations to join in the discussion," Shih recalls. "And I was struck by the number of people who politely declined because, frankly, they couldn't afford to have their company's name, or their own name, involved in the debate."

Why?

"Well," Shih speculates, "I think it gets back to the question, Are the interests of your corporation the same as the interests of the nation? And to me, their refusal to address that question was a tacit admission that the answer is 'No.'"

They can hardly be blamed, for theirs is a genuine dilemma. Although most CEOs are patriotic and want to see America succeed, they also have a binding fiduciary duty to serve their shareholders' interests. If shutting down a factory in California and rebuilding it in China boosts a company's profits and competitiveness, it's hard to fault any one CEO for making such a decision—even if the net effect of similar decisions by many other CEOs harms the United States.

Ironically, if self-interest drove some corporate executives to steer clear of the manufacturing debate, it has certainly spurred one labor leader to embrace it with a consuming passion. Leo Gerard is the president of the 705,000-member United Steelworkers (USW), the largest industrial union in North America. And he says he has been fighting to halt the erosion of U.S. manufacturing ever since the first devastating wave of deindustrialization swept across the nation more than a quarter century ago.

For Gerard, it's not just his members' jobs that are at stake, but America's future. "Back in 1985, when I first got onto the executive board of the union, there was this gentleman named Jim Smith who was the Steelworkers' chief economist," Gerard recalls. "And I remember Jim telling me that there was a battle going on in this country, and that if we lose it, it's going to be terrible. And I, being this young punk, said to him, 'What kind of battle?' And he said, 'There's a battle between those who think they can create wealth by manipulating pieces of paper in the financial community, and those who create wealth by making things. And if those that create wealth by making things lose, we're all of us in big trouble.'"

Gerard lets out a laugh that has no pleasure in it: "Man, was he ever right!"

For Gerard, a key front in the fight to rebuild America's manufacturing sector centers around trade policy—especially trade with China, which he says is pursuing a mercantilist policy aimed at strengthening its own industrial base at the expense of the rest of the world. "We want fair trade, not free trade," insists Gerard. "Free trade doesn't work unless you're playing on a level playing field. So we're not opposed to trade; we're just opposed to trade on an un-level playing field. We filed five trade cases in the last couple of years [with the International Trade Commission]. And we've won every one, because China violates the rules."

Ultimately, however, Gerard shares McCormack's and Shih's belief that the challenge is not so much to block the unfair trade practices advantages of other nations, but to develop a set of tax breaks and other policies that incentivize a rebirth of manufacturing right here at home.

Tax breaks for manufacturers? When have you ever heard a labor leader call for tax breaks for the bosses? Gerard's support for such incentives suggests that on this issue, at least, traditional class and ideological barriers may fall by the wayside if all sides recognize their common interest in a strong manufacturing sector.

What Do They Know That We Don't?

One thing is clear: other countries understand (even if we don't) that manufacturing strengthens an economy and a middle class like no other form of economic activity can. Which is why virtually every one of them offers tax holidays and other meaningful incentives to any company that will locate manufacturing in its territory.

China, for example, offers semiconductor manufacturers a straight-up five-year tax holiday—that's no taxes at all; zero, zip, nada—followed by five additional years of taxation at only half the normal 25 percent rate. Many high-tech manufacturing firms are entitled to a permanent 15 percent tax rate.

Taiwan likewise provides manufacturers with a zero-tax holiday for five years. In Singapore, qualifying firms may be exempt from corporate income tax for fifteen years, followed by five additional years of taxation at rates as low as 5 percent. In India, Malaysia, Korea, and even Vietnam, significant tax holidays and reduced rates are also offered.

Lest anyone think these tax breaks are only available in the emerging low-wage markets in Asia, think again. Germany, Ireland, Israel, and most other non-Asian nations also provide manufacturers with major tax incentives.

What's more, the manufacturing incentives offered by other nations are not just limited to tax holidays or reduced corporate tax rates. Virtually every nation offers a permanent R&D tax credit up to 47 percent of the amounts invested. By contrast, the R&D tax credit in America was only 14 percent—until it expired (again). Congress renewed it for 2011, but failed to make the credit permanent so businesses could reliably plan on it. According to the Organisation for Economic Co-operation and Development (OECD), America's R&D credit ranks a mere twenty-fourth out of thirty-eight nations. In January 2010, the Information Technology & Innovation Foundation (ITIF) reported that raising America's R&D credit to 20 percent, which would put us in the top-ten ranks, would generate 162,000 new or saved jobs and provide the government with $17 billion in additional tax revenues each year. That same month the Milken Institute estimated that such a move would create more than half a million jobs by 2017 and increase our GDP by $206 billion, or 1.2 percent, by 2019.

Then there are incentives for the costs of plant construction. In Dresden, Germany, a few years ago, the federal government and the state of Saxony provided more than $1 billion worth of grants, allowances, and other subsidies toward the construction of a semiconductor fab. In Kiryat Gat, Israel, the Israeli government provided a semiconductor maker with $550 million in outright construction grants for a new semiconductor fab plus an additional $660 million in tax benefits to upgrade a second, older fab to produce more advanced wafers.

According to a Semiconductor Industry Association report, a spokesman for the company stated that his firm "would not have built the fab in Israel" without the incentives.

Manufacturers who keep their operations in the United States, meanwhile, receive no federal assistance and also face the highest corporate income tax rate in the world (save for Japan)—one that's a whopping 50 percent higher than the average corporate tax rate in Europe.

Not only does Washington offer no tax incentives, but those offered by some U.S. states are undermined in value by more than one-third because the federal government continues to impose its federal corporate tax.

I understand that many readers might be skeptical about what they feel may be corporate "whining" over taxes. Twenty years ago, when U.S. business tax rates were much lower than elsewhere in the world, such sentiments would have certainly had some merit. But something happened on the way to the new global economic competition. Most governments realized that any short-term loss of revenues they suffered from reducing taxes for manufacturers would be more than made up for in the long term by the increased wages and economic output generated by a stronger manufacturing sector.

So beginning in the late 1990s, most nations around the world began lowering their tax rates—and they have kept on lowering them ever since. Germany, for example, reduced its corporate tax rate from 38 to 30 percent. The United Kingdom lowered its from 30 to 28 percent, and in 2010 decided to lower it still further to 24 percent by 2015. Israel reduced its rate from 34 to 31 percent in 2006, and then to 29 percent in 2007, 27 percent in 2008, 26 percent in 2009, and 25 percent in 2010. Hungary, New Zealand, Poland, Korea, India, Malaysia—all have cut their tax rates in recent years. Ireland's tax rate is only 12.5 percent today.

Not so the United States, where combined federal and state tax rates now average a whopping 39.2 percent. The Milken Institute estimates that simply reducing the corporate tax rate to the average found in Europe and other OECD countries would generate more than 2 million jobs and increase total GDP by $375 billion, or 2.2 percent, by 2019.

But wait, you say: surely these giant corporations don't really pay the statutory tax rate—not with all their loopholes, right? Fair enough. So let's look at the *effective* tax rates actually paid by U.S. firms, and compare those with the taxes paid by their foreign competitors.

According to a 2009 study conducted by PriceWaterhouseCoopers, Intel paid an average 28.66 percent tax rate on earnings during the years 2004 to 2008. Its competitor Samsung, the Korean semiconductor maker, paid 16.06 percent in taxes for the same period. Intel, in other words, paid 78 percent higher in corporate tax rates than its direct competitor!

A similar story applies in telecom equipment manufacturing. Motorola paid an effective tax rate of 30.11 percent between 2004 and 2008, whereas its foreign competitors Nokia and LG Electronics paid 23.13 percent and 18.49 percent, respectively.

As for the computer hardware industry, Dell paid an effective tax rate of 24.98 percent between 2004 and 2008, whereas its foreign competitors Huawei and Lenovo paid roughly half that rate—12.66 percent and 14.6 percent, respectively.

All of this puts a serious crimp in Intel's and Motorola's and Dell's ability to compete globally. In 2006, former Intel CEO Craig Barrett testified to Congress some of the *disincentives* to locating a manufacturing plant in the

U.S.: "It costs $1 billion more to build, equip and operate a factory in the U.S. than it does outside the U.S. The largest portion of this cost difference (about 90 percent) is attributable to taxes [and] capital grants. Labor cost is not a large difference."

Think about it: The United States is the only major nation on earth that refuses to offer tax holidays, tax reductions, or other meaningful incentives to businesses willing to keep or to locate manufacturing operations within our borders. The only one.

Current Intel CEO Paul Otellini finds this ironic. As he told a meeting of the Council on Foreign Relations, reported by McCormack, "It's not like [offering incentives is] taking away from existing revenue or spending. It's a no-brainer. It funds itself. You put people back to work. You get them off unemployment [and] that starts generating taxes."

So what does the rest of the world know that we don't? They know that such incentives tap into the unique economic force multiplier effects of manufacturing to generate jobs, growth, and a rising standard of living for their people. These benefits extend far beyond the immediate increase in employment, economic output, and sales of products and services.

A World Bank study of the effects of government incentives provided to semiconductor manufacturers locating in Costa Rica, for example, noted that "the period following the investment shows significant GDP growth, staggering increases in exports, and otherwise positive outcomes. [It] is responsible for a shift in the country's top exports, from coffee and bananas to electrical and electronic products. Electronics is Costa Rica's largest sector."

Benefits like these are found not only in relatively underdeveloped nations like Costa Rica. The incentives given to construct those semiconductor plants in Dresden, Germany, for example, have transformed that decaying old rust-belt city into the modern chip hub of Europe.

And in Berlin, where government subsidies for green energy manufacturing enabled Siemens to modernize its hundred-year-old factory to produce new, more energy-efficient and less polluting turbines, "[The Germans] have forged a different path toward recovery. They are making old plants more modern and effective rather than watching workers or companies fall by the wayside." The result, notes the *New York Times,* is that "Germany's economy contracted 5 percent last year, yet its unemployment rate of 7.5 percent is actually down from two years ago. By contrast, the economy of the United States shrank [only] 2.4 percent last year as unemployment doubled, to 10 percent, over the period."

When supposedly "stodgy old Europe," now outperforms nimble and entrepreneurial America in both job creation and in creating a business-friendly tax environment, then you know it's time to wake up and smell the Pilsner.

But let's cut to the chase—can we really compete against China's cheap labor? It's true that China and other emerging nations have a significant cost advantage in labor, although that advantage is getting smaller as Chinese workers organize and even strike for better wages. What most people don't realize, however, is that we absolutely can compete with Chinese labor—and at Western wages, too, as Germany has proved—if only Washington would start providing the same sorts of incentives that other governments offer manufacturers.

Here are the facts, as explained by Louis Vintro, vice president and general manager of the semiconductor product division at equipment maker ESI: "What we see from our data is that China's labor costs are one-third to one-half of U.S. costs depending on the level of expertise. However, there is quite a bit of inflation and also a high level of turnover, which means they have some efficiency problems. But let's just say the net-net right now is that China has a 50 percent advantage in labor costs. Since labor represents an average 7 percent of operating costs across all of the semiconductor sectors, that means China has a 3.5 percent overall cost advantage."

Add in China's tax holiday, and firms locating there get an additional 2.5 percent advantage, if you assume they avoid paying 25 percent tax on a 10 percent operating profit. That brings China's total cost advantage as a manufacturing location to roughly 6 percent.

But what if manufacturers were given a tax holiday in the United States? If you take the roughly 30 percent tax Intel paid on 10 percent operating profit as a guide, that would mean a 3 percent lower cost of operating a plant here. Add in an enhanced, permanent 20 percent R&D tax credit equal to what other nations offer, and China's advantage drops to perhaps 1 to 2 percent.

"And remember," says Vintro, "the U.S. still retains a very high percentage of the R&D centers and the high-tech machinery used in manufacturing. Companies can use the faster time to market they'd get by locating their plants here—and all the benefits of having their R&D closer to manufacturing—to remain competitive with, if not superior to, anything the Chinese can do in the high-tech field. But we've got to have some help from Washington to make that happen."

For me personally, the incentives offered by China and other countries pose a very real dilemma, and I sympathize with those CEOs who Shih said were hesitant to take part in a public debate over the offshoring of manufacturing. I, too, know that a firm's best interests may not always be the same as those of the nation. After all, officers and directors of publicly traded companies are legally obligated to act in the best interests of shareholders, regardless of their personal feelings or patriotic impulses. So at the risk of incurring some criticism, I think all Americans—and especially our leaders in Washington—would benefit from hearing firsthand what American CEOs are really up against in deciding where to locate their operations.

My company, Tessera, is a leader in the field of semiconductor miniaturization. We spend $80 million a year on R&D to figure out how to make electronic devices such as consumer optics smaller and less expensive so they can be deployed in ever-smaller and more powerful computers, cellphones, and cameras. Although we have retained some industrial operations in San Jose, California, along with our corporate headquarters, we now house two-thirds of our employees and facilities in less expensive North Carolina and in several countries overseas.

In February 2010, I visited China, where the mayor of a medium-sized city basically offered me the moon if I would open any type of R&D or production facility there. No tax at all for five years. The land and all construction costs for the facility provided free. All utilities paid for three years. Employee salaries paid for three years. Everything else—all taken care of.

What to do? I want to create jobs in America. I want our country to be prosperous—that's why I'm writing this book. And I want this nation to continue to offer my sons, and their children as well, the same opportunities it gave me, the son of an immigrant factory worker.

But I also have a solemn responsibility under the law to do what's best for my company's customers, employees, and shareholders. If I were to refuse an opportunity to materially grow Tessera's business, increase its profits, and advance our breakthrough R&D efforts by locating a new facility in China, what would I accomplish except to pave the way for Tessera to be less competitive and less successful than it can and should be? If I don't pursue the best course possible for my company, the shareholders and the board of directors would have every right to replace me with another CEO who will.

So as I wrestle with these choices, all I can do is keep building our business and hope that Washington eventually does the smart thing and helps companies like mine create jobs right here at home. That's what every other government in the world does for their own countries, after all.

I want to create more jobs in America. But to do that, I need America's policies to change.

The Flat World Is Tilting Against Us

Will they? It's hard to say, for the dominant view in economics, policy, and business circles remains that expounded by *The World Is Flat* author Tom Friedman—namely, that America need not worry about manufacturing shifting offshore so long as we "specialize in research and innovation," as he puts it, and maintain our lead in R&D and services. This view is only reinforced by techno-utopian notions that, in the Internet age, physical location is irrelevant.

Ah, if only that were true. Unfortunately, there are several things wrong with this theory.

Chief among them is that our R&D and services are being outsourced overseas now as well, along with our manufacturing, and at an ever-faster rate. And if this trend continues unchecked, where will it leave us, exactly—other than in ever-increasing debt trying to pay for the computers, cars, eyeglasses, clothes, and everything else we need to live in this still-quite-material world?

Just ask Gregory Tassey, the chief economist for the National Institute of Standards and Technology (NIST), the agency of the Department of Commerce tasked with promoting innovation and industrial competitiveness in the United States. He calls the proponents of the "R&D and services only" economy the "apostles of denial." And in his groundbreaking 2010 study of manufacturing and R&D in the new global economy, Tassey points to some serious flaws in the "R&D and services only" theory that its advocates ignore.

In the first place, says Tassey, some thirty countries already have policies in place to promote service exports, and they are gaining ground quickly. His claim is confirmed by research from Duke University and PriceWaterhouseCoopers showing that foreign providers of software, legal, and other services are "impacting the market" in ever greater strength, "aided by tax breaks and other financial incentives to attract and nurture outsourcing firms." One example is cited in *Manufacturing & Technology News*: "China has created an outsourcing demonstration city—Hefei—which has already attracted numerous multinational companies to shift work there, including IBM, General Electric, Exxon Mobil, Motorola, and Mitsubishi Heavy Industries."

As for R&D, Tassey points to a stunning contradiction in the view that we don't need manufacturing so long as we "specialize in R&D"—namely, that manufacturing firms conduct 70 percent of all R&D in the United States, versus only 30 percent conducted by service firms.

So what happens to all that R&D if the manufacturing firms that conduct it disappear? We hardly need a NIST chief economist to answer that for us, but here he is anyway. "The large percentage of industry R&D accounted for by manufacturing companies," says Tassey, "means that the demise of a substantial domestic high-tech manufacturing sector would greatly diminish the size and also the efficiency of the U.S. innovation infrastructure."

What's more, he notes, "manufacturing companies employ approximately the same relative share of scientists and engineers as their contribution to national R&D performance"—that is, 70 percent of them. "Under a 'service-sector-only' growth scenario," he explains, "this skilled pool of researchers would be unavailable." Or at least they would be unavailable to the American R&D effort, since they would then be employed by manufacturing firms overseas.

Another problem with the "R&D and services only" theory is that advanced R&D really depends upon close contact with manufacturing for its success, and will follow it if it relocates.

"In most [high-tech] industries, product and process innovation are intertwined," note Pisano and Shih in their *Harvard Business Review* article. "So the decline of manufacturing in a region sets off a chain reaction. Once manufacturing is outsourced, process-engineering expertise can't be maintained, since it depends on daily interactions with manufacturing. Without process-engineering capabilities, companies find it increasingly difficult to conduct advanced research on next-generation process technologies. Without the ability to develop such new processes, they find they can no longer develop new products."

Just a theory? Here's ESI's Vintro again: "You've got to be close to your customers—in our case semiconductor manufacturers—to understand their needs. Otherwise you can't create the next-generation product to meet those needs. And I have to tell you, with semiconductor manufacturing going overseas, it's getting harder for us to do that."

In the long term, write Pisano and Shih, "An economy that lacks an infrastructure for advanced process engineering and manufacturing will lose its ability to innovate."

And, indeed, there is absolutely no doubt that American R&D is increasingly "co-locating" near manufacturing centers overseas. The Semiconductor Industry Association reports that while R&D spending by member firms increased overall between 1997 and 2007, R&D spending *within the United States* declined by 8.4 percent as firms shifted ever more of it overseas. The trade group expects it to decline by an additional 9.3 percent by the year 2013.

Adds Tassey: "[Other] countries' efforts to 'tilt the flat world' [by attracting R&D] is an increasingly frequent phenomenon. Nanotechnology research is a standout example, as global R&D in this area is [now] evenly distributed among North America, Europe and Asia. U.S. R&D spending as a whole is expected to double in Europe over the next five years."

This movement of R&D offshore to follow manufacturing has resulted in a sharp decline in U.S. R&D intensity—the percentage of GDP devoted to R&D—relative to the rest of the world. We used to have the most R&D-intensive economy in the world. Now we're eighth.

The offshoring of R&D has gotten so large, in fact, that the National Science Foundation (NSF) has for the first time started keeping track of it. The NSF reported that in 2008 $58 billion, or one-fifth, of total R&D spending by U.S. firms took place overseas. Depending on the industry, that amounted to anywhere from 19 percent to 39 percent of industry R&D spending.

Said economist Richard Florida about the report: "In key sectors of the economy, innovation appears to be following production off shore."

This situation cannot help but slow hiring and growth here at home, as noted in a September 6, 2010, article in the *New York Times*: "'There's been this assumption that there's a global hierarchy of work, that all the high-end service work, knowledge work, R&D work, would stay in the U.S., and that all the lower-end work would be transferred to emerging markets,' said Hal Salzman, a public policy professor at Rutgers and a senior faculty fellow at Heldrich Center for Workforce Development. 'That hierarchy has been upset, to say the least,' he said. 'More and more of the innovation is coming out of the emerging markets as part of this bottom up push.'"

The most glaring exemplar of this shift of innovation overseas is Applied Materials, the world's biggest maker of equipment used to make semiconductors and solar panels. In March 2010, the firm stunned analysts when it announced that it was opening a new R&D center—its newest and biggest ever—in China to complement its manufacturing operations there.

Even more shocking (and revealing), however, is the fact that the company is relocating its chief technology officer, Mark Pinto, to China as well. As the *New York Times* reported: "Mr. Pinto is the first chief technology officer of a major American tech company to move to China." The *Times* also noted that the company even held its annual shareholders' meeting in Xi'an.

As company spokesman Howard Clabo conceded to none other than Tom Friedman in the latter's April 28, 2010, *New York Times* column: "Roughly 50 percent of the solar panels in the world were made in China last year. We need to be where the customers are."

There it is—the smoking gun that shoots down Friedman's theory that America can just "specialize in research and innovation." Yet the only conclusion Friedman drew at the time from Clabo's stunning revelation was that Congress should pass a carbon tax energy bill. Go figure.

To be fair, someone as perceptive as Friedman will surely adjust his views in the light of new evidence. Only a few years ago, there were few hard indicators that our "R&D and services only" economy was falling into a downward-spiraling innovation doom loop. Today, however, a growing number of pundits and policy makers have clearly seen the writing on the wall.

As Spencer Michaels of *PBS NewsHour* put it, summing up the real lessons of Applied Materials' move: "Silicon Valley is losing steam and perhaps the innovative spirit that made it the economic engine that propelled California and the U.S. into the front ranks of high tech."

The biggest irony in this whole debate over whether or not America needs manufacturing is that it was supposed to have been definitively resolved more than a quarter of a century ago, after David Teece wrote one of the most widely cited articles in the history of economics: "Profiting from Technological Innovation." In it, he demonstrated that no firm or nation could capture the full value of innovation unless it also held certain "complementary assets," such as the ability to manufacture products derived from that innovation, and could therefore create a value chain around that innovation.

"The notion that the United States can adopt a 'designer' role in international commerce, while letting firms in other countries do the manufacturing, is unlikely to be viable as a long-term strategy," Teece argued back in 1986. "In this context, concerns that the decline of manufacturing threatens the entire economy appear to be well founded."

Strangely, many economists appear to have forgotten this core principle, which explains why twenty-five years later none other than the chief of the Defense Advanced Research Projects Agency (DARPA)—the organization whose basic research in the 1950s and 1960s led to semiconductors, PCs, software, and the Internet—had to bring it to Washington's attention again. Testifying before the House Armed Services Committee on March 23, 2010, DARPA director Regina E. Dugan warned that America's thirty-year-long experiment in outsourcing manufacturing has been a failure, not least because it undermined the country's ability to innovate.

"At DARPA, we have developed a short hand for this," she told the committee. "We say, 'to innovate, we must make.'"

Or as I like to put it: a nation that no longer makes things will eventually forget how to invent them.

We Broke It, We Can Fix It

So here's the question for the president, the Congress, and all the policy wonks who watch while our innovative and productive capacity bleeds out of the nation: What have we truly gained from this thirty-year-long flight from our shores of manufacturing—and now of R&D as well? Put all the theory aside. Just look at the real-life results of this loss of industrial capacity for middle-class communities across the country, from Sharon, Pennsylvania, to Silicon Valley.

Since deindustrialization began in 1980, average real weekly wages for all Americans have remained essentially flat. Just between 2000 and 2008, inflation-adjusted median household income in the U.S. dropped 4.2 percent—and that's *before* the current recession set in.

Meanwhile, in that same time period, incomes for the top 1 percent of earners have tripled. In 1973, CEOs like myself were paid on average twenty-six times the median income. Today we receive more than three hundred times the median income. And according to the latest research, the average American is far less likely today to rise from poverty than is a citizen of any European country. Horatio Alger, it seems, is likely to speak French or German nowadays.

Indeed, for the first time in all of American history, "the U.S. economy has been unable to provide a rising standard of living for the majority of its people," says Shih.

Our prosperity has been withering away. But like some giant nationwide Ponzi scheme, it was all covered up first by a dot-com bubble and then a housing bubble and now a debt bubble.

No wonder people feel that upward mobility for the middle class has disappeared. It has!

No wonder two-income families can barely make it today, whereas when I was young a middle-class family could usually do fine on just one income.

And no wonder America used to have money for schools and GI Bills and interstate highways but today can't even repair a few broken bridges without putting our grandchildren in debt.

And by the way, in case you're wondering why the recoveries after each recession feel like they're getting weaker and weaker, it's because they are. The thirty-year deindustrialization process has introduced a devastating new wrinkle into capitalism's normal boom-and-bust cycle. In the first seven recessions following World War II, it took an average of only four months for employment levels to return to normal. But after the offshoring craze began in the 1980s, the recovery from each recession started to take longer—much longer.

Following the 1990–1991 recession, for example, it took nineteen months before positive employment levels were reached. Following the 2000–2001 recession, after even more manufacturing jobs were lost, we needed thirty months to recover positive employment levels.

So how long will it take to recover the 8.4 million jobs lost in the current recession—not to mention the 4.5 million additional jobs that a healthy economy would normally have created over the last three years for our growing population?

Hard to say. One thing seems clear, however: these jobless recoveries wouldn't be happening had we not thrown away the greatest economic force multiplier in history—manufacturing.

Once again, I have to stress that what happened was not the natural or inevitable result of modernization. Nor was it some sort of natural disaster. It was a man-made debacle.

And if we caused it, we can fix it.

I know that many will have trouble believing that we can stop and even reverse the damage. That's because the notion that economic and technological change just *happens* to us and there's nothing we can do about it goes back a long way in our cultural history.

In the 1933 Century of Progress International Exposition in Chicago, for example, visitors to the Hall of Science were met in the foyer by a Louise Lentz Woodruff sculpture entitled "Science Advancing Mankind." Two life-sized figures, male and female, faced forward with arms uplifted. They were dwarfed by the much larger figure behind them, however: a metallic robot, hands at their backs, pushing them seemingly against their will to whatever fate "progress" had in store for them. The ideology of this sculpture—if it can be said to have such a thing —was reinforced by the Exposition Guide-book's official motto, written in large, boldface letters:

Science Finds, Industry Applies, Man Conforms.

No kidding. It really said that.

It's no wonder then that Americans have what historian John Michael Staudenmaier calls "a pervasive societal ambiguity" about technology. We pray it brings "liberating progress," but we bow down to its supposedly autonomous power as if it were some "intimating master." This sort of technological passivity, Staudenmaier writes, "encourages a childish citizenry" that assumes that "the welfare of the body politic is someone else's business."

In truth, however, it *is* our business, if only we would choose to act.

What Can We Do?

We must, as a nation, act like state and local officials in Milwaukee, Wisconsin, did when they recently provided tax credits, loans, and other incentives to the Spanish firm Ingeteam to build a wind turbine factory in the city. Company officials said that the incentives weren't the only lure. It was also the talent and know-how of workers in a city once known as the "machine shop to the world" that led the Spanish multinational to build its first U.S. factory there.

Other states have implemented similar incentives programs in recent years to bring back jobs and manufacturing to their regions. However, these efforts need to be well designed to ensure that job creation rather than corporate welfare is the result. In any case, their success will only be limited at best in the absence of a larger federal effort to incentivize the rebirth of a healthy manufacturing sector nationwide.

And that's the beauty of such incentives. Their benefits aren't just theoretical, nor even really debatable. We know that when properly designed, they work. And every other country in the world knows it, too. There's no doubt that well-planned incentives yield new manufacturing jobs whose force multiplier effects spark more job creation, economic growth, and prosperity for communities and, yes, even whole nations.

All that remains is to act on this knowledge.

We must also cease our shameful dilly-dallying on an R&D tax credit and act now to set a permanent one at no less than 20 percent, as most other nations have done. Since its inception under President Ronald Reagan thirty years ago, the R&D tax credit has been allowed to expire fourteen times by Congress, only to be renewed (as of this writing) thirteen times.

What is the problem here? What do we not grasp that every other major country on earth understands so clearly?

It's also time to offer incentives to get venture capitalists to invest in more manufacturing start-ups, as well as for investment in established capital-intensive manufacturing operations. Capital grants and feed-in tariffs to help support an indigenous market for locally manufactured solar panels and other clean energy solutions are also needed.

Capital equipment purchases by manufacturers should also be allowed a full write-off in the year of purchase from now through 2014, or until economic conditions greatly improve.

We should also reduce the repatriation tax rate of 35 percent to 20 percent for any U.S. business that invests in tangible assets, R&D, or job creation here at home. Right now some $1 *trillion* in U.S. corporate profits are held overseas, where they are taxed at lower rates. As at least two studies noted, the last time this rate was reduced—after the American Jobs Creation Act of 2004—the result was an additional $300 billion plowed into domestic capital investment, R&D, and hiring.

Finally, regarding the issue of unfair trading practices by China and some other nations, there is little doubt that a real problem exists. But the best way to defend American interests here is to focus less on trying to block their manufacturing and export power and more on rebuilding our own.

So let's end this chapter where we began—where *I* began, in fact—in my old hometown of Sharon, Pennsylvania. On February 5, 2010, an editorial in the Sharon *Herald* noted:

"It's not news that the local employment picture has deteriorated over the last three decades. The exodus of manufacturing jobs and its attendant population loss and brain drain has damaged the entire region and turned once-prosperous communities into struggling, near-ghost towns."

The paper went on to concede that some people "may look at the numbers and say it's all over for Mercer County. Stick a fork in us, we're done.

"But," the paper insisted, "there could be an opportunity."

Indeed, there could. And not just in the industrial communities in the Shenango Valley. Manufacturing offers an opportunity to rejuvenate employment opportunities across the nation, especially for the three-quarters of all Americans who do not have a college education.

It also offers an opportunity to save Silicon Valley from slowly but surely losing its innovation mojo and devolving into some sort of Banana Republic of Silicon Valley with no future for "people other than software billionaires and their servants," in *Forbes*'s words.

And most of all, it offers an opportunity to save the once-great American middle class from almost certain death and restore its health and pride.

But we, as a nation, must act.

According to a 2009 study conducted by the Deloitte consulting organization, 70 percent of all Americans say "developing a strong manufacturing base should be a national priority."

Will Washington listen?

Immigration

The Global War for Talent

More than most people, Silicon Valley entrepreneur and start-up incubator Farzad Naimi knows why people all over the world dream of coming to America. And it's not simply because in America no one gets tortured to death, although as Farzad can personally attest, that certainly does have an appeal to anyone who has grown up in a society where a midnight knock on the door can lead to your demise in a government interrogation facility. As a young man growing up in Tehran in the 1970s, Farzad, though nonpolitical himself, often heard stories of political activists and innocents alike being thrown into the city's infamous Evin Prison and tortured to death by the CIA-backed shah's secret police.

More than thirty years later, now a resident of Silicon Valley, Farzad is once again hearing of the torture and murder inflicted upon activists and innocents inside Evin Prison—only this time by tyrannical mullahs who brook no dissent from their medieval policies. This is of more than passing concern to Farzad, of course, because aside from being Iranian himself, some of the students he mentors at Stanford and other universities are Iranians. And given the restrictive U.S. visa policies implemented after the terrorist attacks of 9/11, many of these bright young men and women will have to go back to Iran one day, where their talents will surely be wasted—and in some cases, their lives even lost.

For Farzad, however, there's an even deeper meaning to the American Dream. It's the openness of America, its unmatched responsiveness to individual effort and initiative. Simply put, says Farzad, America is the best place on earth to realize your dreams.

"In America, no one cares where you came from," he insists. "As long as you are truly contributing to society, they welcome you with open arms. Here you can grow something out of nothing, and follow your dreams without any limits. If you have talent and drive, no other country is like America. It's why I came here—why people all over the world still come here."

Whether talented immigrants will continue to come here—and whether those already here contributing to American economic growth and job creation will be allowed to remain—is a question of great importance for American policy makers and citizens alike. For across the globe today, a "world war for talent" has begun. Every nation now understands that its economic strength and future prosperity depends upon its ability to attract, and retain, the very best scientists, engineers, and entrepreneurs on earth—whatever their nationality. Noted the *Economist*, "[Talent] has become the world's most sought after commodity."

But an America driven to distraction by understandable concerns over the flood of illegal aliens across our southern borders seems to have forgotten that its economic success since World War II was in no small measure built by talented *legal* immigrants. Almost alone among other nations today, only America restricts legal immigration by the best and brightest technology professionals. Most other countries welcome them with open arms.

Farzad's own dream took shape, oddly enough, in an iconic American form—building model cars as a boy, marrying his high school sweetheart, working his way through college, and then forging a path to wealth and success by starting a business. Several businesses, in fact.

Farzad's parents were members of the urban professional class. His mother worked in the Foreign Ministry, while his father was CFO for a division of an oil and gas firm. The years of his youth were a time of great upheaval in Iran, especially in the capitol. Although Tehran was a very cosmopolitan city of 3 million—its residents were often referred to as "the French of the Middle East"—it was also a city torn by the challenges of modernity. Tensions brewed between the rising educated elites and a mostly illiterate peasantry swarming into the city in search of work or fleeing various tribal wars in the countryside. The Western-oriented professionals looked to the future and saw a modern and prosperous Iran. The peasants, seeing little place for themselves in that future Iran, bound themselves even more tightly to tradition and Islamic orthodoxy. Farzad's family tried to navigate the divide between the two strata of society.

"When we were kids," says Farzad, "my mother used to take us every month to the poor sections of town where we would distribute high-nutritional food to the unfortunate ones. This is how we were taught to treat these people—not as less than us, but as less fortunate than us. My family had very high standards of humanity and integrity. We were taught to treat every person with respect—this was an absolute, never to be forgotten. Even though we wanted to be modern, my mother insisted we must follow the ancient traditions of courtesy and humility."

He pauses a moment, his voice thickening: "She is still my role model."

Farzad attended Dr. Hashtroodi High School, named after a renowned Iranian mathematician, whose graduates often went on to study at American universities. "I can remember my friends and I would see these educated Iranians returning home from the West," Farzad recalls. "They all got good jobs with high salaries. We could see it was a great advantage to be educated in the West, and so of course this is what we wanted, too."

He was torn, of course, about leaving his high school sweetheart, Farahnaz, behind. But he figured he would find a way to be with her somehow, just as he always had in the past. Indeed, Farzad had always employed a great deal of ingenuity in his courtship of Farahnaz, as he revealed in an interview for *Profiles in Prominence,* a book published by Golden Gate University in San Francisco about some of its more successful graduates.

"The schools [in Tehran] were separate for girls and boys, but I used to stand outside of her school and make sure I would escort her home," he explained. "But there were certain limitations: she had to be home by 7:30 p.m., and when we went out, her sister had to come. And so it was with respect but at the same time a lot of love. It doesn't matter what culture or customs, I think love [just] happens."

Sometimes love has to be put on hold, however. After graduating from high school in 1976, Farzad received a coveted F-1 visa to study electrical engineering at Cogswell Polytechnical College in San Francisco. His decision to go to America would radically change his life, of course, and within a decade thrust him into the front lines of the global telecommunications revolution. But three years after his arrival in the U.S., another revolution broke out first—the Iranian Revolution. It was 1979, and Farzad went home to rescue the woman he still calls his one true love.

"I proposed to her . . ." He pauses. "Actually, I proposed to her parents, as this is the custom in Iran. And I promised them that I would take good care of her. They were very hesitant, of course, because we were both so young—I was twenty-one, and Farahnaz was only eighteen. But they were also very worried about what was happening in Iran. So I made a solemn promise to her parents that I would get her out of Iran and see that she was educated at an American university."

With the wedding set for two weeks ahead, Farzad went to the U.S. Embassy in Tehran to renew his student visa, which had expired the moment he left the States to come back to Iran. Although Iranians were at that time among the largest recipients of foreign student visas, it was next to impossible to even get inside the embassy to pick one up because of the thousands lining up outside hoping to escape the new revolutionary government. Fortunately, Farzad had a friend who worked in the embassy, who took him through the crowds and inside to meet a consular official, who quickly renewed his visa. Farahnaz, however, would have to wait two weeks until she had an actual marriage certificate in hand before she could obtain a spousal student visa.

Then, seven days before the wedding, militant Iranian students seized the U.S. embassy in Tehran and took sixty-six people hostage, fifty-two of whom would remain prisoners for 444 days. The State Department stopped issuing any new visas to Iranians.

Farzad and Farahnaz got married as planned, but what followed was no honeymoon. Farzad decided the only realistic plan was to leave Farahnaz behind in Iran, in the care of her parents, while he returned to the United States and pursued a visa for her. This is what he did, spending the next year and a half writing the State Department and American consulates all across Europe pleading for a humanitarian exception to the visa ban so that his wife could join him in the U.S. For her part, Farahnaz traveled to Greece and then France in vain attempts to secure a U.S. visa on her own. The separation from his bride and worry over her fate was agonizing for Farzad.

In Iran, meanwhile, what had begun as a popular revolution against dictatorship waged by a broad coalition of all anti-shah forces in society was soon transformed into a fundamentalist power grab by obscurantist mullahs. Ayatollah Khomeini, who at first denied any interest in ruling, swiftly consolidated power. Within eighteen months of the start of the revolution, all opposition parties had been banned and the moderate president Abolhassan Banisadr had been impeached. Things began to get ugly in Iran. The Islamic regime started arresting, torturing, and executing democratic opposition figures by the thousands. In her letters to Farzad, Farahnaz tried to maintain a positive attitude, but he could tell she was scared. So was he. Time was running out for her—and for them.

Finally, in June 1981, Farzad found a sympathetic consular official in Vienna who agreed in principle to grant a spousal visa to Farahnaz on humanitarian grounds. The catch was that Farzad had to request the visa for her in person, with Farahnaz at his side. The instant he left the States, of course, his own student visa would automatically expire with no guarantee that he would ever be allowed back in to the U.S.—with her or without her.

He had no choice. He packed everything he owned, in case he was denied reentry into the U.S. and he and his wife were forced to either return to revolutionary Iran or seek refuge in Europe. Then, with plane fare borrowed from a sister who also lived in the States, Farzad flew to Vienna and met Farahnaz. They went immediately to the U.S. embassy for their interview.

"It was a very tense moment," Farzad remembers. "I was a good student, so I was not worried about the academic side of things. But we knew this one man's decision would change our lives forever, either way. I did not want to be without my wife, so I decided that if her visa was denied, I would not go back to the U.S. without her. Our whole future together—either with freedom in America, or in Iran under the regime of the mullahs—depended upon this one man."

He does not remember the man's name. What he does remember, though, is his manner. "He asked only a few questions," Farzad recalls. "Mostly, he just listened."

Finally, the consular official leaned back in his chair and cleared his throat. Farzad and Farahnaz exchanged a quick glance and braced for the worst. There was a long pause as the man sat there, thinking. The couple held their breath. Then the official leaned forward on his desk, picked up both of their passports, and stamped a U.S. visa inside each of them.

"I almost could not believe my eyes," Farzad recalls. "I looked over at my wife and she was already starting to cry. I don't remember what we said at that moment. But I hope to God we thanked this kind man for giving us the chance for freedom. All I remember is that as soon as we left his office, Farahnaz and I both burst into tears. We could not stop crying. Then we started laughing, then crying again. We ran out of the embassy like this, laughing and crying."

Finding Horatio Alger

A week later, Farzad and Farahnaz began their new life in San Francisco. The screeching political turmoil in Iran had begun to recede into a muffled revolutionary dreariness that was reflected in the many letters they received from their parents. Their financial support had stopped, because both the Iranian and U.S. governments had banned the transfer of funds between the nations. They therefore had to work to pay for their education and living expenses. But the couple found that despite the Iranian hostage crisis, most Americans were very willing to help them, often going to great lengths to do so. Farzad was back at Cogswell Polytechnic, finishing his engineering degree, while Farahnaz studied computer science at San Francisco State. With his job teaching swimming at the Marines Memorial Club in downtown San Francisco, they survived on barely $800 a month. But they were together. That was enough.

A photo from that time shows Farzad and Farahnaz standing together in front of the Palace of Fine Arts in San Francisco. His arms are casually wrapped around her, both of them staring at the camera with the weary contentment of people who have endured a difficult trial but are now safe. There is a confident strength in her pose, her chin proudly upturned, and an almost defiant quality to her gaze—as if at that moment she had been thinking, "We did it!" As for Farzad, he is the optimism to her endurance. His dark wavy hair and open, boy-next-door smile remind you immediately of the young Tom Hanks in the movie Big.

The next four years were a blur of school and work, work and school. By 1985, Farzad had gotten his degree in electrical engineering as well as a master's in business administration from Golden Gate University. To realize his dream of starting a business, however, he needed two things he did not have: business experience and a green card so he could stay in America.

He found both when in 1985 he met Fred Glynn, the founder of a San Francisco start-up called Centex Telemanagement. Following the break-up a year earlier of the century-old AT&T telephone monopoly, telecommunications ventures had begun to spring up everywhere. Centex had developed a technology that offered businesses huge savings on their in-state calls.

"I told Fred, 'Listen, it doesn't matter how much you pay me. I just want to learn the business. You sponsor me, you get me a green card, and I will work my ass off for you—excuse my language.' And Fred, who still is a great friend of mine, he agreed to hire me. I was still teaching swimming at night, but during the day I came in and did the programming and whatever else they needed. I made $6.25 an hour. But as the number-five employee, I also got stock."

He laughs. "I didn't even know what stock was. All I cared about was the green card, so I never paid any attention to the shares they were giving me. But after two and a half years, the company went public for $500 million. That's when I found out what stock was!"

No kidding. Suddenly, for the first time in his life, Farzad had real money. And he had gotten his first taste of the start-up life.

"From there I started consulting," he explains, "so I could learn more about business and about product differentiation. I was especially interested in e-commerce and electronic payment systems, which were just being developed. This was before the Internet. Anyway, after a number of years, I went to Visa International with a software idea for how to differentiate their customer support services from MasterCard's. But they didn't want to get into software development. So instead I went to Prestige International, which ran the call centers for big Japanese banks and other businesses that served ten million customers. They really loved my idea."

His idea was an early version of what we now call computer-telephony integration, or CTI. He and his two partners, Greg Shenkman and Alec Miloslavsky, developed a way to link incoming telephone calls with computerized customer databases to improve call center service and make it far more efficient while also reducing call center costs.

Prestige International paid for development and in return received the technology at cost, while Farzad and his partners retained ownership of the technology. They assigned their seminal patents—including "apparatus and methods for coordinating telephone and data communications" (U.S. Pat. 6130933) and "methods and apparatus for implementing a network call center"

(U.S. Pat. 5825870)—to their new start-up company, Genesys, which marketed the systems worldwide and eventually went on to employ more than a thousand people.

In July 1997, Genesys went public on the NASDAQ stock exchange for $800 million. This time, Farzad had founder's stock, so he was now rich. Three years later, he and his cofounders sold Genesys to Alcatel Telecommunications for $1.6 billion.

This was not Farzad's last IPO. In 2009, a South American e-commerce and retail banking venture he cofounded—VisaNet Brazil, a consortium of Visa International and four major Brazilian banks—went public. Raising $4.3 billion, it was the largest IPO in the world that year.

Not bad for an immigrant kid.

Today, Farzad Naimi is a naturalized U.S. citizen and runs his own venture investment and start-up incubation firm called Rona Holdings, which is part of the NAIMIgroup. He and his partners—including the former head of technology at Stanford University's Human Genome Center, Mostafa Ronaghi—have funded and launched over a dozen start-ups in the medical, biotech, renewable energy, and mobile communications industries that have already generated more than a quarter of a billion dollars in returns. The NAIMIgroup also sports a philanthropic arm that it says supports organizations "taking big bets towards enriching the value of human life," as well as an arts studio that "pools together the talents of its in-house creators along with artists from around the world to exhibit their works and realize potential commercial applications of their artistic achievements."

Farzad also served as a member of the adjunct faculty at Golden Gate University, teaching MBA students in the School of Technology and Industry. He is also an active participant and teacher in the entrepreneurship programs at Stanford University, Golden Gate University, and the National University of Singapore. Never forgetting his own roots as a young foreign student seeking opportunity in America, of course, Farzad today spends roughly one-third of his time mentoring students at various Silicon Valley universities and helping them launch their careers.

Sometimes these mentorship duties assume the character of a humanitarian mission, as in the case of one young Iranian woman for whom he recently waged a campaign to get a visa.

"Out of the two-and-a-half million Iranian students who took the university examinations in Iran last year, this lady ranked number 10," Farzad explains. "Her professor back in Iran, who I know, he recommended her to me. But the government here, you know, it is so afraid of terrorism now. Anyone from a Muslim country they think is a terrorist. So I arranged with some friends to join me, and then I spoke to the authorities, explaining that this woman and others like her are truly brilliant minds who can do so much for America. Let us educate her, let us train her, I said. We will sponsor her, pay for her, take responsibility for her."

When, on April 10, 2010, this woman—to protect her identity, we will call her Rabia Balkhi in honor of a great Persian poet of a thousand years ago—received the news that she would be issued a visa and be admitted to Stanford in the fall, she wrote to Farzad.

"Dear Mr. Naimi," she wrote in her best English. "I am more than happy now! It was a dream for me to study at the best education school of the world at Stanford University. What you and Dr. Tabrizi did for me were so valuable to me. I send this letter in order to thank you for all your kind helps. What you did will change my life. I wish to thank you by doing my very best, and I hope to open a new way for Iranian students to this excellent school. Best Wishes, Rabia."

Rabia is not the only young person—foreign or American-born—who benefits from Farzad's generous support. In researching his story, we came upon an online blog entry dated August 2008 that had been written by a young Chinese student studying at Stanford. "Every month, just after I meet with Farzad, I am so confident and motivated because I seem to be infected by his passion for life," this young student wrote. He then retold a story he had heard about how Farzad had found new jobs for every one of the employees he was forced to lay off after investors pulled the plug on one of his start-ups after the 9/11 terror attacks. Farzad apparently called contacts throughout the entrepreneur community and said he had some very talented people they should hire. None of the new employers asked to see resumes. Instead, they hired every one of Farzad's people on the spot, such was their trust and confidence in him.

One friend, Mahni Ghorashi, explains the source of people's faith in Farzad: "He has adapted to a Western way of networking without losing his old-world tradition of courtesy and hospitality. He has charisma, but more than that, he is always a gentleman, always courteous to others. I've never met *anyone* who didn't immediately like Farzad upon first meeting him." One can almost hear his mother's early teachings in this description of Farzad's manner.

What's in It for America?

So now we come to the real question at the heart of Farzad Naimi's immigrant success story: Why should we care? He may be a prolific innovator, a very successful businessman, even an all-around wonderful human being. But what's he done for America lately?

The question is not as facetious as it sounds, for a huge debate now rages in our nation over whether we should allow more—or fewer—talented legal immigrants like Farzad into our country. Unfortunately, this debate has been muddled and distorted by the public's legitimate concerns over the influx of millions of *illegal* immigrants across our southern border.

Some political leaders insist that the United States must tighten its post-9/11 restrictions on F-1 student and H-1B work visas. They claim that educated and skilled foreigners take high-paying jobs away from qualified Americans. Although this is a claim that is only true in some situations, as we will explain shortly, H-1B critics do make a fair point when they note that even though our Statue of Liberty proclaims "Give us your tired, your poor, your huddled masses yearning to breathe free," we simply cannot as a nation provide a home or a job for every foreigner in the world who wants a better life. We must be pragmatic, they rightly point out, and look out for the interests of our own citizens, and our own nation, first.

Fair enough. Let's dispense with any bleeding-heart sentimentality here and instead look at this issue solely from the hard-nosed standpoint of national interest. What does America get by letting skilled foreign-born engineers and entrepreneurs like Farzad legally come here?

In Farzad's case, his contributions to American economic and technological strength have been significant. In addition to his CTI technology—now used by over half of all customer support call centers on the planet—the innovations Farzad and his partner Mostafa Ronaghi helped to develop have greatly reduced the cost of gene sequencing and brought closer the day when medical treatments can be tailored to one's own body, boosted the power of hearing aids as well as military and covert intelligence listening devices, enhanced the efficiency and reliability of online payment processing, improved voice-over-IP and mobile communications technology, boosted data center performance through the use of new composite materials, and invented new ways to produce low-cost sustainable energy.

Can we put a precise dollars-and-cents value on Farzad's economic contribution to the United States, other than the millions of dollars in taxes he has already paid into the U.S. Treasury? Not exactly. But we can provide one real-world measure of Farzad's value to the U.S. economy that most citizens will readily relate to during these times of high unemployment.

"If you add up all my ventures," estimates Farzad, "I have created about ten thousand jobs."

Ten thousand jobs.

How many of the politicians who complain about "foreigners taking American jobs" have themselves ever created ten thousand jobs? Or ten jobs? Or even one job?

Farzad, of course, is only one of the more than a million immigrants, many of them from China and India, who contribute to our economy today. In fact, wrote author and economist Richard Florida in his 2005 book *The Flight of the Creative Class,* immigrants "helped power America's economic growth engine since the dawn of the republic."

In the 1930s, this took the form of physicists and other scientists such as Enrico Fermi and Albert Einstein fleeing the rise of fascism in Italy and Germany. And after World War II, Florida notes, "America's rise to preeminence in the high-tech age would have been nearly unimaginable without imported talent." He cites famous immigrant path-breakers who changed the business and economic landscape of America, such as David Sarnoff, who built the electronics giant RCA and founded the NBC network when television appeared on the scene, and Georges Doriot, who created America's very first venture capital firm—the most successful financial tool for stimulating innovation ever devised—and funded the pioneering minicomputer firm Digital Equipment Corporation. The semiconductor industry, meanwhile—the heart of the $1.1 trillion worldwide consumer electronics business—was largely built by immigrants William Shockley of Britain, Jean Hoerni of Switzerland, and Eugene Kleiner of Austria. Kleiner later cofounded the world's preeminent venture capital firm, Kleiner Perkins Caufield & Byers, which midwifed nearly three hundred start-up companies, including icons such as Amazon, Google, AOL, Sun Microsystems, Intuit, and Genentech. As for Intel, whose chips power most of our computers, it was built into the industry giant it is today by Hungarian immigrant Andy Grove.

To be sure, immigrants have not only founded start-ups; they are also a major presence in the top ranks of corporate America as well. According to author Florida's research, 10 percent of America's top five hundred companies in 2005 were led by CEOs who were born outside the United States.

Immigrants' role in small technology start-ups, however, is of far greater concern to us here because it is within these firms that virtually all job-creating, economy-building innovations take place. Take German-born Andy Bechtolsheim and Indian-born Vinod Khosla, two of the four founders of Sun Microsystems in the early 1980s. Or Sergey Brin, the Russian-born cofounder of Google in the late 1990s. Then there's Yahoo! cofounder Jerry Yang of Taiwan, Hotmail cofounder Sabeer Bhatia of India, and Finnish-born Linus Torvalds, who created the Linux operating system as well as the open-source model of collaborative software development. And don't forget Ukraine's Max Levchin and South Africa's Elon Musk, who cofounded PayPal—since acquired by Iranian immigrant Pierre Omidyar's eBay for $1.5 billion. Elon Musk, of course, went on to found the private space exploration enterprise SpaceX as well as, more recently, Tesla Motors, until recently the world's only manufacturer of mass-market, highway-capable, all-electric cars. In June 2010, Tesla Motors conducted one of Silicon Valley's few successful IPOs in recent years.

These are some of the more outstanding immigrant contributors to U.S. economic success. But what about the aggregate impact of all the foreign-born students and high-tech workers legally in the United States today? Is their presence here, overall, a plus or a minus for America?

On the issue of whether immigrants lower wages for—or even take jobs from—native-born Americans, the evidence is in dispute. As the *New York Times* noted in April 2009, "there is longstanding criticism among some labor groups that workers on such visas suppress engineering salaries and actually make it easier for employers to move more jobs to low-cost countries like India."

Some studies have found that immigrant engineers working on H-1B visas may be holding down wages for native-born technology professionals. Other studies, however, such as one conducted in 2010 by Sunil Mithas and Henry Lucas, professors at the University of Maryland, report that foreign-born technology professionals actually earn more than their native-born colleagues.

"[Information technology (IT)] professionals without U.S. citizenship earn approximately 8.1 percent more than those with U.S. citizenship," noted the University of Maryland study, while "IT professionals on an H-1B or other work visa earn approximately 7.9 percent more than those with U.S.

citizenship [and] IT professionals with a green card earn approximately 13.6 percent more than those with U.S. citizenship or work visa holders."

Then there are those who insist that the number of H-1B visas—currently sixty-five thousand each year—is simply too small to truly affect wage levels among the 3.5 million or so IT professionals in the U.S. They argue that it's actually the strict caps on H-1B visas that drive some companies to shift jobs overseas, where wages are irrefutably much lower.

So what's the truth about the role H-1B workers play in American society? One highly regarded chief technology officer with wide-ranging experience in the start-up community offers a perspective that seems to cut to the heart of the issue:

"It's true that a number of H-1B visas holders are not real intellects or innovators. They're just folks with rubber-stamp overseas computer science master's degrees who are hired to be drones at some big corporate 'software sweatshop.' They will do very little, if any, real innovation."

The challenge, he says, is to distinguish between the people he calls "drones" and the real technologists and innovators. "I've interviewed hundreds of H-1B applicants in my time, and hired many of them. So I've gotten to the point where I can tell in a few minutes if they fit into the 'drone' category or not. The drones have usually all done the same school projects and know all the same things. They've all had classes in enterprise Java programming and basic net-working, but no real-world experience outside these areas. And they've had no self-actuated experience—no personal projects or open source work—which is inexcusable in today's world. So they make poor start-up employees. They aren't the ones we need to be attracting because we can grow good middle-class, midlevel computer science developers here at home. It's the entrepreneurial types like Farzad who we need to attract, as well as the real technologists and the science and engineering rock stars. I've had terrific experience with those people. In fact, I just hired an Indian PhD who's clearly going to be a rock star."

Despite this problem with some types of H-1B workers, however, the research clearly demonstrates that taken as a whole, immigrant technology professionals and entrepreneurs boost start-up formation, innovation, and economic growth in the United States.

Research published in January 2009 by Jennifer Hunt, a professor of eco-nomics at McGill University, and Marjolaine Gauthier-Loiselle, at Princeton, shows that immigrants who first entered the United States on a student visa or a H-1B work visa make a greater economic and scientific contribution to the nation, in terms of wages, patenting, commercializing and licensing patents, and writing scientific books and publications, than native-born citizens. Immigrants patent at double the rate of native-born Americans, in fact, and are also overrepresented among members of the National Academy of Sciences and the National Academy of Engineering, as well as among the authors of highly cited science and engineering journal articles. These educated legal immigrants are also far more likely than native-born Americans to start a successful company and create jobs.

Other research discovered that foreign nationals residing in America were inventors or co-inventors of one-quarter of all the international patent applications filed in the United States.

All told, say Hunt and Gauthier-Loiselle, for every one percentage point increase in the number of immigrant college graduates in this country, there is a corresponding increase in the per capita patenting rate in the U.S. of between 9 and 18 percent. For the period from 1990 to 2000, therefore, when the share of educated immigrants rose from 2.2 percent to 3.5 percent of the total U.S. population, the per capita patenting rate increased by 12 percent to 21 percent.

Research by Gnanaraj Chellaraj, Keith Maskus, and Aaditya Mattoo, meanwhile, found that a 10 percent increase in foreign graduate students in this country would raise the number of patents issued to universities by 6.8 percent and the number of nonuniversity patents by 5 percent.

Bottom line, using patents and scientific publications as proxies for innovation, we see a dramatic effect by immigrants upon U.S. technological progress. And this "immigrant effect" is reflected in increased U.S. GDP output, say Hunt and Gauthier-Loiselle. They found that the influx of educated immigrants into the U.S. over the last twenty years has increased the nation's per capita GDP by 1.4 to 2.4 percent. That's an increase of approximately $1,000 in GDP output for every man, woman, and child in America—a truly astonishing number—that occurred just because of the presence of these talented immigrants in our country.

Even more recent research by William Kerr and William Lincoln at Harvard and the University of Michigan, respectively, indicates that fluctuations in the numbers of H-1B visas granted affected the amount of invention in the United States. When H-1B visa grants declined from a hundred ninety-five thousand early in the last decade to only sixty-five thousand by the mid-2000s, the rate of patenting declined.

Overall, they report, a 10 percent growth in the H-1B visa population increases total invention (as screened through patent counts) by up to 2 percent. Interestingly, half of that increase, or 1 percent, was due to a patenting increase by native English speakers apparently stimulated to be more creative themselves simply by the presence of talented immigrants in their schools and workplaces.

"Clearly," writes *The Flight of the Creative Class* author Florida, "foreign inventors have become a key feature of the U.S. innovation system. Without them, the level of innovation would be much lower."

The problem with economists' data, of course, is that it can seem like such an abstraction. Besides, economists haven't exactly inspired a lot of confidence in their abilities lately, given their failure to warn of the dangers of the housing bubble or deindustrialization. Which probably explains the continued popularity of that old joke about economists:

"How does an economist open a can of soup? First, assume a can opener."

So why should we believe the economists' statistics about how great these immigrants are for the American economy when our own instincts tell us that if an immigrant engineer gets hired by Google, then that is one less job available for American engineers?

Because there wouldn't even be a Google, or a Yahoo!, or an eBay, to hire any engineers in the first place if it weren't for their immigrant founders. And these founders would never have gotten the funding to launch their ventures if it weren't for immigrant venture capitalists such as Doriot, Khosla, and Kleiner.

You really want to talk about American jobs for American citizens? Then consider this little-known but rather astonishing fact: immigrants founded over 25 percent of all venture-backed technology companies in the United States between 1995 and 2005—and over 50 percent of all those in Silicon Valley!

One study notes that in 2005 alone, these companies generated $52 billion in revenue and employed four hundred fifty thousand workers—a number greater than the total number of H-1B workers in all technology sectors hired over the prior ten years combined.

The National Venture Capital Association (NVCA), however, states that all venture-backed start-ups in America today collectively employ more than 12 million people and contribute $3 trillion to the U.S. economy. That's 21 percent of U.S. GDP and 11 percent of the nation's private-sector employment. So if we take a straight-line percentage, the hundreds of immigrants who were responsible for founding 25 percent of all those start-ups actually created, more or less, 3 million American jobs and produced over 5 percent of the nation's GDP.

In other words, these immigrants don't take jobs. They create them—possibly by the millions!

As Kauffman Foundation researcher Dane Stangler was quoted as saying, immigrants are "a virtually free source of job creation for the United States."

Shooting Ourselves in the Foot

A world war for talent is now under way that "promises to radically reshape the world in the coming decades," argues Florida. "No longer will economic might [depend on a nation's] natural resources, manufacturing excellence, military dominance, or even scientific and technological prowess. Today, the terms of competition revolve around [each] nation's ability to mobilize, attract and retain human creative talent. Every key dimension of economic leadership, from manufacturing excellence to scientific and technological advancement, will depend upon this ability."

Unfortunately, national security concerns and the radioactive politics of illegal aliens have somehow induced us into denying to ourselves the contributions of many of the world's best and brightest technology professionals. We deny entry to many thousands—seventy-eight thousand in 2008 alone, according to one report—and drive away many thousands of others, with the result being that these highly skilled immigrants benefit the economies of *other* nations rather than our own.

According to research out of Duke University, more than 500,000 highly educated and skilled immigrants—plus another 126,000 who already have job offers—were waiting for permanent resident visas either here in the States or abroad. Together with their family members, that means nearly 1.2 million people are waiting for visas—a wait that can last fifteen years. Only around 120,000 visas are available for skilled immigrants in the key employment categories each year.

As for the world's brightest students, author Florida found a steep drop in the number of student visas issued after 9/11—a 20 percent drop in 2002 and another 8 percent slide in 2003—which represents the largest declines ever recorded since the government began tracking student visa statistics in 1952.

He also reported that the rate of rejection of student visas shot up after 9/11 to 34 percent in 2002 and 35 percent in 2003. In 2004, 90 percent of the graduate schools responding to a June 2004 survey reported a major decline in admission applications. Bear in mind that in the United States today, nearly 60 percent of all engineering doctorates are awarded to foreign students, as are more than 50 percent of doctorates in mathematics, physics, economics, and computer science, according to the National Science Foundation (NSF).

Looking at all visa categories together, the American Immigration Lawyers Association (AILA) estimates that the total number of people waiting for student, temporary employment, or permanent residence employment visas is more than 4 million, including family members.

As for the most controversial of these visas—the H-1B visa for temporary immigrant workers—only sixty-five thousand are allowed to be issued each year (universities and government research centers are exempt from that limit). No more than 7 percent of these visas may be allocated to citizens of any one country. As a result, immigrants from large countries such as China and India that produce millions of highly educated scientists and engineers are only eligible for the same number of H-1B visas as those from Iceland. In 2009, the annual quota of sixty-five thousand H-1B visas was reached in only one day—on January 2, the first business day of that year.

What's worse, an amendment in the $787 billion stimulus bill of 2009 prevents any firm receiving stimulus funding from hiring immigrants on H-1B visas for one year. Add to that a memo issued by the United States Citizenship and Immigration Service (USCIS) in February 2010 mandating a host of new restrictions on the kinds of work that H-1B workers can engage in, and according to AILA first vice president Eleanor Pelta, "the assault on H-1Bs is not only offensive, it's dangerous."

First of all, argued Pelta in an AILA blog posting, "H-1Bs create jobs—statistics show that five jobs are created in the U.S. for every H-1B worker hired." Second, she said, "the anti-H-1B assault dissuades large businesses from conducting research and development in the U.S. and encourages the relocation of those [R&D] facilities to jurisdictions that are friendlier to foreign professionals." Finally, she insisted, H-1B restrictions "chill the formation of small businesses in the U.S., particularly in emerging technologies," which is something at which foreign-born professionals particularly excel.

Combined with the national security restrictions on legal immigration imposed by the Patriot Act of 2001, the Enhanced Border Security and Visa

Entry Reform Act of 2002, and the Visa Mantis and similar terrorism-related reviews of more than a million visa applications since 9/11, these policies have created what the NSF calls a "chilly climate" for highly skilled foreign-born students and workers. According to the scientific journal *Nature Biotechnology*, "H-1B visas for high-skilled workers and international applications to American graduate programs decreased significantly" after 9/11.

How ironic that by curtailing student visas in the name of national security and reducing H-1B worker visas in the name of protecting American jobs, we are actually achieving exactly the opposite: we are *harming* national security and *weakening* American job creation. The notion of America picking up the rock of immigration policy only to drop it on its own feet might almost seem funny were it not so dangerous to our nation's future.

This is not the first time that the United States has shot itself in the foot after being blinded by overexcited national security fears. Take the Cold War case of H. S. Tsien (also known as Qian Xuesen), one of the original founders of the Jet Propulsion Laboratory at the California Institute of Technology in 1943, who went on to become one of this nation's top rocket scientists.

During the anticommunist hysteria of 1950, Tsien was accused of having communist sympathies and his security clearance was revoked, despite the evidence as well as the unanimous pleas of Caltech president Lee DuBridge and other colleagues on his behalf. He was blacklisted, and then summarily detained by the federal government at the U.S. naval facility and federal prison on Terminal Island, just offshore from Los Angeles. For five long years he was held there—unjustly, we now know—and then deported to China along with his wife and two American-born (and therefore citizen) children in 1955. There, Tsien went on to create and lead the Chinese rocket program. He developed the Dongfeng and Silkworm missiles, and his research was the foundation for China's first manned space launch in 2003. He died in Beijing on October 31, 2009, at the age of 97.

"It was the stupidest thing this country ever did," conceded Dan A. Kimball, the undersecretary of the navy at the time of Tsien's arrest, many years later: "He was no more a communist than I was, and we forced him to go."

In his novel *2010: Odyssey Two*, science fiction author Arthur C. Clarke named the ill-fated Chinese spaceship Tsien after him.

To be sure, although many immigrants still clearly want to work here, those numbers appear to be dwindling as other nations become more attractive to innovators and entrepreneurs and as America's own start-up ecosystem becomes more costly and restrictive. It's a more competitive marketplace now for talent, and other countries are not making the same mistakes we are.

Author Florida quotes the New Zealand minister for science and technology as saying, "We no longer think of immigration as a gate-keeping function, but as a talent-attraction function necessary for economic growth." Many other nations, from Asia to Europe, also actively recruit top scientists and engineers, including students in those fields, to come and work or study in their countries. China, for example, now offers recruitment bonuses of $150,000 to any U.S.-educated scientist or engineer who opts to return to China.

In decades past, notes Vivek Wadhwa, a highly regarded scholar at Duke, Harvard, and the University of California–Berkeley, over 90 percent of U.S.-educated Chinese PhDs chose to remain in the U.S. But now, he says, "when I talk to my Chinese students, most are buying one-way tickets home. When my team at Duke, Berkeley and Harvard surveyed 229 students from China during October, 2008, we found only 10 percent wanted to stay permanently. Fifty-two percent believed that their best job opportunities were in China."

Shi Yigong, for example, was a Princeton University molecular biologist whose cell studies had opened up a new line of research into cancer treatment. Shi had lived in the United States for eighteen years when, in 2008, he was awarded a prestigious $10 million grant from the Howard Hughes Medical Institute. But Shi's colleagues were shocked, reported the *New York Times,* when he abruptly declined the grant, resigned from Princeton's faculty, and returned to China to become the dean of life sciences at Tsinghua University in Beijing.

A similar exodus of highly educated Indian scientists, engineers, and entrepreneurs is also occurring. Whereas in past decades 75 percent of all graduates of India's top Institute of Technology ended up living in the U.S. today the number is less than 10 percent, and falling.

What is going on?

America's Loss Is the World's Gain

To find out, Wadhwa and a team of first-class scholars backed by the Kauffman Foundation conducted a six-month survey in 2008 of 1,203 Indian and Chinese immigrants who had worked or received their education in the United States and then returned to their home country. To their surprise, they discovered that although America's restrictive immigration policies certainly did cause some immigrants to return home, "the most significant factors in their decision to return home were career opportunities, family ties, and quality of life."

How do they know that? Because 27 percent of the Indian and 34 percent of the Chinese respondents had permanent resident status or were U.S. citizens. Yet still they went back!

One can understand the pull of family ties. It's a little harder to swallow the notion that many of these highly educated professionals would find the quality of life better in India or China, although one can imagine how much further a dollar—or a hundred thousand dollars—goes in China or India than it does in the States. But professional opportunities? What could be better for one's career than working or starting a business in the most technologically advanced and prosperous nation on earth?

Wadhwa explains: "A return ticket home really put their careers on steroids," he said. "About 10 percent of the Indians polled had held senior management positions in the U.S. That number rose to 44 percent after they returned home. Among the Chinese, the number rose from 9 percent in the U.S. to 36 percent in China."

Apparently, it wasn't only because they could be bigger fish in a smaller technology leadership pond back home. To ensure that the researchers weren't simply hearing the self-justifications of those who had already returned, they surveyed an additional 1,224 foreign students who were then still studying in the United States. Even among these people, the majority said they felt that the U.S. was no longer the best place to build their professional careers or entrepreneurial businesses, and that they planned to return home.

In fact, only 6 percent of Indians, 10 percent of Chinese, and 15 percent of Europeans planned to settle in the United States. Historically, the "stay rates" of students and professionals from China and India had been 92 percent and 85 percent, respectively, according to the NSF.

As Wadhwa warned in the Spring 2009 edition of *Issues in Science and Technology*, "Perversely, now that China and India are becoming formidable competitors, the United States seems inclined to enhance their economic productivity by supplying them with an army of U.S.-trained scientists and engineers." This "reverse brain drain," as he calls it, will see more than a hundred thousand skilled technology professionals leave the U.S. for their native lands.

The Indian technologist and entrepreneur Velchamy Sankarlingam explains the appeal that India has for so many of his U.S.-trained countrymen these days. Born and raised in India, Sankarlingam got his undergraduate degree in electrical engineering before coming to the States for graduate studies in 1988, where he earned two master's degrees. At first, he worked for large companies—IBM and then Accenture—which is fairly typical for early-career information technology professionals. But after he had a number of years of work under his belt, he bolted for a start-up called Presenter. (Wadhwa's research suggests that it takes an average of fourteen years before most Indian technologists act on their entrepreneurial urges and get involved with a start-up.) After several years at Presenter, the firm was acquired by another start-up called WebEx, which offers technology for Web-based business meetings, and Sankarlingam became vice president of engineering at the new firm. In 2007, WebEx was itself acquired by Cisco Systems, a large technology company in Silicon Valley, for $3 billion.

"I see a lot of Indians going back now," says Sankarlingam. "The difference in salary between India and the U.S. isn't as great as it used to be, but still the living costs are much lower. And the other thing is that the modernization of the country has come a long way in the last twenty years or so. So the quality of life is not that different in many ways."

Why are Indians leaving Silicon Valley to go back home?

"There are basically two types of people going back," he believes. "One group is because, you know, their kids are growing up and they're not comfortable with the culture here. And the other group is going back because they want to start a company and the opportunities for doing that are much better now in India—at least for certain kinds of businesses."

For one thing, says Sankarlingam, "it's going to cost me much less to start a business there. Here in Silicon Valley, to start a business, it will cost you maybe $150,000 per employee. So to hire twenty people and run the business for a year, you need $3 million."

In India, however, the costs are basically one-tenth of that. "You can run a company in India with the same twenty employees for maybe $15,000 or $20,000 a month. That's $300,000 or $400,000 instead of the $3 million it takes here. The Silicon Valley work environment is still better, of course, with the universities and all the other start-ups here. But India is catching up."

As for how U.S. immigration policies affect talent flows, Sankarlingam believes it is definitely a problem for students and professionals wanting to come to the States. But he suspects that most of those going back to India are doing so voluntarily, for the reasons he cited.

A firsthand view of the "reverse brain drain" is offered by Hao Zhou, who was born and raised in China and earned his bachelor's degree in electrical engineering at Beijing University in 1985. At the time, China was just beginning its modernization and market liberalization efforts, and Zhou saw few opportunities for exercising his ambition to achieve.

"I told my mom that we had to get out of China," Zhou recalls. "I didn't want to deal with the communists."

So he applied to Louisiana State University in Baton Rouge and was accepted. He spent six years at the campus, earning first a master's and then a doctorate in physics. His thesis adviser and mentor, Martin Feldman, had studied high-energy particle physics at Cornell University and later worked at AT&T's fabled Bell Labs, where he made a number of inventions related to silicon semiconductor manufacturing.

"The main thing he wanted me to do was to challenge authority," Zhou remembers. "He wanted me to have the equal footing with him when we talked about science and technology. He wanted me to know that what anyone said, well, it may not be true. You have to think independently. Be willing to challenge authority, you know?" Zhou pauses, to emphasize his point. "This was a big shock to me. A very big shock. This is not how we were taught back home. But right away, I realized that this is the core strength of American culture. This is why America still leads in technology."

After getting his doctorate, Zhou spent the next decade working in Silicon Valley and Southern California for firms such as Cypress Semiconductor and Conexant Systems. Then he had the idea to build a business around manufacturing imaging sensor modules, but he couldn't convince any of the American companies he worked with to back him.

Meanwhile, Zhou noticed that after fifteen years away from home, new opportunities had opened up in his native country. So he decided to go back and start his business there.

He quickly got a government loan—the Chinese government was and remains very serious about promoting technology development—but soon realized the downsides to that arrangement. "When the government is your major shareholder," Zhou explains, "the first thing you find out is that they don't want to take many risks. Not only because this is the government's asset, this money. But also because the officials, the ones who are managing this government asset, they don't want to be blamed if something goes wrong and the asset starts shrinking."

In other words, for all the vaunted vitality of Chinese industry in recent years—and it truly has been a marvel to behold—there is still the ancient gravitational pull of an obedient culture weighing down the entrepreneurial mind, says Zhou.

"In the past, nobody encourage you to challenge authority," Zhou explains. "They actually discourage you doing it. All the time you grow up, you are told to follow your parent, you know, obey your teachers, your manager, your government. Nobody will tell you that, hey, your boss might be wrong. Or that maybe you can do it better."

One of Zhou's new initiatives at the firm didn't pan out as expected. In the United States, where a large percentage of new products fail in the market, that wouldn't be such a big deal necessarily. Learn your lessons and move on to the next project. But that's not always the view in China.

So Zhou left to start his own company, Qtech—this time with no government money. It was June 2007, and Qtech's business plan was to produce imaging sensor modules for large camera and cellphone manufacturers. With no government funding handcuffing him, Zhou was able to take the sorts of big risks that can lead to equally big success. He licensed very advanced "wafer-level packaging" technology from my own company, Tessera, that enabled him to place thousands of image sensors on a single silicon wafer. Being able to deliver camera modules in a smaller form factor to manufacturers would give him an edge, he believed.

He was right. Today, Qtech offers original equipment manufacturing services for brand-name customers such as Samsung, Toshiba, and STMicroelectronics. Zhou says he expects to capture 70 percent of the global wafer-level imaging sensor market by 2014.

As you'd expect, Zhou is happy to be doing business in China, happy about his own success, and quite pleased with China's overall progress on the economic and technology front. But he appreciates how far China still has to go in developing a start-up culture comparable to that in America.

"In America, you are not afraid of failure," he says. "For you, failure is just a learning experience. And you are always challenging the top people, asking if there is a better way. This is almost expected in America."

Can China develop that sort of risk-taking culture? Zhou believes it can, but the process will take time. "Think about it," he notes. "The freaking guy here, he has spent the last thirty years being told to obey authority. How is he going to change that overnight? The problem is not the communist government. It's the culture. And cultural change takes time."

Another overseas Chinese immigrant who found China a changed country from the one he left behind many years ago—and a more attractive place to start a new business—is Hongyu Ran, a brilliant PhD in mechanical engineering from Caltech who was a valued employee here at Tessera. Ran says that he always planned to remain in Silicon Valley—until, that is, he attended a conference for overseas Chinese in Guangzhou in 2008.

"It was fifteen years since I left," Ran recalls, "and I could see right away that the environment in China had become much more friendly to entrepreneurship. Everyone is more open minded. The working conditions are much better. They also now have many kind of books and magazines and even TV shows like your *Apprentice* that teach the people about risk and failure and starting a business. Even the communication between people is changed. It used to be more subtle, less confrontational, so as not to be rude. But now so many people like the American way of communicating, especially in business. It's much more straightforward."

In contrast to the bright new prospects in China, says Ran, he saw that the environment in Silicon Valley had gotten much more difficult for entrepreneurs. "It's very tough to get angel funds there now, very tough to get venture capital. And the expense is very great. For a half-million dollars, I could hardly do anything in Silicon Valley. Maybe I can rent a small space. But I cannot hire any people, any good engineers. But for the same money—which the city of Suzhou in China's Jiangsu Province offered me—I can go back to China and the government will give me free office rent, free utilities. And I can hire a lot of very talented people. For half a million, I can run a real business for more than two years."

So in February 2010, Ran went back to China to found Being Technology, an environmental systems business, with three friends, each of whom has an advanced degree.

"The problem of pollution is what we will address with our business," Ran explains. "Fluid dynamics, atmosphere dynamics, advanced technology—this is what we know. We can help solve China's environment problem and build a good business at the same time."

Entrepreneurs and Geniuses Welcome!

If only America's "environment problem" could be solved by technology. Unfortunately, the problems we're most concerned with in this book are largely regulatory, legal, economic, and political. But these, too, can be solved fairly quickly if America would just put its mind to it. We can liberate small start-ups from the shackles of ill-advised tax and regulatory policies. We can fund the patent office properly and get it working to promote innovation again. We can rebuild a healthy manufacturing sector. And we can revitalize an old-fashioned venture capital industry and IPO market so that they build great companies, new industries, and hundreds of thousands of middle-class jobs for all citizens again, rather than simply make the super-rich even more super-rich.

No matter what we do, however, America can never go back to the days after World War II when we were the only nation on earth with world-class science and technology capabilities. Now we have multiple rivals for technology leadership all over the world, including nations such as China that are churning out more scientists and more job-creating IPOs than we are. This is fine, of course—Americans tend to thrive on healthy competition.

But as Wadhwa put it, "The United States is no longer the only place where talented people can put their skills to work. It can no longer expect them to endure the indignities and inefficiencies of an indifferent immigration system."

So let's be smart here. We have to transform our immigration policy from a club that drives good people away into a carrot that attracts the best minds of tomorrow.

How do we do that? It's actually not all that mysterious.

We must increase the numbers of visas for bright students.

We must greatly speed up visa processing times.

We must offer many more—but much smarter—job-creating H-1B visas. This means the H-1B visa process should be revised to start selecting for proven skill sets rather than simply educational levels. We should also limit the number of H-1B visas going to any one company. And as Vivek Wadhwa suggests, we should eliminate the restrictions that prevent H-1B workers from switching jobs, traveling, or getting promoted—which only keep them captive to low-wage employers. All three of these measures would greatly reduce the likelihood of immigrants with cookie-cutter college degrees but little or no genuine advanced technology skills being hired for low-wage jobs in corporate "software sweatshops."

Instead, our nation would likely attract more "technology rock stars" like Belgacem "Bel" Haba, a longtime Tessera employee who spearheads many of our most important advances in the miniaturization of memory, optical, and communications technology. Born in the isolated date-farming oasis of El-Meghaier in Algeria, Bel is today one of the world's foremost experts in materials science. With 131 issued U.S. patents to his name (and more than 100 more pending), Bel is among the top one-tenth of 1 percent of all American patentees.

Can we be certain that H-1B workers will never be hired into "software sweatshops" or depress wages even slightly for any sector of the U.S. technology workforce? No. Large corporate H-1B employers may abuse the system. But even if they do, it would be unwise in this current economic crisis to give priority to concerns about wage suppression over the need for job creation. No one disputes the fact that immigrants found a large percentage of all our technology start-ups, which is where virtually all new U.S. job growth takes place. It doesn't take place in large companies, which is where most H-1B abuses are likely to occur.

We must also pass the Startup Visa Act of 2010 introduced by Senators John Kerry (D-MA) and Richard Lugar (R-IN), which provides a two-year visa to any immigrant entrepreneur who secures $250,000 in capital from American investors. After the two years are up, the immigrant could obtain permanent resident status if his or her venture has created five full-time jobs in the United States, raised an additional $1 million in capital, or earned in excess of $1 million in revenue.

We must also remember that our national security is hardly served by sending the world's top scientists and engineers to work for *other* countries instead of our own.

Indeed, if we really want to bolster America's economic strength and innovation prowess, we should hang a big bold sign at every border crossing in the country: "Geniuses and Entrepreneurs Welcome!"

We began this chapter by talking about the American Dream. But do you know where the term actually comes from? It was coined in 1931 by historian James Truslow Adams in his book *Epic of America*. It is instructive to read what Adams himself meant by the term:

The American Dream, that has lured tens of millions of all nations to our shores in the past century, has not been a dream of material plenty, though that has doubtlessly counted heavily. It has been a dream of being able to grow to fullest development as a man and woman, unhampered by the barriers which had slowly been erected in the older civilizations, unrepressed by social orders which had developed for the benefit of classes rather than for the simple human being of any and every class.

My father never read *Epic of America*. But he certainly knew what the American Dream was. He came to the United States from Germany without even a high school diploma, yet he lived to see his two sons go to college, serve America in time of war, and build happy and successful lives for themselves. As a father with two sons of my own, I now understand how important that must have been to him.

Farzad Naimi also never read *Epic of America*. Yet in describing what he loves most about America, he used almost the same words as James Truslow Adams: "In America you can grow something out of nothing, and follow your dreams without any limits."

If we close the door on the dreams of people like Farzad, we may destroy our own.

Government-Funded
Research

Getting Smart, for a Change

On May 13, 2010, Steven Aftergood, director of the Project on Government Secrecy of the Federation of American Scientists, finally received the letter for which he had long been hoping. It was from James P. Hogan of the Department of Defense (DoD), which had previously denied Aftergood's Freedom of Information Act request for a document known as the JASON report, which was marked "for official use only." Aftergood had appealed the denial, and in the interim, it seems, the powers that be had apparently decided that the DoD was better off letting Aftergood have the JASON report than continuing to try to stonewall him. This may have had something to do with Aftergood's reputation as a dogged piercer of government secrecy—not the secrecy that government employs to protect the nation's security, just the secrecy it uses to protect itself from embarrassment. Whatever the impetus, Hogan was now writing to inform Aftergood that he could have a copy of the JASON report after all.

What is the JASON report? And just as interesting, who are the JASONs? You will not find out much about them, no matter how hard you search on Google. What little we do know about this secret group of elite scientists comes mostly from a 2002 letter that Congressman Rush Holt (D-NJ) wrote to key members of Congress protesting the decision by the Defense Advanced Research Projects Agency (DARPA) to fire the JASONs.

"JASON was founded in 1958," the congressman wrote. "It consists of an evolving group of approximately fifty academic scientists who convene semi-annually to study selected scientific issues for the military and other federal agencies. The important feature of JASON is that, even though it is funded by DARPA and other agencies, JASON acts independently of the Department of Defense and these agencies. This ensures that the advice that JASON gives is unbiased."

Their dismissal, wrote Congressman Holt, himself a former physicist, occurred after JASON members refused to allow DARPA management to select three new JASON members.

"For forty-four years," Holt explained, "the current members of JASON have selected the new members. This selection process maintains JASON's autonomy and ensures that their decisions are not based on any obligation to the Department of Defense. Allowing [DoD] to choose JASON's members would compromise the objectivity and independence of the group's advice."

The few other bits and pieces of information we have about the JASONs suggests that their advice has, indeed, often been strikingly independent. In 1967, for example, the JASONs were asked by a war-weary DoD to assess the impact of using nuclear weapons to try to end the war in Vietnam. They advised that a nuclear attack on Vietnamese insurgents would "offer the U.S. no decisive military advantage" but that its political effects "would be uniformly bad and could be catastrophic." Thankfully, DoD and the White House took JASON's advice to heart.

As for where they got their name, apparently the group was originally called Project Sunrise when the DoD established it in 1958. The wife of one of the founders, however, felt that this was a rather unimaginative name, and suggested they instead adopt the name of the Greek mythological hero Jason, who led the quest for the Golden Fleece.

In any event, Congressman Holt's 2002 letter apparently achieved the desired effect, for funding was restored to JASON and its independence of thought and action maintained.

All of which brings us back to the JASON report, and why the DoD didn't want anyone to see it. Entitled *S&T [Science & Technology] for National Security,* the May 2009 report is a damning assessment of the effectiveness of the DoD's basic science research program. Basic research is defined as "systematic study directed toward greater knowledge or understanding of the fundamental aspects of phenomena" without any preconceived applications or uses in mind. This sort of research is essential for scientific and technological progress, but is rarely pursued by the private sector because of the decades-long time frames often required before its results can be translated into useful new innovations. The laser, for example, was first researched in the 1950s based on theoretical principles developed by Einstein in 1917, but it took decades before any applications of laser research—fiber optic communications, laser printers, barcode scanners, DVD players, and laser weapons—were ever developed. Similar research in physics and electrical conductivity, information technology, and communications theory in the 1950s and 1960s, most of it funded by DARPA, led to the birth of four of the most powerful industrial innovations in human history: semiconductors, personal computers, software, and the Internet. In short, basic research is vital to our economic prosperity and national security. And by necessity, government has always been the primary sponsor of it.

According to the May 2009 JASON report, however, a once-visionary and wildly successful American research effort has, in the words of the investigators, "morphed during the past decade into a tightly-managed effort with a shorter-term and more [limited] character."

During the lost decade of the 2000s, the JASONs found, funding for basic research has "declined steadily" and is "currently at or near all-time lows." What's more, they noted, "we have seen significant change in focus from long-term basic research to short-term deliverable-based research." The result, said the JASONs, is that "basic research funding is not exploited to seed inventions and discoveries that can shape the future." In fact, "new technology is [seen as] high risk and routinely avoided." What's more, the report noted, "the bureaucracy associated with DoD research has grown to consume ever more time and has diverted program managers" from their proper sponsorship and oversight of quality research.

Overall, said the JASON report, "DoD does not generally focus [basic research] funding on research of the highest caliber carried out by individuals with the potential to provide new paradigms for science and technology." This, the JASONs warned, "is reducing the potential for true breakthroughs."

The JASONs had one additional concern:

> *Over the past decade, there has been an exodus of scientific and technical exper-*
> *tise from the U.S. government and, in particular, from the DoD [basic] research*
> *enterprise. Gone are many of the technically literate program officers who plied*
> *the streets of the scientific community to find those remarkable people who could*
> *help shape the future. Gone too are many of the scientists and engineers in the*
> *academic community [who were supported by DoD basic research contracts] and*
> *who contributed to revolutionary advances that changed the landscape of mod-*
> *ern war fighting. And most importantly, lost is the opportunity to develop the*
> *next generation of scientific talent who would otherwise have been trained and*
> *capable of carrying the research enterprise forward.*

Bottom line, according to the JASONs: "DoD basic research programs are broken to an extent that neither throwing more money at these problems nor changes in procedures will fix them."

The JASON report obviously has troubling implications for national security. But the revelations of a U.S. basic science program that has lost its way, adrift in short-termism and bureaucracy, raises disquieting concerns over this nation's innovation leadership as well.

How can we revitalize America's basic research program so that it once again pioneers breakthrough scientific and technological discoveries that help us meet the awesome challenges we face in energy, national security, economic growth, and public health?

How can we recreate the élan and spirit of discovery that fueled DARPA's research efforts during the immediate years after the shock of Sputnik so that it seeds new technologies that can be commercialized to create whole new industries, millions of new jobs, and a rising standard of living for the broad masses of the American people?

And what is the proper role of government itself—the right balance of public interest and private incentive—that can help this nation stop spinning its economic wheels and finally tackle the urgent challenges of innovation, job creation, and economic growth?

This is not the first time that concerns have been raised over federal support for basic research. A large number of prominent individuals and organizations, including the American Mathematical Society, the American Institute of Physics, and the American Association for the Advancement of Science (AAAS), have raised concerns about the decline in basic research funding over much of the past decade. Although fiscal year 2011 funding showed a slight uptick in one part of the basic research budget, overall trends have been flat or down since 2004, says AAAS. This holds true for non-defense-related funding for such organizations as the National Institutes of Health, National Science Foundation, and the Department of Energy as well. In contrast to the golden age of DARPA in the 1950s and 1960s, basic research nowadays seems almost an afterthought in governmental funding priorities, to the chagrin of thoughtful people across the political spectrum.

For some perspective into these issues, perhaps it would be useful to find someone who was part of DARPA during its glory years in the 1960s and can offer insight into why it worked so well back then. Someone, perhaps, who was at DARPA when the key breakthroughs that led to the semiconductor, PC, software, and Internet industries were made. How about DARPA's chief scientist, the man who led the research that produced what eventually became—along with fire, the wheel, and the printing press—one of the greatest inventions in human history?

Meet Larry Roberts, the father of the Internet.

Actually, there were three other fathers of the Internet. Leonard Kleinrock of UCLA developed the theory of packet switching that enabled the speedy and effective transmission of information between remote computers on a network. Robert Kahn helped design the Interface Message Processors (IMPs) that connected these computers to the network, and also created the basic Transmission Control Protocol (TCP) that enabled the computers to talk to each other over the network. And Vint Cerf worked with Kahn to codevelop the TCP/IP enhancement of that protocol that today enables people all over the world, using their disparate computers and operating systems, to communicate with each other over the Internet.

Larry Roberts, however, was the guy who in 1967 designed the project to build the ARPANET prototype of today's Internet, brought the talent and brainpower together to build this first-ever interactive computer network, and then led the team to their first successful test of real-time communication between two remotely located computer centers on October 29, 1969.

(Almost exactly twenty years later, British engineer and computer scientist Tim Berners-Lee would become the father of the World Wide Web when he devised the first system for communicating visual Internet content using the hypertext transfer protocol.)

At seventy-three years of age, Larry Roberts's memory of his DARPA days is remarkably fresh. Perhaps that's because Roberts, as founder and CEO of a new start-up called Anagran, is still actively developing enhancements to the network that he helped to create nearly forty-five years ago. As the recipient of a $12 million grant from DARPA to study traffic flow, authentication, and other network issues, he has the unique perspective of someone who has been a DARPA administrator, DARPA program manager, and a DARPA grantee or "principal investigator."

Roberts himself is an unusual mix of personality traits. He is first of all a very practical man. It's not that he's uninterested in the science or theory of things. He simply has a need to put what he knows to real-world use in some way. As a boy, he built a Tesla coil and a working television on his own. While an electrical engineering student at MIT in 1958, he designed a telephone network for his parents' girl scouts camp. Roberts says that his phone network was the first in the world to employ transistors rather than read-relay contact switches. Sure enough, AT&T's Web site says that it didn't deploy its first electronic switch until 1965.

Yet for all his practicality, there is still a certain ethereal quality about Roberts. When I worked for him as vice president of marketing at his start-up, Telenet, from 1979 to 1981, we all used to call him "Dr. Packet" because of his distracted professorial manner.

At one computer trade show that we attended together, however, I discovered a wickedly mischievous side to Roberts when I saw him gleefully employ his programming talents to a project dear to many Americans' hearts: beating the house in Las Vegas.

"I devised a program based on the high-low system of card counting that computed the precise probability of winning at blackjack for any set of casino rules and any counting system," Roberts recalls. "Ed Thorp's system, which he published in 1962 or so, only worked for one or two decks. That's why the casinos switched to four decks. Well, my counting system allowed you to count even with four decks, which the casinos thought was impossible. So Len [Kleinrock] and I did extremely well for ourselves for quite a few years. I probably made over $20,000 myself, and could have made much more, but I kept myself to a loss limit of $1,000 to $2,000."

On one occasion, this got him kicked out of a casino. "Oh, yeah . . . that time!" Roberts laughs. "Well, the situation was that the count showed that the deck was full of aces and tens—very positive for the player winning. So my wife and I increased our bets from $25 to $100 each. Then an ace turned up for the dealer, and I decided we should protect our hands as the count showed he had a high chance of Blackjack. Normally, a good player—and by then the dealer knew we were good—would never take insurance since it's generally seen as a bad bet (unless you're counting cards like we were). Well, the dealer got Black-jack, but the insurance saved us. Unfortunately, the fact that we had bought insurance told the casino that we were likely counting. As we found out later, a casino security person started watching us from a camera in the ceiling, count-ing with us to see if our bets moved with the count. They did, and so they asked us to leave. We went to another casino and quickly made another $2,000 there."

All these personality quirks—and, of course, the great good fortune to be an engineering wizard at the critical moment in history when the field of information technology was just being born—combined to put Roberts at the nexus of one of humanity's half-dozen or so greatest technological advances. It was an extraordinary opportunity for Roberts, yet it was also one that he resisted at first.

"I had gotten my doctorate and was working at [MIT's] Lincoln Lab," Roberts recalls. "This was about 1966, and I was happy just doing my research. But then the head of the group left—some sort of dispute about the lab not letting him operate on cats or something—and suddenly there was no head of the group. So I just sort of took over, unofficially, and started telling everybody what ought to be done. I managed the activity there, and got a contract from DARPA (then known as ARPA) to do some research about networks. And so because I was running the contract and also because I was the one who seemed to know what kind of research needed doing, I sort of took over managing that group. That was my first management activity, just out of grad school. But it was very happenstance. And mostly I just wanted to do my research."

Roberts had by then already met the great visionary psychologist and man–machine theorist J. C. R. Licklider, who everyone called "Lick," and been inspired by Lick's vision of an interactive communications network composed of linked computers. In a much-talked-about 1963 memorandum that Lick wrote to the staff at DARPA, Lick proposed the notion of an "Inter-galactic Computer Network." This idea was quite a few orders of magnitude grander than anything yet proposed within military or civilian science.

"Consider the situation in which several different centers are netted together [via an integrated computer network], each center being highly individualistic and having its own special language and its own special way of doing things," Lick wrote. "The problem is essentially the one described by science fiction writers: How do you get communication started among totally uncorrelated sapient beings?"

It should be noted, incidentally, that prior to 1965 there were no U.S. universities granting doctorates in computer science. Licklider and his DARPA successors funded the research needed to create university graduate programs in computer science at the University of California–Berkeley, Carnegie Mellon University, MIT, and Stanford. The first PhDs in computer science were awarded in 1969.

In any event, Roberts was inspired by Lick to study ways of linking disparate computers together and sharing resources and capabilities, and he soon received a contract from DARPA to do just that. Roberts didn't particularly like having management responsibilities at Lincoln Lab; he preferred simply to do research. But he did both because there was no one else to do it.

Apparently, his skill at both management and research got noticed, for the head of DARPA's Information Processing Techniques Office (IPTO), Ivan Sutherland, asked Roberts to come to DARPA and lead the effort to build Lick's integrated computer network.

"Ivan asked me to come do the DARPA project but I said no," Roberts explains. "And then later, Bob Taylor [who replaced Sutherland as IPTO chief] asked me as well. Again I said no. Finally the top guy, [DARPA director Charlie] Herzfeld, put pressure on the head of the Lab, who then convinced me it would be good for my career to go to DARPA."

Roberts pauses. "I was still somewhat reluctant, but I went on to DARPA because he kept telling me 'We'll take you back if you don't like it,' and so on. So I joined DARPA as chief scientist in December of 1966 or thereabouts. And I found to my surprise that it was actually quite attractive to have the resources to get done the things I thought ought to be done and not have to do it all myself. I had $50 million worth of research I was managing [$330 million in today's dollars], which is like running a company. I could lay out the plan, and lay out the concept, and get all the researchers to work on it together. And that was quite attractive."

In April 1967, Roberts organized an "ARPANET Design Session" at a meeting of IPTO principal investigators in Ann Arbor, Michigan. The various research challenges were discussed, from how to identify users and the protocols and methods of transmission to be used to the operating system software and the means of connecting each computer to the network. By the spring of 1968, Roberts had developed a comprehensive plan for building a working version of the network. He handed in his plan, entitled "Resource Sharing Computer Networks," to IPTO chief Bob Taylor on June 3. Taylor approved it on June 21, and the implementation work began. When Taylor left DARPA fifteen months later, Roberts took over as IPTO director.

It's always interesting to find out what the people involved in historic, world-changing events or inventions thought at the time. In most cases, the principals involved never fully appreciate the scale or depth of the changes in society they are about to unleash. They certainly never foresee all the myriad ways that their inventions will be used. Henry Ford did not foresee the emergence of highway motels, although in retrospect they were inevitable. Steve Jobs did not expect that spreadsheet programs like VisiCalc 123 would be the principal driver of personal computer use in business. Roberts certainly did not imagine that one day hundreds of millions of people would share details of their personal lives on Facebook.

But give him credit—he did suspect that his network would change the world. "After talking to Licklider and getting the concept," Roberts recalls, "I really started thinking about it. And I saw that basically man went from language, which allowed him to communicate face to face, to the printing press, which let him speak to and educate others far away over a period of months or years. But what if we could do this in seconds rather than months? Instantly, no matter how far away you were? Well, that would change the pace of research, of business, and really of everything. And that's what I saw—more or less the World Wide Web facet of the Internet today. I didn't know whether people would be working with terminals or computers or what they would be using. But I knew that ordinary people would be using this computer network to get their information and conduct business and to send basic communications to each other. I knew what we were doing would really change things."

Did he have any inkling that a whole new $4 trillion industry in e-commerce would emerge from the network and employ millions of people worldwide?

"No, I didn't. I thought it would change the way people did the work they already do, and let them do it easier and faster. And I thought it would greatly increase the pace of business and scientific research. Deep down, I knew it would change the world."

He pauses a moment. "Looking back on it, I think that's what the biggest motivation was for me to leave Lincoln Labs and go to DARPA. I really wanted to change the world, and I just couldn't see that what I was doing at the Lab was going to be very impactful. You know, I was doing graphics research, and Ivan [Sutherland] and I did a bunch of virtual reality back in the early '60s. But I just couldn't believe that this was going to ever amount to much even in thirty years, because no one would have the money to buy the machines that would be needed."

In the intellectual ferment of the 1960s, with the challenge posed by Sputnik demanding new breakthroughs in American science and technology, DARPA provided the perfect setting for the best and brightest minds of the period to put their imaginations to work. "I wanted to make a difference," Roberts explains, "and I knew I couldn't do it alone. I mean, maybe I could invent some of the ideas for the network. But to make it actually happen, you know, to really create this network, it was going to take a lot of people. So if I really wanted to make as big an impact as I possibly could, then DARPA was where I needed to be."

Interestingly, while some ARPANET participants may have sensed the world-historic nature of their work and perhaps even alluded to it among themselves, none of the myriad memos, proposals, reports, or presentations to conferences written by the principals explicitly talks about the network's larger impact on society. With one exception. On July 3, 1969, UCLA issued a press release announcing that, under the direction of engineering professor Leonard Kleinrock, it would in a few months become the first station in ARPANET's nationwide computer network linking computers of different makes and machine languages.

"Creation of the network represents a major step forward in computer technology and may serve as the forerunner of large computer networks of the future," the press release observed. It then closed with a prediction from Kleinrock: "As of now, computer networks are still in their infancy. But as they grow up and become more sophisticated, we will probably see the spread of 'computer utilities,' which like the present electric and telephone utilities, will service individual homes and offices across the country."

When Kleinrock made that prediction, I was a young U.S. Marine captain in Vietnam. Twenty-six years later, I became CEO of one such "computer utility," Concentric Network.

Changing the World

Before any of that could happen, of course, someone had to turn ARPANET into a publicly available communications network for individuals and businesses. In 1973, Roberts approached AT&T about taking over the network. He had no idea what he wanted to do himself after AT&T took it over, but he figured AT&T might want him to stay and manage it.

"I tried to get AT&T to take over the network, but they actually decided not to. This was a major decision on their part—and a disaster for them. I told them I'd give them the whole network, and they could charge us for it while they built it up for commercial use. They had this big committee of executives consider the idea, but they eventually came back and said, 'It's not compatible with our telephone networks or our philosophy.'"

It was not the first time AT&T discounted the possibilities of a new technology. A few years earlier, an AT&T committee had studied the commercial potential of cellphones and concluded there would never be more than nine hundred thousand people worldwide who wanted mobile phone service.

"So then I went to the [Federal Communications Commission] and I said, 'What am I going to do? I need to make this a commercial business,'" Roberts recalls. "They said, 'Start a carrier.' So I did." He launched a start-up called Telenet in 1973, the first packet-switched communications network. It got funding from newly emergent venture capital groups—the only other venture-funded company in 1973 was Federal Express—and went public with an IPO a few years later. Telenet was acquired by GTE in 1979 and subsequently became the data division of Sprint.

Of course, that meant that someone had to take over leadership of the IPTO at DARPA. "Larry was such a strong leader," Kahn recalled to one interviewer. "It was not that easy to find someone to replace him. [Finally] Licklider agreed to come back and take the job. As soon as Larry learned that Licklider had agreed to do it, then he left [without concern]."

At Telenet, Roberts got hooked on the entrepreneurial life. Over the next two decades, he started and sold several more companies focused on networks. Not all were successful, but such is the entrepreneurial life. You have to tolerate uncertainty, not be (too) afraid to get knocked down a few times. Still, Roberts probably likes the comfort of working with his alma mater, DARPA, even if DARPA is much changed today.

It also gives Roberts a wholly unique perspective on government support of basic research in America, as both a former director and now a current recipient of DARPA funding. And what the JASONs saw from the outside looking in, Roberts sees from the inside out.

"When Licklider and I and all the others were there back in the 1960s," Roberts points out, "DARPA was heavily investing in basic, or 6.1 research, as it's called in DoD. You know, 6.2 and 6.3 are more in the realm of developing specific applications to meet specific DoD needs. But 6.1 is basic research, the kind of research that led to the first computers and lasers and the network. It doesn't have any requirements in terms of 'build a better whatsit' or 'solve this or that problem.' The only requirement is to explore a field, like computing, and make any discoveries or advances you can that seem important and compelling."

But how did DARPA decide what areas of research might be worth pursuing?

"It had to be something that, if the research was successful, would make a qualitative difference for the country," says Roberts. "We funded artificial intelligence [AI] research. We didn't have any particular goal in mind, but we knew if we made progress it could lead to all sorts of things, from smart defense systems to smarter phone systems. So we funded principal investigators at universities who we knew did a good job and could attract the best students to work with them. We funded [AI researchers] John McCarthy and Marvin Minsky and let them do what they wanted. We knew they were good and that the research would be important someday."

He offers another example. "We also did speech recognition, because we knew that if we had a semantic breakthrough, it would lead to a lot of useful applications in industry and the military. Which, of course, it has. So we funded the best people at the best universities who wanted to work in that area, and didn't impose any requirements in terms of results."

The point of basic research, Roberts insists, is that it's supposed to be open-ended. You weren't supposed to be constrained by what you thought was going to be immediately useful.

Would DARPA have ever funded research into far-out ideas like, say, levitation?

He laughs. "Well, levitation might not qualify because it's too far out. But actually, if a program manager thought that it was even a remote possibility, yeah, he might fund it. I mean, we funded some pretty strange things that later turned out to be valuable."

Like what?

"Well . . ." A long pause. "I'm just not sure if the things I'm thinking of are classified or unclassified. So maybe . . . "

Fair enough.

"But the important thing," says Roberts, "is that we didn't fund anything unless it was way beyond what industry would do—much more long-term and open-ended than industry would ever do. And it had to offer the possibility of radical or fundamental breakthroughs."

Sometimes the research ideas proposed were intriguing yet so far out of the mainstream that he had to fund them with "borrowed" money from other, already-approved projects just to see if they could be developed into projects credible enough to get funding of their own.

DARPA's positive impact was felt not just in the funding of basic research, but also in federal procurement policies. Unlike in Europe, where research and procurement policies helped reinforce the leadership of entrenched incumbent firms, U.S. federal procurement policies for semiconductors, computers, and software were deliberately designed to nurture the formation and growth of start-ups like Texas Instruments, Fairchild Semiconductor, and other new players. Federal procurement policy thus encouraged an *entrepreneurial* bent in these critical information technology industries that was not seen in their European cousins.

In a chapter entitled, "The Federal Role in Financing Major Innovations: Information Technology during the Postwar Period," in *Financing Innovation in the United States: 1870 to the Present*, Kira R. Fabrizio and David C. Mowery wrote, "In contrast to Western European defense ministries, the U.S. military awarded substantial procurement contracts to new entrants such as Texas Instruments with little or no history of supplying the military. [This] increased the diversity of technological alternatives explored by individuals and firms. These public R&D and procurement programs enhanced the innovative dynamism and competitive strength of the [American] IT sector."

Much of that innovative dynamism seems to have bled out of the federal R&D effort. "The main problem now," argues Roberts, "is that there's virtually no 6.1 basic research any more. Which means that there's also very little basic DoD research at the universities—and therefore no way for bright graduate students to do any basic research. University people are constantly complaining that the funding is just not there anymore."

So what sorts of research will DARPA fund today?

"They come up with a particular goal first now," he says. "I need a better thing, a faster computer. Or, in the case of the research we're doing for them, they want to be able to secure the network, make sure that all of the users are authenticated and no one who's unauthorized can get through—and also give priority to, say, a general in the field or to an emergency service when the system gets overloaded. Basically, they want us to see if we can make all of the nodes in the network aware of where the traffic is coming from, and ensure that no one is spoofing it."

Applied research and development always tend to take precedence over basic research during times of war, and the wars in Iraq and Afghanistan and the post-9/11 struggle against jihadist terror have certainly placed urgent demands upon federal research for everything from anti-improvised-explosive technology to smarter electronic surveillance systems. But the tendency to minimize the longer-term value of basic research has been criticized at least since the 1970s, when the escalating Vietnam War effort produced the Mansfield Amendment of 1973 that explicitly limited appropriations for defense research to projects with direct military application.

Some critics believe that the amendment devastated U.S. science, since DARPA provided major funding for basic research projects at the time and the National Science Foundation never picked up the slack. And sure enough, as a percentage of GDP, federal support for research in both engineering and the physical sciences declined by more than 50 percent over the next two decades. On the plus side, perhaps, the resulting brain drain from universities that had lost funding spurred many young computer scientists to flee to start-up companies and private research labs such as Xerox's Palo Alto Research Center. Overall, though, basic research has never regained the funding strength or political support it enjoyed in the 1950s and 1960s.

What's more, the support DARPA does provide for basic research is undercut by the high level of bureaucracy at the agency now, says Roberts. "It used to be that you'd fund the *person*. You'd know what his reputation was, what his area of research was. There was no requirement as to what he was looking for or what he might produce. If it was someone we weren't familiar with, or a university we didn't know much about, then we'd go out and meet with them and see if they were capable and had good graduate students working with them, that sort of thing."

But now, he says, "Everything has to go through BAA"—a Broad Agency Announcement of a problem distributed to any and all—"and they've lost their relationships with the best researchers. Plus it has to go through this whole complicated process nowadays and the red tape has just increased so much."

DARPA's more constrained and bureaucratic approach affects every other agency. "DARPA set the tone for everyone else," he says, "because they had the best programs and the biggest successes. So other agencies tried to do like we did—talking to the right researcher, putting a proposal together and getting it funded in just a few days. Now? Forget it."

He sums up DARPA's problem today: "Their research is much more short term and directed to some purpose or need nowadays. Which by itself is fine. We need that. But we also need the more fundamental open-ended research, or we'll never make the breakthroughs that open up whole new possibilities for us to explore and exploit."

The budget numbers (and the JASON report) confirm Roberts's impression. During the golden age of DARPA, when fundamental advances in the 1950s and 1960s led to the birth of computers and semiconductors and communication networks, basic research constituted more than 26 percent of DoD R&D funding. Today it represents barely 12 percent of total DoD R&D funding, or about $2 billion in 2011. That's only a quarter of Microsoft's R&D budget. The AAAS says that federal support for basic research has been in "free fall" since the late 1990s and today represents only 0.38 percent of GDP.

Roberts spoke to DARPA's original mission in an interview with Arthur L. Norberg, past director of the Charles Babbage Institute at the University of Minnesota:

"The biggest decision factor [in funding] was whether it was going to affect the nation significantly. Could I look at it in five years and be proud that this country had done it? Because anytime you are just leading industry by a few years, you're not changing the world that significantly. That is the biggest benefit of such a program—being able to go out and do something which [results in] a major shift in thinking."

Today, says Roberts, DARPA thinks small, not big: smaller projects, safer projects, and not enough vision and imagination to really move things forward in a big way.

Also lost is the positive influence DARPA once had on the university system. "We had a big impact on the universities," Roberts told Norberg. "We produced excitement so students went to those departments [where DARPA funded basic research]. The people from those projects are [now] the leaders of industry, and the basis for the progress of the United States."

Indeed, as we pointed out earlier, graduate studies in computer science didn't even exist in the United States until DARPA funded it. Unfortunately, as the JASON report made painfully clear, basic research's secondary mission to train the future leaders of science and industry in America seems to have been forgotten in today's DARPA.

Overall, the government percentage of total U.S. R&D expenditures—basic, applied, and development—has been in decline for decades. In 1964, at the height of DARPA's effectiveness, federal funds composed 67 percent of total R&D expenditures in the United States. Industry contributed just 33 percent. Today those numbers are reversed, with the feds picking up only one-third of the tab of total U.S. R&D funding.

According to a May 2010 report by the U.S. Congress Joint Economic Committee, this level of federal investment in R&D—and especially in basic research—"may only be half of the optimal level." It noted that basic research "generates the greatest economy-wide returns" of all forms of R&D and "plays a critical role in sparking innovation."

At least it has until now. Besides government funding that led to semiconductors, lasers, information technology, and the Internet, DARPA grants for university research also produced such standout advances as GPS, satellites, advanced composite materials, and stealth technology. Somebody had to make breakthroughs in our understanding of physics and materials before others could develop the specific technology applications we now see all around us.

As for federal funding of small business R&D under the Small Business Innovation Research (SBIR) and Small Business Technology Transfer (STTR) programs, the approach has been rather schizophrenic over the past decade. These programs, administered by the Office of Technology at the Small Business Administration, funnel competitive grants from eleven federal agencies (including the DoD and the National Institutes of Health) for R&D performed by start-ups and other small businesses.

Doing so makes perfect sense, since small firms employ 38 percent of all scientists and engineers in America—more than are employed by either universities or large businesses—and produce five times as many patents per dollar as large firms do. And don't forget, as we demonstrated in chapter 1, small firms are the exclusive developers of the kinds of breakthrough technological innovations that lead to the birth of whole new industries and millions of new jobs.

Says the National Small Business Association, "As the nation's largest source of early-stage research and development funding, SBIR has provided a way to meet the nation's technology needs using the proven innovative power of small, technology-based companies."

Indeed, the Information Technology & Innovation Foundation (ITIF) recently concluded that the SBIR program produces as much as 25 percent of the nation's most important technological innovations each year—and more than sixty thousand patents in total since the SBIR program was established twenty-five years ago.

Yet despite their vital importance to the entire fabric of R&D in the United States, small businesses receive only 4.3 percent of the federal government's total R&D funding. And that funding—now $2 billion allocated through all eleven federal agencies—is continually threatened by the possibility that Congress might let the program lapse.

It's time for Congress to exercise leadership and permanently authorize as well as fully fund the SBIR program, which has been praised for its outstanding effectiveness by every agency and independent review of its operations. If ever there was a government program that worked, this is it.

This lack of leadership is also clearly reflected in the abysmal state of science and technology education in the United States today. More than 60 percent of all U.S. doctorates in science and engineering now go to foreign-born students. About 17 percent of all U.S. undergraduate degrees were awarded to students in the hard sciences; in China, that figure is 56 percent. America will educate about seventy thousand engineers this year. China will field six hundred thousand, and India three hundred fifty thousand.

These figures represent the tip of the iceberg waiting to sink America's once-titanic innovation leadership. A broader worry is that whereas just a decade ago the U.S. led the world in the number of twenty-five- to thirty-four-year-olds with college degrees, now we rank a mere twelfth among thirty-six developed nations, according to the College Board. Without enough human talent to invent the future, American prosperity could eventually become a thing of the past.

We have deliberately chosen not to delve deeply into the problems with America's educational system. In part this is because the problems in education, from kindergarten through college, are so complex and so enmeshed in a dizzying web of other social and economic problems as to defy the wisdom of even the most astute educational experts. It is an issue that the innovation expert John Kao calls a "wicked problem," resistant (at least so far) to solutions.

Yet my instinct tells me that, at bottom, this is a problem of political will more than a lack of understanding of the basic problems involved. As a high school student in 1958, I remember the sense of purpose, the concerted new emphasis on math and science in our curriculum, that came to my school in the aftermath of the Russian Sputnik launch. Suddenly everyone wanted to be an engineer. Or an astronaut.

These are less innocent times today, that is for sure. But Americans are not a suicidal people, and I am confident that at some point in the future we will deal with the problems in our education system—because we will simply have to in order to survive.

How Not to Build a New Industry

Any discussion of federal support for basic research inevitably raises the larger question of government's overall role in nurturing innovation. Some in the United States advocate that we borrow a page from the Chinese playbook and launch a massive federal program to develop and support clean technology industries. Others say just the opposite—that *any* government intervention in the marketplace or in promoting new technologies is doomed to fail.

The history of DARPA demonstrates clearly that strong government support for basic research, followed by private entrepreneurial development of the technologies that emerge from this research, can yield outstanding economic results. But how much government support is too much? At a time of growing concern over America's competitiveness in the world and the erosion of its innovation leadership, people rightly wonder how far government should go—or not go—in supporting innovation and the emergence of new industries.

To help answer this question, let's revisit the birth of high-definition television (HDTV) in the 1980s, a time with many similarities to our own. Then, as now, many Americans worried about a seeming juggernaut of economic power emerging out of Asia, only then the worry was Japan, whereas now it is China. Then, as now, many also felt government should play a more direct and powerful role in sponsoring the development of new industries, as the governments of our economic adversaries were clearly intent on doing. And then, as now, thoughtful people asked, "What is the proper role of government in supporting innovation?"

HDTV had its origins in Japan in the early 1970s, when the Japanese broadcaster NHK developed a set of standards known as the MUSE system that promised to more than double the 525 lines of resolution typical in standard TVs and make other improvements that would render television more brilliantly realistic and captivating than ever before. The most noteworthy aspect of the Japanese MUSE system, however, was not the old-fashioned analog technology it employed, but the fact that NHK managed to secure government backing for it through an alliance that included Japan's Ministry of International Trade and Industry (MITI)—now called the Ministry of Economy, Trade and Industry, or METI—and the country's leading TV-set manufacturers. They called their combined efforts the Hi-Vision project.

For the Japanese, who would ultimately pour over $1.5 billion in government and private R&D money into the Hi-Vision project ($6 billion in today's dollars), the high-definition television effort promised to cement Japan's dominance over the global consumer electronics business. It also offered them the opportunity to take the lead in emerging markets for new kinds of semiconductors, new displays, new satellite transmission technologies, and new medical imaging products that would ultimately be built around the technologies developed for HDTV.

To achieve all this, however, Japan's HDTV system had to be accepted globally. So after more than a decade of research and investment, the Japanese took their Hi-Vision project on the road. At a crucial meeting of the International Radio Consultative Committee in Dubrovnik, Yugoslavia (now Croatia) in 1986, the Japanese formally proposed that their analog, satellite-based, 1,125-line HDTV system be adopted as a world standard.

To be sure, the notion of a single global standard for high-definition television did have a certain appeal. The fifty-year-long history of standard television, after all, had always been complicated by the existence of three competing standards: the NTSC standard used by the United States and Japan, the PAL standard common in most of Europe and the developing world, and the SECAM standard employed in France, Russia, and some of the former French colonies. Adding to the frustration over television's historic Tower of Babel, new complaints were now being voiced over a similar lack of standards in the emerging world of computers, operating systems, and data communications.

With these concerns in mind, the U.S. delegation voted—naively, said some critics—to support the Hi-Vision project. However, the Europeans were not nearly so sanguine about Japanese intentions. They recognized that adoption of the Japanese Hi-Vision standard would not only bar alternative HDTV technologies from any real chance to compete in the market but also would help Japanese manufacturers dominate HDTV markets by enabling them to use uniform designs rather than retooling their products to meet the engineering standards of each local market.

"HDTV was Japan's ultimate weapon," insisted one European delegate at the meeting, "an instrument with which to squeeze their European competitors and blitzkrieg the wide-open American market—in short, move in for the kill. Dubrovnik was to be the new Verdun."

Hoping to protect their industrial competitiveness from what they felt was a Japanese Trojan horse, the European delegates voted to block the Hi-Vision HDTV plan and create a nine-nation European consortium known as Eureka Project 95—led by Dutch electronics giant Philips and Thomson of France, and backed by a billion dollars in government and industry funding—to promote a new HDTV system, known as HD-MAC, using 1,250 lines of resolution.

The director of Europe's Eureka Project, P. Bogels, would later offer a surprisingly honest view of the stakes in the battle over a global HDTV standard: "Of course, we think our standard is technologically superior to the Japanese standard. But the essence of the issue is strategy, not technology."

In other words, standard setting often has little to do with picking the best technical solution. It's often about advancing your own interests over those of your competitors—and what better way to do that than to get the government involved on your side?

Nowhere were those interests more pronounced, of course—or the stakes higher—than in the U.S. market for high-definition television. The United States, after all, was where the majority of TV sets in the world were then sold. It was where the world's leading broadcasters and TV networks, which would ultimately need to spend billions to upgrade their transmission and production systems to handle high-definition programming, were based.

And it was where the world's largest number of TV stations operated, which by one estimate would each need to spend $38 million simply to upgrade their transmission systems to handle HDTV broadcasts.

Clearly, America was where the battle over HDTV would ultimately be decided—and where, not surprisingly, any decision by the Federal Communications Commission (FCC) over which HDTV standard to embrace would have the greatest impact on the bottom lines of Japanese, European, and American electronics companies, broadcasters, and TV manufacturers.

Yet, despite (or perhaps because of) the fact that the stakes were so high, the American response was, at least by Japanese and European standards, astonishingly confused. Indeed, an almost-comic interplay of overheated political posturing, self-interested maneuvering by competing broadcasters and electronics companies, and plain old-fashioned head-in-the-sand myopia would align itself with a providential technology development to not only deny victory to either the Japanese, European, or indeed *any* of the existing players in the HDTV competition, but also to doom analog HDTV itself to the scrapheap of history's obsolete technologies.

Some of the most important forces affecting the HDTV competition in the U.S. were, of course, political. That's because in the years between the 1986 Dubrovnik meeting and the FCC's final ruling on HDTV in June 1990, U.S.–Japan issues had become highly politicized, with a widespread fear among Americans that a predatory mercantilist Japan, Inc., was trying to rob the United States of its presumed birthright to technological and industrial leadership in the world.

By the late 1980s, after all, a flood of superior-quality imports from Japan had already gutted large portions of the American electronics and automobile industries, and in the TV industry itself, nine of ten sets sold in the U.S. were by then being built in foreign-owned plants (and Zenith, the sole remaining American producer, had already shifted its production and most of its jobs overseas). This contributed, of course, to a loss of American jobs and productivity, as well as to a huge and growing trade deficit with Japan.

Indeed, there was a sense among some in the United States that the Japanese financial and industrial juggernaut was quite literally taking over America. This was a time, after all, when Japanese electronics giants were buying up American movie studio icons such as MCA and Columbia Pictures for then unheard-of billions of dollars. And Japanese golf magnates were buying up the majority of golf courses in Hawaii and had just acquired the classic Pebble

Beach Resort for close to a billion dollars. And when even stodgy Japanese insurance companies were paying eight-figure sums for French impressionist paintings to hang in their hallways—and Japanese ice cream parlors were serving (for a price) flecks of real gold on their scoops of vanilla.

So perhaps it's no surprise that some influential policy makers called upon America to emulate Japan's potent industry–government partnership and create an "industrial policy" of its own. Thus we were treated to the spectacle of Commerce Secretary Robert Mosbacher testifying before a 1990 Senate hearing on HDTV in support of an electronics industry–backed proposal for over $1 billion in government research grants, loans, and loan guarantees—only to have him called to the White House the next day and chewed out by such staunch opponents of government intervention in the market as chief of staff John Sununu, economic adviser Michael Boskin, and budget director Richard Darman.

As Oregon Democratic Congressman Les AuCoin described it to one reporter, "It was like a vaudeville show. They yanked Mosbacher with a hook."

In the end, none of the government-backed efforts of the Japanese or the Europeans—and none of the maneuverings by either proponents or opponents of American industrial policy—counted in the final determination of HDTV's fate. Why? Because something happened that no one—and I mean literally *no one*—could ever have predicted: the accidental genesis of an entirely new technology by an innovative little American firm called General Instrument (GI).

The company, a maker of satellite gear and cable TV converters, had noticed that none of the twenty-three different analog HDTV proposals submitted to the FCC (later winnowed down to four) would be compatible with its existing products. So it initially put its crack team of engineers to work on a digitally based conversion process that would enable its cable TV boxes to handle HDTV signals.

"We really weren't interested in HDTV per se," recalled Mat Miller, who was then GI's chief technology officer. "For us, HDTV was just an in-house stalking horse for speeding up the work we wanted to do anyway on digital video and compression."

Indeed, GI had not even planned to submit an HDTV proposal to the FCC, not least because it didn't think it was worth the $250,000 it would have to pay for FCC testing of the system. But at literally the eleventh hour—late in the evening before the final June 6, 1990, deadline for filing with the FCC—GI's little band of Davids decided to fire their slingshot at the government-backed media Goliaths of Japan and Europe by filing a proposal of their own. The proposal outlined the specifications for the world's first all-digital HDTV system.

The shock of the first-ever workable technology for digital television was felt around the world. Within months, all the other contenders—including Europe's HD-MAC project and Japan's Hi-Vision project—had dropped their original analog HDTV proposals and either retreated or come back with all-digital versions of the technology themselves. But it was no use. All the money, and all the concerted efforts of the best minds of government and industry working together in Europe and Japan, had come to naught.

Eventually, General Instrument combined forces with the remaining U.S. digital HDTV proponents in a group called the Grand Alliance to employ the best attributes of each system. The high-definition television we all watch today is the fruit of their efforts, especially those of General Instrument—"the little engine that could" in the world of HDTV.

There are many ironies in this story. First of all there is the irony of a Japan that spent twenty years of effort and billions of dollars on a government-mandated technological standard only to wind up feeling perhaps like the nineteenth-century builders of America's transcontinental railroad might have felt had they hammered the last spike in the last stretch of track only to look up in the sky and seen a passenger jet flying overhead.

Then there's the irony of General Instrument coming out of nowhere at the last minute with an entrepreneurial innovation that propelled it to the top of the HDTV mountain. Even more ironic, it turned out that HDTV itself was the *least* valuable result of its effort. By unlocking the secret of digitizing television signals, this company accidentally gave birth to the digital technology revolution and its trillions of dollars in commerce.

Finally, there is more than a little irony in the fact that America had managed—through a combination of entrepreneurial innovation and laissez-faire economics rather than European- or Japanese-style industrial policy—to end up in the leadership of the digital technology revolution. In so doing, the United States regained a position of technological and industrial leadership in the world.

Today, America faces a new economic challenge not unlike that which we faced in the 1980s. Our innovation engine has slowed, our economy and political institutions are gridlocked, and an Asian economic juggernaut is surging ahead in cleantech, advanced materials, and many other critical industries of the future. The temptation is great either to overestimate other nations' capabilities and throw up our hands or to follow the example of strong government intervention and central planning seen in some parts of Asia, and launch a kind of cleantech Hi-Vision project of our own.

It would be a mistake, however, to underestimate the awesome regenerative power of America's entrepreneurial inventiveness, or to overlook the generally sad history of centrally planned corporate and governmental R&D programs in the past.

For history shows us, again and again, how the best-laid plans of even the wisest government officials and corporate executives can be undone by the fickle hand of fate—or by a couple of guys tinkering in a garage.

Absolutely we must have concerted government support for basic research in science and technology. But then we must let start-up entrepreneurs take the fruits of that research and build from it a better tomorrow.

Back to Basics

It's time for government to step up to the plate and fully support the kinds of research programs that have been proven to generate outsize returns for society.

We must enhance our funding of basic research through all appropriate federal agencies.

We should aim high in our basic research, and fund projects that will make a big difference in the country if successful—projects that are orders of magnitude ahead of what industry is currently capable of, yet that will also eventually have commercial potential.

Government should learn from private industry and invest research funds just like a venture capitalist invests start-up capital—that is, it should invest in people and teams first of all, especially those who can attract bright graduate students to participate.

Government agencies such as DARPA should get back to the practice of acting quickly and decisively, eliminating complex approval chains and other red tape.

Finally, Congress should fully and permanently fund the terrific SBIR program offering competitive grants for early-stage research to small businesses— the proven source of all breakthrough innovation and job creation in America.

A good way to do that is to pass S.B. 3362 from the 110th Congress, or its successor bill.

Government can be bureaucratic, wasteful, infuriating, and dumb as a brick. So when we finally do create a government program that works—and I mean really works, like the federal funding of basic research—we should care for it and treasure it like a tiny little flower amidst a patch of weeds.

The trick lies in knowing when government should step forward, and when it should step back.

Epilogue

Do We Still Need Government?

A bout a year into the current economic downturn, the Nobel Laureate economist Edmund Phelps wrote an essay about the almost-religious manner in which some people view the free market. "The market is an instrument—an imperfect and failure-prone instrument," he observed, "whose purpose is to deliver social benefits. It is not an object of worship, nor should it be."

I know exactly what he means. I have been an entrepreneur all my life, and have built a fair number of start-up companies into industry leaders, creating six thousand jobs and returning $8 billion to investors in the process. And I absolutely know that the free market is the most powerful engine for change and the betterment of human society ever devised by man. It is the beating heart of all social and economic progress, the proving ground of all innovations in technology, the sole and indispensable engine for the creation of broad social wealth.

But the free market is not everything. It does not contain the sum total of all human knowledge and experience, nor does it encompass and reflect all human needs and concerns.

This is why, for thousands of years, human beings have created governments in the first place—so that citizens can act together, consciously and with purpose, to shape the spontaneous economic and natural processes going on around us.

There is a difference between a bazaar and a civilization.

Government, too, is an imperfect instrument. It can successfully correct a certain kind of "market failure" (as economists call it), as it does when funding the basic scientific research that no private enterprise, pressed to demonstrate to shareholders some returns from its R&D expenditure, ever will. It can even, on rare occasions, intervene more directly in the economy to correct another type of market failure—the one we call "monopoly."

Indeed, whenever we make a cellphone call or send an e-mail or log on to the Internet today, we are the direct beneficiaries of these two types of government interventions in the free market: funding the basic research in the 1960s that led to ARPANET, and breaking up the old AT&T monopoly in 1984 to free the logjam of innovation in telecommunications.

I am also mindful of the positive role that government has played in my own life. I am the son of immigrants who, quite literally, had nothing when they came to America. Yet I, their son, was privileged by my country to attend good public schools. Competing on merit, I won an appointment to the U.S. Naval Academy and received a world-class college education tuition-free. I later attended graduate school at George Washington University thanks in part to the GI Bill, which over the years has returned $5 in economic growth and $1.83 in new tax revenues for every dollar spent on the benefits it provides. And many of the technologies my companies commercialized were born in labs funded by government agencies such as DARPA.

So no one needs to tell me how much I owe my country and our government. I have tried to repay these gifts by serving in the Marine Corps and by helping to build businesses that provided jobs and wealth for the whole community.

Like any large corporate enterprise, however, government is slow-footed and dim-witted when it comes to responding to rapid changes in technology or the marketplace. To ask it to pick the next winning technology or to manage the development of some new cleantech industry is to ask it to do what it was never meant to do—and, in point of fact, has never successfully done.

Still, for all its high costs and political and economic failings, government still remains the only society-wide institution we possess with sufficient scope and legitimacy to represent the public interest and to intervene in the flow of history to give it shape and direction.

That is why I decided to get involved in the innovation policy debates in Washington as well as at the state and local level. True, I am only a businessman, an ordinary citizen, not a policy expert or politician. But I know something about creating jobs and wealth. And when I saw that government was setting policies that hamstrung the nation's ability to create jobs and social wealth, I thought it was time to get involved and try to serve again.

Obviously, I don't have all the answers. But I do know this much: the answer is neither the "big government" of the radical left nor the "no government" of the radical right—it's the "smart government" of the commonsense middle.

It's a government that, in all its policies and laws, distinguishes between the entrenched interests of Big Business and the critical needs of small start-ups.

It's a government that steps in where no private venture will go to fund the basic research that unlocks the science behind new technologies benefiting all mankind—and that educates and inspires the next generation of university scientists and engineers.

But it's also a government that then gets out of the way and lets entrepreneurs make what they can out of the new scientific knowledge and skills that result.

Smart government is one that does all it can to incentivize the revitalization of our high-tech manufacturing sector, for that is the engine of a vibrant middle class and the vehicle through which the wealth created by innovation spreads through all of society. Smart government knows that a rising tide of wealth only for the few will drown us all.

It's also a government that clears the logjam at the patent office so that innovators can once again obtain the legal and financial assets they need—patents—to start new businesses and bring their new products, services, and medical treatments to the American people.

And it's a government that recognizes that with tough competition today coming from almost every corner of the globe, the best and brightest minds will be our most precious resource no matter their land of birth. Immigration policy must become "recruitment policy."

Most of all, it's a government that clears away the tax and regulatory roadblocks standing in the way of start-up business growth and success—for entrepreneurial start-ups are the engine of job creation and economic growth in America.

If there is a silver bullet in economic life, then start-ups are it. They're the only future we have, and we'd better start acting like it.

Notes on Sources

The stories and incidents described in this book came from a large number of interviews conducted November 1, 2009, to February 7, 2011, and, where not specifically cited, also from accounts in newspapers and magazines—particularly the *New York Times, Wall Street Journal, Milwaukee Journal-Sentinel, Sharon Herald, Bloomberg BusinessWeek,* and a great many other business, general interest, and specialist media.

Other sources that proved immensely helpful in our research include the treasure trove of academic research and working papers maintained by the Social Science Research Network, the tremendous library of studies offered by the U.S. Small Business Administration, the National Institute of Standards and Technology, the United States Patent and Trademark Office, the Ewing Marion Kauffman Foundation, Information Technology & Innovation Foundation, Milken Institute, the U.S. Census Bureau, and the Community Library of the Shenango Valley.

—Henry R. Nothhaft
February 2011

Index

About the Authors

Henry R. "Hank" Nothhaft is a highly successful serial entrepreneur and tireless advocate of smart innovation policies in Washington, D.C. During his thirty-five-year career leading high-tech start-ups, Nothhaft participated in some of the key technology breakthroughs of the postwar era—from the first public e-mail and data networks (Telenet) and nationwide Internet service providers (Concentric Network) to the creation of the mobile Internet and the first smartphone with social networking capability (Danger). Today he is Chairman and CEO of Tessera, a company at the forefront of semiconductor miniaturization technologies. A U.S. Naval Academy graduate with an advanced degree from George Washington University, Nothhaft served as a young Marine captain in Vietnam. He may be reached at hank@greatagain-thebook.com.

David Kline is a Pulitzer Prize–nominated journalist, author, and communications strategist who has been the first to report on some of the world's most dramatic stories over last thirty years—from the conflict in Afghanistan and the "Coca Nostra" drug wars in Bolivia to the plight of family farmers and the digital technology revolution in the United States. He has also authored several highly regarded books on innovation policy, including the bestselling seminal work on intellectual property strategy, *Rembrandts in the Attic.* He may be reached at dkline@well.com.

Please be sure to visit **www.greatagain-thebook.com.**